THE FUTURE OF AMERICA'S ALLIANCES IN NORTHEAST ASIA

Edited by
Michael H. Armacost
and
Daniel I. Okimoto

ASIA-PACIFIC RESEARCH CENTER

THE ASIA-PACIFIC RESEARCH CENTER (APARC) is a unique Stanford University institution focused on the study of contemporary Asia. APARC's mission is to produce and publish Asia Pacific–focused interdisciplinary research; to educate students, scholars, and corporate and governmental affiliates about the importance of US-Asian relations; to promote constructive interaction to understand and resolve the region's challenges; to influence US policy toward the Asia-Pacific; and to guide Asian nations on key foreign relations, government, political economy, technology, and social issues.

Asia-Pacific Research Center
Stanford Institute for International Studies
Stanford University
Encina Hall
Stanford, CA 94305-6055
tel 650-723-9741
fax 650-723-6530
http://APARC.stanford.edu

The Future of America's Alliances in Northeast Asia may be ordered from:
Brookings Institution Press
Department 029, Washington, DC 20042-0029, USA.
Tel. 1-800-275-1447 or 202-797-6258.
Fax: 202-797-2960 Attn: Order Dept.
Online: bookstore.brookings.edu

First printing, 2004.
ISBN 1-931368-06-6

CONTENTS

PREFACE

Daniel I. Okimoto

When the Berlin Wall fell, symbolizing the end of the Cold War, the global balance of power shifted from a tense military standoff between the world's two superpowers—the Soviet Union and the United States—to one of American dominance. The end of the Cold War, which had gripped the world for nearly a half-century, transformed the parameters and dynamics of international security. For the United States, the disappearance of the communist threat meant that the nature, goal, and missions of America's far-flung network of alliances needed to be reassessed within the context of new threats posed by the post–Cold War security environment. The cohesion supplied by the Soviet threat dissipated and alliance solidarity inevitably weakened. The United States came to rely, increasingly, on ad hoc "coalitions of the willing," going outside the framework of alliance networks to deal with pressing security contingencies. In addition, the revolution in military technology and the proliferation of advanced weapon systems prompted defense planners to review the effectiveness of US bases and force deployments overseas.

Just as the fall of the Berlin Wall symbolized the end of one historic era, the events of September 11, 2001, signaled the start of a new era for the United States and its allies: namely, a high state of mobilization to prosecute the war on global terrorism. A small but dedicated group of terrorists had demonstrated that subnational organizations could inflict serious damage on the financial center and the capital of the world's mightiest power. Long protected by the enormous stretch of the Atlantic and Pacific Oceans, the United States, no longer feeling safe from direct attack, scrambled to redefine its national security strategy. Out of this reassessment came a new post–9/11 doctrine, one explicitly asserting America's right to take preemptive action. Here again, the ever-shifting parameters and dynamics of international security raised questions about the missions and role of America's alliances in the global war against terrorism.

In Asia, several developments since 1993 have raised questions about the operational readiness and political sustainability of America's defense alliances with Japan and South Korea, the twin pillars of the security architecture in Asia. Specifically, the prospect of nuclear proliferation on the Korean peninsula and North Korea's development of Nodong and Taipodong missiles gave rise to two serious crises. The first, in 1993–94, was temporarily resolved through the signing of the Framework Agreement. The second occurred in 2002, after the Framework Agreement broke down. The outbreak of yet another security crisis in East Asia—that between China and Taiwan—also raised troubling questions about the operational complexities and political fallout associated with the mobilization of American forces on US bases in Asia, in order to conduct combat missions against China in the Taiwan Strait.

Major changes have also taken place in the domestic political systems of South Korea and Japan since 1993. South Korea has passed through a remarkable transition from military rule to participatory democracy, marked by the emergence of a robust civil society. The political party of conservative military generals like Park Chung-hee—the Grand National Party, which had occupied the Blue House for decades—gave way to the opposition, the Millennium Party, headed by the human rights activist and political dissident Kim Dae-jung.

Between the first and second nuclear crises in Korea, President Kim reoriented South Korean foreign policy from one based on military deterrence of the North Korean threat to a more conciliatory approach based on diplomatic-socioeconomic engagement, known as the Sunshine policy. The huge and growing gap in capacity and output between the economies of South and North Korea—acutely evident in North Korea's dysfunctional system of self-reliance, or *juche*—boosted the confidence of South Koreans and diminished their perception of the security threat posed by the North. Many South Koreans came to view North Korea, their once-feared enemy, as a crippled and cornered outcast state, more deserving of sympathy and pity than fear and foreboding.

Moreover, South Korea's demographic composition underwent a decisive generational shift, as the younger generation born after the Korean War (1950–53) came to constitute the majority of the population. This generational transition has given rise to a gathering sense of nationalism, reflected in a deep-seated desire for national autonomy and greater freedom from foreign dependence and external interference in domestic affairs. The conjunction of these structural developments—the emergence of an active civil society, the end of domination by military leaders and by the old conservative ruling party, the rise of liberal opposition forces, North Korea's economic implosion, the yawning gap between the economies of South and North Korea, the political implications of generational turnover, and the perceived waning of the security threat posed by North Korea—have rendered the bilateral management of the US-ROK alliance significantly more complicated and difficult than was the case as recently as the first nuclear crisis in 1993–94.

Significant changes have also taken place in Japan's political system, but in ways that have facilitated US-Japan defense cooperation (in contrast to South Korea, where domestic political changes have generated rifts in the bilateral alliance). In 1993, the conservative ruling party, the Liberal Democratic Party (LDP), which had controlled majorities in both branches of the National Diet for nearly four decades, fell from power when a dissenting faction split, formed a new party, and entered into a coalition with the Japan Socialist Party (JSP). Although the LDP returned to power in 1994, it was forced to govern in a coalition with other political parties, including, initially, the JSP. Once the JSP joined the majority coalition, and especially after a Socialist became prime minister, the JSP abandoned its long-standing policy of "unarmed neutrality," eliminating the ideology of pacifism as an alternative policy platform from Japan's security discourse. The policy dialogue in Japan has shifted toward pragmatic realism. As a result, Japan has ratified several key pieces of legislation, including one for international peacekeeping, paving the way for Japan to contribute actively to the war on terrorism, the campaign in Afghanistan, and the noncombat support for the war in Iraq. It would have been hard to imagine these actions prior to 1993, as evidenced by Japan's reluctance to contribute anything but hard cash during Desert Storm.

Yet, the overwhelming concentration of US bases in Okinawa continues to be a source of underlying tensions. Local resentment over the presence of US troops finds expression in political protests triggered by certain dramatic events, such as a military plane crash, fatal traffic accident, or an outrageous crime committed by American soldiers. For example, the rape of a Japanese schoolgirl ignited a firestorm of protest in 1996, leading to the announcement of plans to close down certain base facilities (such as Futenma), relocate others to different parts of Japan or Okinawa, and redeploy troops there. To date, progress in implementing the plan has been slow.

Taking note of the powerful impact and far-reaching implications of the historic developments alluded to above—specifically, the end of the Cold War, the first nuclear crisis on the Korean peninsula, the rise of China, and the China-Taiwan conflict, Professor Michel Oksenberg took the initiative to organize and direct a multiyear study at the Asia-Pacific Research Center (APARC) at Stanford University. The project focused on the history, current status, and future viability of the US-Japan and US-Korea alliances as viewed from the perspective of the major actors in the region—the United States, Japan, South Korea, China, and Southeast Asia. A distinguished group of scholars and policy analysts were invited to write papers. The Smith Richardson Foundation provided generous funding to cover the costs of field research, short-term visits, two major conferences, and publications. All of the individual papers were published in APARC's Occasional Papers Series, and the collected papers were to be edited by Dr. Oksenberg and published as a single volume. Dr. Oksenberg, the organizer and intellectual driving force behind the project, had started to write the conclusion, integrating central themes, summing up major findings, and setting forth policy recommendations about ways to adapt the alliances to recent changes. Dr. Oksenberg's unexpected and untimely passing, however, meant that this key chapter was never completed.

Several years later, when Dr. Michael Armacost rejoined the core faculty at APARC, he was asked to review the manuscript and consider writing a new conclusion. After reading the papers carefully, Dr. Armacost concluded that the pace of events had overtaken the manuscript. Between Dr. Oksenberg's passing and Dr. Armacost's arrival, several seminal events had occurred—the terrorist attack on September 11, the new doctrine of preemption, the wars in Afghanistan and Iraq, democratic change in South Korea, major shifts in Chinese foreign policy, and the second nuclear crisis on the Korean peninsula. These historic events had once again altered the nature of America's military alliances with Japan and South Korea. Dr. Armacost recommended that a fresh set of papers be written.

Under his leadership, and with the financial support of Walter H. Shorenstein and the Shorenstein Forum at APARC, the Center APARC convened a follow-up conference in January 2004. A different but equally distinguished group of scholars and policy analysts wrote papers and participated in the conference proceedings. This updated manuscript is the result.

APARC is grateful to Dr. Michael Armacost for taking the initiative to bring the alliance project to completion. Special thanks also go to the Smith Richardson Foundation, especially to Dr. Marin Strmecki, for their patience and the generosity of their support. We wish to thank the staff of APARC for their role in organizing and executing all the logistics related to the America's Asian Alliances conference, held at Stanford in January 2004—specifically to Shiho Harada Barbir, Claire McCrae, and Debbie Warren. We owe a special debt of gratitude to Neeley Main, who proved herself to be, once again, a superb conference organizer. In completing the burdensome task of editing the manuscript in record time, and with professional competence, Victoria Tomkinson and Megan Hendershott also deserve an explicit word of thanks. And to our beloved colleague, the late Dr. Michel Oksenberg, APARC dedicates this book with appreciation, respect, and a profound sense of loss.

INTRODUCTION

THE FUTURE OF AMERICA'S ALLIANCES IN NORTHEAST ASIA

Michael H. Armacost

There are obvious similarities between America's alliances with Japan and Korea. The United States provides a security guarantee to both, and maintains forward based forces in each country. Tokyo and Seoul have sized and shaped the composition and deployment of their military forces with US support in mind. Local ambivalence about the presence of foreign troops has long been a staple of politics in both countries.

The two alliances are strategically connected. The United States would have difficulty supporting its commitments to South Korea without access to bases in Japan. Japan would find it more difficult politically to sustain support for United States bases if it were America's only ally in the region. Both deterrence and "compellence" vis-à-vis North Korea are facilitated by trilateral cooperation among the United States, Japan, and South Korea. Washington has been the midwife of regular trilateral security consultations.

Yet there are also profound differences between these two American defense partnerships.

- As a global, maritime, trading nation, Japan shares broad strategic interests with the United States that extend well beyond its home islands. US forces in Japan—mainly naval, air force, and marine amphibious units—are available for missions outside Japan (e.g., protecting sea lanes or responding to regional contingencies).
- The scope of the US alliance with the ROK is narrower; its focus has been essentially on North Korea. The United States retains an infantry division north of Seoul to perform a "tripwire" deterrent function. And as a peninsular power, South Korea has fluctuated between "continental" and "maritime" orientations toward grand strategy.
- China (PRC) is perceived by many Japanese as a potential rival; by South Koreans it is regarded as a source of leverage with Washington among some, and as a strategic alternative to the United States among others.
- South Korea is a "normal" nation without constitutional or political prohibitions on the nature of its forces or their use. Japan has long considered itself a "civilian power," with significant legal and institutional constraints on its defense policy.

• At a time when the US-Japan alliance is expanding in scale and redefining its missions, the future of the US alliance with South Korea is beset by uncertainties.

US-Japanese security relations currently thrive. That could not have been said a decade ago. Washington and Tokyo got a wake-up call in the early post–Cold War era that prompted both governments to reconsider the fundamentals of the alliance. Fortunately, they took decisive action to reaffirm its enduring importance and to redefine its rationale and supporting arrangements. Kurt Campbell played an important role within the Clinton administration in promoting these adjustments, and his essay in this volume offers an assessment of the US security posture today.

The US-ROK alliance has yielded mutual benefits for more than half a century. Recurring, and occasionally acute, frictions were a familiar feature of the relationship in the past, but a shared sense of danger from North Korea facilitated the timely accommodation of differing perspectives and diverging interests, when they arose. Today, conflicting perceptions in Washington and Seoul of Kim Jong-il's North Korean regime and how to deal with it raise more basic questions about the future of the US-ROK alliance.

A mid-1990s crisis in US-Japan relations was treated as an opportunity to reshape and update the alliance in the face of changing circumstances. It remains to be seen whether current US-ROK difficulties can be overcome in a similarly salutary fashion.

The Post–Cold War Challenge to US-Japan Security Cooperation

The US-Japanese defense partnership was sorely tested in the 1990s. The disintegration of the Soviet Union undermined the principal motivation and rationale for US-Japan security cooperation. Requested by Washington to share the risks as well as the costs of the Gulf War, Japan punted. Neither its legal framework nor the existing political consensus allowed a prompt, forthcoming response—for which Tokyo paid a steep political price, despite its ultimately generous financial support. The Clinton administration, which had campaigned in 1992 on the slogan "It's the economy, stupid," took off the gloves in bilateral US-Japan trade negotiations, and the resulting tensions threatened to spill over into the field of security cooperation. When Japan spurned economic sanctions as a means of responding to North Korean nuclear activities in 1994, Washington was reminded of the alliance's limited efficacy for dealing with operational contingencies, even in Japan's own backyard. And a brutal rape case involving American marines in Okinawa triggered such an explosive reaction in Japan that many wondered whether public support for the alliance could be sustained.

Fortunately, neither Washington nor Tokyo was prepared to let matters drift. The Pentagon's 1995 East Asia Strategy Report—incorporating the policy premises of what became known as the "Nye Initiative"—articulated a firm defense of the alliance. US force levels in the Pacific were frozen at existing levels—roughly 100,000. A timely accommodation was struck in bilateral trade negotiations over auto parts.

More importantly, Pentagon and Japan Defense Agency (JDA) officials purposefully tackled the immediate issues complicating bilateral defense cooperation. The United States promised to interpret the criminal jurisdiction provisions of the Status of Forces Agreement more flexibly, and agreed to create a new committee—the Special Action Committee on Okinawa (SACO)—to review ways of reconfiguring the US base presence on the island. Japan in turn pledged to negotiate revised Guidelines for US-Japan Defense Cooperation.

Fortuitously, a planned visit by President Clinton to Japan, originally scheduled for late 1995, was aborted by a budget crisis in Washington. Before the visit was rescheduled, the PRC, responding to President Lee Teng-hui's 1995 visit to the United States and his subsequent bid for re-election, undertook provocative military exercises off the coast of Taiwan. This offered Japanese and Americans alike a timely reminder of the alliance's value as an insurance policy whose premiums were relatively modest. Prospects for security cooperation turned up, and have followed a generally smoother path ever since.[1]

Toward a More "Normal" Alliance

During the Cold War, when "over the horizon" security problems loomed, Tokyo generally expected Washington to handle such challenges; Tokyo extended compensation in the form of increased financial support for US troops stationed in Japan. In the post–Cold War world, however, Japan discovered that it could not sit out conflicts which pitted "outliers" like Saddam Hussein against the international community without risking severe international criticism and diminished self-respect.

This realization prompted Tokyo to undertake adjustments in its strategic division of labor with the United States. Since 1993, Japan has gradually embraced a more balanced pattern of "responsibility sharing" in the field of international security. Peacekeeping operations legislation, passed by the Diet in 1993, was a first step down this road. Revisions in the bilateral US-Japan Guidelines for Defense Cooperation to allow rear-area support for US forces in Japan constituted a second. The assumption after 9/11 of "out of area" responsibilities as an offshore, noncombat provider of logistics and other services in support of the UN-authorized campaign against the Taliban in Afghanistan was a third. And Japan's decision to send combat personnel to Iraq to participate in efforts by the US-led "coalition of the willing" to foster economic reconstruction and political development is the most recent manifestation of Japan's more proactive contribution to international security.

As Self-Defense Force (SDF) involvement in distant peacekeeping and counterterrorist operations has become more frequent and routine, Japan has begun to procure defense equipment which is gradually extending its capacity to project power over greater distances. Aegis destroyers, Standard missiles, aerial refueling tanker aircraft, and a helicopter carrier all fall into this category. None gives Japan "invasion potential"; all promise to augment its defensive strength and improve its ability to perform missions farther from its home islands.

Anxieties about North Korea's nuclear ambitions and missile tests have prompted Japan to expand collaboration with the United States on ballistic missile defenses. These concerns also encouraged Tokyo to align its diplomacy toward North Korea more closely with Washington's. In addition, Japan has joined other maritime nations in supporting the US Proliferation Security Initiative, and it is currently participating in joint naval exercises aimed at impeding the transfer of nuclear-related materials and other contraband goods by "rogue nations."

Domestic constraints on Japanese defense activities are being gradually modified. A long-standing policy proscribing overseas security responsibilities has been modified to permit noncombat peacekeeping, disaster relief, and counterterrorism missions. Tokyo's recent dispatch of military personnel to Iraq, moreover, places its troops in a country where it is difficult to differentiate between combat and noncombat zones, where the UN's role is both modest and somewhat ambiguous, and where Japan's support is being provided to a US-led occupation regime. The realities of joint US-Japan ballistic missile defenses are impelling Tokyo to reconsider a long-standing ban on arms exports. Political inhibitions against exercising Japan's inherent right of collective self-defense are gradually fading. And Prime Minister Koizumi and opposition leaders are now actively promoting amendment of Japan's postwar constitution, including Article 9, though disagreements persist on the content of proposed revisions.

Adjustments such as these[2] have allowed Japan to extend its military missions, enhance its defense capabilities, and gradually modify institutional and political constraints on its defense policy. They also contribute to a more balanced US-Japan alliance that is acquiring broader geographic scope.

To be sure, some extremely important features of Japan's defense policy have not changed. Its nonnuclear principles remain firmly in place. Limits imposed by Article 9 of the constitution have been loosened, but not abolished. Leading politicians have expressed their intent to revise the constitution, but that will be a lengthy, painstaking process. The government has long affirmed its possession of an inherent right of collective self-defense, but remains reluctant to exercise it. Tokyo is in the process of rearranging its defense spending priorities in the light of new security concerns, yet the level of its defense expenditures, as a percentage of GDP, has changed little.

These residual limitations on its defense efforts notwithstanding, the aggregate changes in Japan's defense efforts and its expanding security role within the alliance have been quite remarkable. How can one explain them? The realization that Japan lives in a tough neighborhood, and confronts genuine security challenges—most immediately from North Korea—is the most significant contributing factor. The bitter aftertaste left by the Gulf War experience is another. A third is Japan's readiness to tackle a more ambitious international role in the fields of peacekeeping and counterterrorism: missions which have a certain resonance with its public and promise political rewards in its dealings with foreign friends. A fourth is the realization that the emerging generation of Japanese, for whom becoming a more "normal" nation seems an appropriate ambition, is more comfortable shouldering a broader array of "shared responsibilities" within the US-Japan alliance. Older voters, too, appear to welcome a more active global role, so long as it is compatible with the spirit of prudential limits that Japan has cultivated during the past half-century.

The Bush administration has made steadfast efforts to enhance the cohesion of the alliance. From the outset, key administration officials pointed to the US-UK "special relationship" as an apt model for the long-term evolution of its defense partnership with Japan. They have consistently and subtly encouraged a more expansive Japanese understanding of its international security responsibilities. Deputy Secretary of State Richard Armitage suggested that the Japanese "show the flag" in the Afghanistan campaign, and put "boots on the ground" in Iraq. But he and others have voided heavy-handed public pressure campaigns.

For his part, President Bush has cultivated close personal ties with Prime Minister Koizumi, praised his forthrightness in tackling tough foreign policy challenges, and taken his diplomatic counsel seriously. At the same time, the administration has managed bilateral economic issues deftly, playing down disputes and foreswearing gratuitous public advice on macroeconomic questions. It has sought, in short, to foster a constructive, comfortable relationship with Japan in which defense cooperation could flourish.

It remains to be seen whether the current direction and pace of change in the alliance can be sustained. Some items on the future agenda seem clear. For Japan, these include identifying conditions in which to exercise the right of collective self defense; amending current laws to recognize that international operations are central rather than peripheral missions; adjusting budgets and force structures to downgrade past priorities (e.g., countering an invasion of the home islands, the likelihood of which is extremely remote) and finance new requirements (e.g., creating the infrastructure and operational arrangements needed for ballistic missile defense); and further revising the rules of engagement for Japanese troops participating in international peacekeeping ventures. For America, they include refining US force and base structure in Japan in the light of current global security realities, coordinating approaches to regional challenges in Korea and the Taiwan Strait, and bolstering a new division of labor in the struggle against counterterrorism, which capitalizes on Japan's substantial capabilities in the field of "state-building."

While US-Japanese defense cooperation has been expanding impressively, one cannot blithely assume that the current trajectory is fixed and unalterable. The present path could be disrupted by large-scale Japanese casualties in Iraq or Al Qaeda terrorist attacks in Japan, crises with unexpected twists in the

Korean peninsula or Taiwan Strait, insensitive conduct by the United States, or the emergence of more assertive nationalism in Japan.

Even without such developments, it would be imprudent to expect or press Japan to become "the UK of the Orient" within the coming decade. Japan's nonnuclear norms have deep roots. So does its reluctance to participate in peacemaking, as opposed to peacekeeping, ventures. In these respects particularly, Japanese policy reflexes are decidedly different than those of the British. The concerns of Japan's neighbors about Tokyo's expanding security responsibilities, moreover, while currently muted, have not disappeared. And Japan remains a conservative society in which policies tend to change through the almost imperceptible accumulation of nuance, rather than through crisp debates and bold decisions.

Still, Tokyo is on a course, as Ralph A. Cossa suggests in this volume, which may permit it to assume within the foreseeable future the kind of international security role that Germany has embraced over the past decade. Americans should welcome that eventuality. Without articulating that specific aim, the other papers in this section—written by Ambassador Takakazu Kuriyama, Ambassador Rust M. Deming, Ralph A. Cossa, General Noboru Yamaguchi, and Professor Hiroshi Nakanishi —suggest ways to foster a more balanced and more effective alliance enjoying wider domestic support in both countries.

The US-ROK Alliance

Current prospects for the US-ROK alliance are less clear and less encouraging. It is marked by diverging perceptions of the principal threat, difficulties in aligning our respective policies toward North Korea, disagreements over supporting arrangements, (e.g., troop deployments, command relationships, and the Status of Forces Agreement), and a significant erosion of public support for the alliance among elites in both countries.

These developments are as surprising as they are troubling. The US-ROK alliance, which celebrated its fiftieth anniversary last year, is widely and appropriately considered a great historical success. It not only helped safeguard ROK independence for half a century; the secure environment, which it helped to create, facilitated South Korea's remarkable economic growth and its impressive transition to a robust, pluralistic democracy. By fostering peace on the Korean peninsula, the alliance has become a central feature of Northeast Asia's security architecture.

But for several years—and especially since early 2001—the alliance has been adrift, a hostage to diverging perspectives.

- American officials have branded the DPRK a rogue state; South Korean authorities view it as a potential partner in peninsular peacemaking.
- Arresting nuclear proliferation has become a top Washington priority, and Pyongyang is recognized as perhaps the most dangerous proliferator. Seoul,

on the other hand, seems more worried about US reactions to North Korea's nuclear aspirations than about Pyongyang's nuclear activities.

• As fears of North Korea abate, moreover, the value many South Koreans attach to the alliance and to the US military presence on the peninsula seems correspondingly to diminish.

• Americans still regard the North-South conflict as the major rationale for the alliance. However, key ROK officials now believe the core dispute on the peninsula pits North Korea against the United States, and they appear to covet the role of mediator—a stance Americans view as akin to declaring neutrality between an arsonist and the fire brigade.

It is possible to exaggerate these differences. Since President Roh Moo-hyun's inauguration in February 2003,[3] he has publicly hailed the alliance, visited US bases, pursued bilateral negotiations over the future redeployment of US units, and sent ROK troops to help in Iraq's reconstruction. The United States also has sought to avoid imposing additional strains on the alliance by consulting frequently with ROK officials, putting the discussion of troop redeployments into regular diplomatic channels, expressing a willingness to offer security assurances to Pyongyang under the proper conditions, downplaying talk of military options vis-à-vis North Korea, and deferring efforts to raise the DPRK nuclear issue in the UN Security Council.

Despite these efforts at damage control on both sides, however, palpable elements of distrust are visible in the US-ROK relationship. A January 2003 public opinion survey revealed that 39 percent of the South Koreans polled considered the United States to be the greatest threat to ROK security; only 32 percent regarded North Korea in that light. Foreign Minister Yoon Young Kwan was recently sacked, ostensibly for being too pro-American. With respect to North Korea, American and South Korean policies remain poorly synchronized; indeed, in some respects they seem mutually incompatible. The United States seeks to build a common diplomatic front to pressure Pyongyang to dismantle its nuclear program; Seoul appears eager to sustain a business-as-usual approach without much reference to Pyongyang's nuclear activities. Conversely, South Korea urges Washington to "engage" with the North by offering it tangible inducements to freeze its nuclear activities; the Bush administration dismisses such suggestions as "rewarding bad behavior." Whatever the respective merits of these competing approaches, their juxtaposition encourages Pyongyang to drive wedges between its adversaries, rather than confront the baleful consequences of its nuclear activities.

How can one account for the emergence of these conflicting perspectives within one of America's most durable and successful alliances? A number of factors are involved. The following seem most significant.

1. South Korea's Declining Fear of the North

Diminished South Korean fear of the North is perhaps the most notable development. Since the 1970s, there has been a dramatic shift in "the correlation of forces" on the peninsula. The South's economy has grown steadily and dramatically, permitting Seoul to finance a growing military budget even as the share of GDP devoted to defense declines. By contrast, the North Korean economy has stagnated—indeed, contracted—over the past decade. Acute shortages of food and fuel have paralyzed the North's industry, imposed extraordinary hardships on its people, and atrophied its military strength. The North's former allies, Russia and China, ceased providing subventions to the DPRK, and cultivated close political and economic ties with Seoul. Meanwhile, the ROK continued to enjoy US military backing, Japanese diplomatic support, strong commercial links with the world, and growing respect within Asia and the wider international community.

Against this backdrop, Kim Dae-jung, following the June 15, 2000, North-South summit, declared that the dangers of North-South conflict were a thing of the past. This was a convenient conclusion for the architect of the Sunshine policy. It also reflected and reinforced a widespread (if far from universal) consensus among South Koreans, particularly younger people. The recent revival of Pyongyang's nuclear program has undoubtedly been unsettling to South Korea's people and its leaders, but it has scarcely produced a general sense of public alarm.

Some South Koreans openly accept the legitimacy of North Korea's quest for nuclear weapons. Others seem to regard it as Pyongyang's search for bargaining leverage to be used in negotiations with the United States. Few register a significantly heightened perception of risk. Perhaps this is because Seoul is already hostage to devastating North Korean artillery attack in the event of war. Perhaps most South Koreans cannot imagine Pyongyang targeting such horrific weapons against "blood kin." Perhaps confidence that reunification will eventually be achieved, on South Korean terms, allows many to expect that the ROK will eventually inherit a nuclear deterrent of potential value against powerful neighbors.

Whatever the reasons, South Korea's current leaders appear not to be obsessed by dangers from the North. They are anxious to avoid backing Pyongyang into a corner, even inadvertently. They remain hopeful that magnanimous gestures will induce gradual reforms in North Korea. At the very least they trust that such gestures may postpone Pyongyang's collapse—with all the financial burdens that eventuality would pose for Seoul.

Needless to add, leaders in America—or for that matter, in Japan and China—do not view the resumption of the North's nuclear activities, and its acquisition of long-range ballistic missiles, with such benign diffidence.

2. South Korea's "New Nationalism"

A new spirit of nationalism has appeared in South Korea over the past decade. It has undoubtedly been spurred by pride in the nation's economic success. Hardships experienced during the 1997 financial crisis reinforced such sentiments, and gave them an anti-foreign and anti-American edge. Incidents involving US Olympic athletes and military troops, Bush administration criticisms of Kim Dae-jung's Sunshine policy, a perception of US "hegemonism," and the visible presence of American bases in the national capital may have broadened South Korean susceptibility to such attitudes.

This "new nationalism" has fostered sympathy for the North, and heightened ambivalence toward the United States. It has encouraged pan-Asian sentiments among South Koreans, increasing their sense of identity with China, while reinforcing their resentment of US "unilateralism" and US-led "globalization." It has deepened divisions between the Roh administration and its predecessors, since the mixture of pro-democratic, pro-labor, anti-American, nationalistic sentiment it reflects conflicts with the anti-communist, pro–United States, pro-business views of much of the Grand National Party's constituency. These differences in outlook tend, moreover, to reflect and exacerbate the pronounced and growing division between older and younger generations in contemporary Korean politics.

How durable this new brand of nationalism will be is unclear. It is stirred by events, and emotions tend to cool as memories of specific incidents fade. It is also marked by pragmatism, and underscores the "Korea first" attitudes of people who have always maintained a certain aversion to outsiders. For some South Koreans, this implies a foreign policy more independent of the United States. For others, it suggests a more balanced alliance with the United States, consonant with Korea's growing stature in the world.

Anti-American nationalism in Korea naturally evokes reactions in the United States. What is particularly noteworthy in this connection is that conservative commentators who have long supported the alliance with South Korea—e.g., William Safire, Dick Allen, Ken Adelman, and Charles Krauthammer—have expressed sharp criticism of recent ROK policies.

3. America's Post–9/11 Grand Strategy

The September 2001 terrorist attacks on the World Trade Center and Pentagon triggered profound changes in US grand strategy. This has altered, among other things, the way American leaders view US commitments, forces, and bases in Korea. For Washington, the "main enemies" were readily identifiable after 9/11: international terrorist groups "with a global reach," and the states that extend them safe haven or support. The "fulcrum of international politics" shifted away from Europe and Northeast Asia to the Middle East and other regions in which Muslim populations predominate. Formal alliances were not necessarily downgraded, but traditional allies were valued mainly as potential enlistees in "coalitions of the willing" targeted against new foes—above all, terrorists and nuclear proliferators. The current deployment pattern of US military forces and bases around the world is under review in the light of these new dangers.

From Washington's vantage point, in recent years South Korea's commitment to the war on terrorism has appeared tepid, its seeming indifference to North Korean nuclear activities mystifying, and its evident preference for the role of mediator or broker between Pyongyang and Washington perverse. With US forces now stretched thin to handle mopping-up campaigns in Afghanistan and Iraq, the Defense Department has hinted at reductions in the size of the US presence in Korea, and declared its misgivings about leaving the 2nd Infantry Division in static positions to perform a "tripwire" function that South Korea is capable of shouldering. Some reports suggest the United States might be prepared to relinquish operational control over ROK forces in wartime out of deference to South Korean political sensibilities.[4] Ironically, evidence of US flexibility on these matters has apparently inspired second thoughts among ROK officials, some of whom now worry that such steps might be misread in Pyongyang and elsewhere as heralding a hasty US retreat from security responsibilities on the peninsula, and others fear might allow the United States greater flexibility to consider coercive options against the DPRK.

4. China's Pivotal Role

These diverging perspectives have been reinforced in some respects by China's emergence as a key player on Korean issues. Until the spring of 2003, Beijing exhibited surprising passivity about Pyongyang's nuclear ambitions. The Chinese tended to consider Washington's assessments of the North's nuclear prowess as exaggerated. They discounted PRC political influence in Pyongyang, and they urged the United States to resolve its concerns through bilateral negotiations with the DPRK. In spring 2003, however, Beijing abandoned its aloof stance.

One can only speculate on the reasons for this change of perspective. Certainly the North's withdrawal from the nuclear Non-Proliferation Treaty (NPT) had a major effect. China had to worry anew about a neighbor, inclined to "brinksmanship," equipped with nuclear weapons. The possibility that North Korea's nuclear activities would encourage other Northeast Asian nations— above all, Japan—to emulate them inspired even greater apprehension. The United States, moreover, had made clear it had no intention of tackling this problem by itself; it insisted that it was a regional security issue. Nor could the Chinese rule out the possibility that if diplomacy failed, the United States might consider coercive options.

Whatever its motivation, during the past year China has become the principal broker of Six-Party Talks on the North Korean nuclear issue—a diplomatic format that Pyongyang initially resisted. Beijing has reportedly communicated China's own "red lines" to the DPRK leadership with clarity and precision. Coincidentally, as the thoughtful papers in this volume by David M. Lampton and Jing Huang make clear, the PRC has ceased public criticism of US alliances in Northeast Asia.

Two rounds of Six Party Talks on the North Korean nuclear issue have been held. Little substantive progress has been made. Further discussions are expected. All parties appear willing to "buy time" in hopes of avoiding a crisis. Local political concerns are driving decisions in the key capitals. But time may not be the answer, since the North Koreans are presumably continuing their development of nuclear weapons.

In the negotiations, China's substantive and tactical instincts appear at times more akin to Seoul's than Washington's. That is scarcely surprising. Both fear a military conflict more than the proliferation of nuclear weapons, and seem to prefer "buying off" the North rather than confronting it. Each is anxious to avoid Pyongyang's collapse—an eventuality Washington would welcome—because of the consequences they might face, including massive emigration, possible civil-military discord in the North, and new financial burdens.

Moreover, Sino-ROK relations have expanded dramatically in recent years. China is now Seoul's largest export market, and South Korea invested more in China in 2003 than it did in the United States. Leaders in both countries exhibit a keen interest in Northeast Asian economic cooperation, and political consultations have flourished.

This robust Sino-ROK relationship no doubt gives South Korea wider diplomatic flexibility in pursuing its preferred approach to North Korea. Korea's historical and cultural affinity for China is well established, and some South Korean officials may even regard reliance on China as a plausible and attractive alternative to long-standing dependence on the United States. In short, both Seoul and Washington are paying greater attention to Beijing. Ironically, this reflects some frustration in both capitals with the US-ROK alliance.

5. Democratization in South Korea

South Korea's democratization has brought huge benefits. In the long run, shared democratic values surely strengthen relations between states. That has been seen in US-ROK relations over the past decade and a half. Yet the results of elections—in both the ROK and United States—may on occasion complicate the coordination of bilateral diplomacy toward the North. American and South Korean politics periodically slip out of sync. President Bush leads the most conservative US administration in several decades; the Roh government is South Korea's most liberal. Their divergent perspectives certainly pose an obstacle to joint diplomatic initiatives toward Pyongyang. Since elections are looming in both countries, new leaders—in one or both capitals—might find it easier to harmonize existing differences, and develop a concerted strategy toward the North.

- The decisive constituency which swept President Roh Moo-hyun into office in February 2003 consisted of voters under the age of forty-five. They possess scant recollection of the US role in defending ROK independence. Many—particularly those in their late thirties and early forties—are inclined to regard the United States less as a liberator than past patron of authoritarian regimes; an accomplice of the ROK military at Kwangju; a bully in trade negotiations; and a predator seeking to buy up ROK assets at fire-sale prices during the 1997 Asian financial crisis. Harboring little apparent fear of the North, many of these voters tend to regard US military forces in the country as, at best, an unnecessary inconvenience, and, at worst, a slur on ROK sovereignty. A training incident in 2003, in which two young girls were killed by American soldiers, crystallized their outrage, which was intensified when the offenders were acquitted by a US military tribunal. The resentments generated by that incident, and the displays of hostility it inspired against US troops, have never fully dissipated.

- Among the salutary effects of the ROK's transition to democracy has been enhanced civilian control of the military. This has been accompanied by a steady decline in the policymaking influence of South Korea's uniformed services. A possibly inadvertent by-product of this development has been diminished institutional support within the ROK government for the alliance with the United States.

- Divided government is among the potential consequences of South Korea's mixed constitutional system. At present the legislative branch is controlled by the Grand National Party, which recently impeached the president. The current political deadlock in Seoul—however it is resolved—seems destined to stymie virtually all legislative initiatives for some time.[5] This in turn will inevitably divert attention away from needed adjustments in the alliance. Needless to add, fundamental differences within the Bush administration over policy toward North Korea have posed an obstacle to policy coordination with Seoul.

6. Globalization and Its Skeptics

Despite the benefits that "globalization" has brought to South Koreans, many still regard the financial "contagion" that forced the ROK to the brink of bankruptcy in 1997 as a symptom of globalization's dark side. That memory, among others, encourages some South Koreans to bolster the nation's defenses against globalization. Regional integration in Asia offers one such defense, and this may explain efforts invested in the rapid expansion of trade and investment links with China, the ROK's interest in negotiating a free-trade agreement with Japan, Roh Moo-hyun's enthusiasm for transforming Korea into the hub of a Northeast Asian economy, and South Korean enthusiasm for ASEAN Plus

Three (and the closer consultations among China, Japan, and the ROK which its frequent meetings encourage). None are necessarily inimical to US interests; all serve as potential or actual counterpoints to Seoul's long-time reliance on the United States.

Redefining the US-ROK Alliance

The concatenation of these developments has generated deep concerns about the future of the US-ROK alliance. As the papers in this volume attest, this has prompted officials on both sides to turn their attention away from managing the defense partnership toward redefining its terms. It is about time.[6] The forces, deployments, and command relationships supporting the alliance remain strangely fixed, despite profound changes in the balance of power on the peninsula, and the shifting contours of American and South Korean domestic politics and foreign policy priorities. This situation is not sustainable.

The chapters in this volume by William M. Drennan, Donald P. Gregg, Lee Chung-min, Kim Won-soo, Victor D. Cha, and General Kim Jae-chang all address the need for change in the alliance. Each offers suggestions for accomplishing such change. Collectively, they provide the basis for a healthy discussion that is long overdue. I shall not argue the merits and demerits of specific proposals, but applaud the fact that Washington and Seoul have begun to discuss such issues in a serious way.

> • Proposals for the consolidation and eventual redeployment of US forces south of the Han River are well defined, and have been extensively discussed between the US and ROK governments.
> • Plans for upgrading US deterrent capabilities in Korea, even as they are being redistributed geographically, are appropriate and timely. ROK forces are well qualified to shoulder those military roles and missions that heretofore have been performed by US troops stationed north of Seoul.
> • The US-ROK Status of Forces Agreement was amended in 2000 to assure its comparability to similar agreements with Japan and Germany. It remains to inform the South Korean people more widely about the changes agreed upon, and to demonstrate that Seoul and Washington can interpret its terms with greater flexibility.

Parallel command structures, as the United States learned in Japan, are compatible with a healthy alliance. A return of wartime operational control to the ROK would unquestionably pose significant challenges in the face of tough military contingencies. But there are good reasons to reconsider the current command arrangements. Timely adjustments would place responsibility for South Korea's defense where it properly belongs, bolster the cohesion of the alliance, and undercut North Korean propaganda which defames the ROK military as "puppets of the Americans" and dismisses the ROK government as a consequently unworthy interlocutor on security issues.

High-level efforts by Washington and Seoul are essential to underline the enduring importance of the alliance. Even more important is the task of refining its purpose. Deterrence is a necessary but insufficient aim. Associating the alliance more clearly with the task of enhancing future prospects for reunification—an aim virtually all Koreans ultimately share—could enhance its durability and augment political support.

Yet the most immediate policy task remains clear. Only if we can develop a shared US-ROK analysis of the current North Korean challenge, and a common strategy for combating it, will the alliance retain the relevance and reflect the promise that marks the US-Japan alliance today. Given the stakes, one must hope that Washington and Seoul will muster the necessary political will to address current problems purposefully and promptly. This volume seeks to offer practical suggestions to assist policymakers in accomplishing that goal.

NOTES

[1] While an April 1996 joint communiqué signed by President Clinton and Prime Minister Hashimoto reaffirmed the importance of the alliance as an instrument for defending shared interests and promoting shared values, the United States continued to experience occasional ups and downs on security matters. Japanese doubts about American intelligence on North Korean missile testing, and/or the US disposition to share that intelligence in a timely way, prompted Tokyo to develop its own autonomous satellite surveillance capability following the Taepodong test in August 1998. There was also acute discomfort in Japan when the Clinton administration began to characterize its relationship with Beijing as a "strategic partnership," a description which invited questions such as "partnership for what?" and "against whom?"

[2] Japan recently passed "Emergency Laws," which languished in the Diet for more than twenty-five years. They strengthen Japan's defense posture by establishing a National Security Council, and clarify the central government's authority vis-à-vis local authorities in the event of an attack on Japan.

[3] He was impeached by South Korea's legislature in March 2004, but whether the courts will uphold this decision appears problematic.

[4] Peacetime operational command was returned to the ROK in 1994.

[5] At least until the legislative elections on April 15, 2004.

[6] Post–Cold War adjustments in other alliances occurred more promptly. In the 1990s, NATO was expanded; US bases were withdrawn from the Philippines; and the US-Japan alliance was reaffirmed and its strategic division of labor adapted to changing times.

America's Asia Strategy during the Bush Administration

Kurt M. Campbell

The United States has for decades asserted central, strategic interests in maintaining peace and stability in the Asia-Pacific region and in preventing the region from coming under the domination of any power. This core US interest is not merely rhetorical but has been tested repeatedly, including in four major conflicts in Asia during the latter part of the twentieth century—against the Imperial Japanese Empire, on the Korean peninsula, in Vietnam, and during a long twilight struggle against the Soviet Union involving a sustained military buildup and near continuous preparations. For generations, the United States has not shirked the prospect of spending blood or treasure in pursuit of these national objectives. The Bush administration came to power at a moment when American power and position were unrivalled in the world and the United States was at the very center of the Asia-Pacific region's political consultations, commercial and trade developments, financial interactions, and military affairs.

This predominant position was neither preordained nor inevitable. Indeed, only a decade ago, conventional wisdom situated the United States in the midst of an inevitable and irrevocable decline spurred by wasteful Cold War preoccupations, and with Japan as the beneficiary. Yet, reports of the US demise were greatly exaggerated. As America's power and influence staged a comeback in the 1990s, nowhere was that influence more clearly felt and understood than in Asia. American staying power was a consequence of a resurgent economic performance, a bipartisan commitment to maintaining a substantial military presence in Asia, a continued nurturing of key bilateral relationships in Asia broadly, and a generally accepted view in the region that despite Washington's occasional unpredictability, the United States remained the only honest broker in the region.

It is probably not an exaggeration to say that despite a generally strong US position in the region for the time being, each of the above attributes associated with American power is now in play in ways almost unthinkable just a few years ago. The United States has gone from being a strong status quo power in most senses to one that now promotes a vision of change. In this sense, the

Bush administration approaches Asia in some ways as a revisionist power, bent on promoting its own vision of change.

The general belief on September 10, 2001, the day preceding the terrible attacks against the American homeland, was that US attention was shifting gradually but inexorably from a traditional preoccupation with Europe toward new strategic challenges in Asia. For the first time in modern history, every major challenge to peace and stability was now located on the Asian subcontinent, rather than on the European landmass. The Korean peninsula was dangerously divided and increasingly militarized, with a deeply unpredictable leadership in the North. China was seen by some prominent Bush administration members as a "strategic competitor" to the United States and the cross-strait dynamic with Taiwan was taking on dangerous military dimensions, given the PRC's continuing investments in missiles and power-projection capabilities. There was also the worrisome nuclear dynamic to the competition between India and Pakistan, which threatened to escalate with little or no warning. For these reasons and others, it was thought the Bush administration would focus like a laser on Asian developments and take extraordinary steps to revitalize America's traditional security partnerships in the region, particularly in Northeast Asia.

September 11, 2001, in retrospect if not immediately at the time, has altered expectations about American perceptions and performance in Asia more than perhaps in any other region with the possible exception of Latin America, where it was expected that President Bush would usher in a renaissance in hemispheric relations. The changes in Bush administration Asia policy as a result of the war on terrorism are perhaps more consequential, however, than elsewhere, with reverberations possible for generations to come.

The most important feature of American power and policymaking in the last two-plus years is the essential preoccupation with developments in the Middle East and South Asia, often to the disadvantage of the Asia-Pacific. The wars in Afghanistan and Iraq have sucked up most of the available bandwidth of the senior members of the administration, and to the extent there has been sustained diplomacy in Asia, it has been conducted through the singular lens of the war on terrorism. There has been intensive diplomacy directed toward the region, but mostly in service to the wider pursuit of gaining support for American initiatives in the global war on terrorism.

In this respect, one of the most intriguing new features of Bush administration policy in Asia is its determination to enlist various Asian states in out-of-area pursuits, military and otherwise, in the Middle East and South Asia. This approach has been more welcome and successful with some states than others, but in most of Asia it is seen as a choice between lending assistance to a peculiarly American pursuit and joining a grand coalition based on a shared sense of struggle. Although it would be going too far to characterize this American preoccupation as strategic neglect, virtually all Asian statesmen have sensed the "engaged elsewhere" quality of their interactions with senior American policymakers in recent years. Americans are not as attuned to specific Asian concerns and region specific worries, and the major interactions of Asian leaders with President Bush tend to be dominated by one topic: terrorism.

Another feature of Bush administration diplomacy and security policy felt strongly in the region is the deeply divided quality of the administration's internal foreign policy deliberations. This would not normally complicate the ultimate execution of American foreign policy, but the current discord is so acute that it has compromised the US ability to communicate clear and consequential messages. Normally, the major political battles are between the two political parties, with each vying to present a coherent international strategy that promotes security and prosperity. In the past few years, however, the most interesting and intense debates have been internal to the Republican party, with a small but well-coordinated cohort of neo-conservatives punching well above their weight in policy debates. Rarely before have there been such major ideological and political divisions housed within one administration. The unfortunate consequence of this divide is an overriding bewilderment in Asia and elsewhere as to the true red lines and bottom lines when it comes to American policy on a range of major policy challenges, such as over North Korea and Taiwan currently and on China policy at the outset of the administration.

North Korea is truly the land of lousy options, but the Bush administration's tortuous path to a slow-motion multilateral engagement of Pyongyang has taken years simply to launch, with every step of diplomacy fought over relentlessly among the various factions inside the administration. After another prolonged review of the options for dealing with North Korea, ranging from the simply unpalatable (engagement), to the unattainable at least for now (regime change), and finally to the unimaginable (war), the administration appears to have settled on the first, with occasional hints that its real policy preference may be none of the above.

The conundrum over North Korea policy has had several consequences. First has been the almost complete alienation between Seoul and Washington, a state of affairs to which both countries have contributed substantially, and which shows few signs of moving toward reconciliation or easing significantly. The second consequence has been the empowering of China in the regional diplomacy over North Korea. China is currently playing the honest broker role on the peninsula, a mantle normally reserved for the United States. This is a role that Beijing did not actually seek, but one that was thrust upon it by Washington. The surprise has been just how effectively China has performed at the pinnacle of diplomatic pressure and the extent to which other countries are beginning to look at China as a stabilizing actor in Asia. While the Bush administration has no doubt viewed China's role on the peninsula as useful in moving the ball forward in the short run, there is perhaps a lack of awareness about how well China's recent actions have set it up for the long term. Beijing's relations with Seoul, in sharp contrast with Washington, are good and improving, and China is well positioned for major strategic changes on the peninsula that sooner or later will arrive.

A further problem posed by North Korea is the apparent contradiction between how the United States is prepared to deal with a potential proliferation problem posed by Iraq (by preventing war) as opposed to an actual proliferation challenge in North Korea (by essentially stalling). The inclusion of North Korea in the "axis of evil" taxonomy was absolutely accurate, but it probably unnecessarily complicated joint United States, South Korean, and Japanese efforts to work with a thoroughly unpredictable regime in Pyongyang.

If the Bush administration has struggled mightily with how to deal with North Korea, it deserves very sincere credit for its handling of several key bilateral relationships, notably with Japan, China, Australia, the Philippines, and Singapore. Much of the rationale for improving relations is ostensible cooperation in the war on terrorism. Even if these countries did not share exactly the new American preoccupation with fighting terror, they could certainly hum a few bars and fake it. Nevertheless, the Bush administration has advanced true military cooperation and interaction, with these states and others, faster and further than at any time since Vietnam.

The United States has worked tirelessly in recent years to encourage Japan to play a more prominent role in regional security and global affairs. Now Japan may well be on the verge of both a modest economic recovery and a new assertiveness in the formulation and execution of its security policies. US relations with China during the Bush administration have risen like a phoenix from the ashes and most in the region are genuinely pleased to see greater comity between these two important though occasionally combustible partners. Although the United States by most measures dwarfs China's power, a funny thing happened while America went to war. China's influence in diplomatic situations, in boardrooms of corporate power, in military councils, and in multilateral settings has risen inexorably and exponentially. This is probably the most significant strategic development in Asia in over a decade, the importance of which cannot be underestimated, but there is little real recognition in the United States of the ground moving under their feet in Asia.

The Bush administration has also made enormous efforts to upgrade relations with Australia, the Philippines, and Singapore, and has also engaged deftly with Indonesia during a delicate stage in their democratic development and in their own internal struggle with Islamic fundamentalism and home-grown terrorism. The Bush team has also moved smartly to develop much closer ties with India and to draw it more energetically into the dynamic economies of Asia and away from its zero-sum calculations and political machinations with Pakistan. In another major strategic initiative, the Bush administration has moved toward greater clarity in terms of the traditional US policy of strategic ambiguity in cross-strait relations. The manner of communicating US intent was in the grand tradition of American clumsiness in these matters, the ultimate import of a change in US policy that both opposes Taiwan independence and promises to rally against any future PRC military adventurism is extremely significant.

These intensive diplomatic forays reveal a strong Bush administration penchant for acting bilaterally at a time when Asia is beginning to put much greater store in the conduct of its multilateral interactions. And here, US preparations and proclivities have not fared as well, while China's efforts at the ASEAN Regional Forum (ARF) and elsewhere suggest a greater comfort with and commitment to multilateral engagement.

Economic and trade policy has also been partially subsumed under the larger banner of the war on terrorism. The most notable Bush administration initiative has been the use of bilateral free-trade agreements to reward loyal allies in the global struggle with violent Islamic fundamentalism. What has been missing is a serious financial or trade agenda designed to promote further market opening and economic integration among the Asia-Pacific countries on a larger scale. Indeed, the Bush administration's stealth efforts to transform APEC into a security forum—in a sense replicating the actual mandate of the ARF—again reflect a preoccupation with terrorism and security pursuits. While these issues are doubtless important, the United States must also appreciate how central economic concerns continue to be among the leaders of the region. China's leaders now talk more about Asia's economic prospects and promise and their words are turning heads in Asia.

The Defense Department—without much internal coordination or examination—is now contemplating dramatic changes in where and how US armed forces are based overseas. Changes being considered for Asia include moving forces away from the Demilitarized Zone in South Korea, new access and deployment arrangements in Southeast Asia, and possibly substantial reductions over time in Japan. American defense planners want to create a global network of bare-boned facilities that could be expanded to meet crises as they arise. Taken together, the adjustments now under consideration—in where bases are located, in the arrangements Washington makes with host countries, in troop and ship deployments, and theaters of operation—will constitute the most sweeping changes in the US military posture abroad in half a century, greater even than the adjustments made after Vietnam and at the end of the Cold War. It would not be an exaggeration to suggest that these ambitious American plans will come as an almost complete surprise to most everyone in the region. While many of these moves may be commonsensical from a narrowly operational standpoint, they are raising profound anxieties in Asia. The new defense deployments will be designed to meet the new challenges of the global war on terrorism; the worry is that the traditional mission of promoting peace and stability in Asia may be compromised in the process. These anxieties have been exacerbated by a substantial lack of consultation on a matter of deep interest to strategic planners and politicians alike in the region.

Given the importance and power of the United States, virtually every strategic document is pored over and analyzed to glean insights into strategic shifts and policy priorities in Washington. There are several important texts to consult from the Bush era to get a sense of just how Asia fits into Washington's plans. Then-governor Bush's Citadel speech, the 2001 Quadrennial Defense Review, the 2002 National Security Strategy, and the Pentagon's report on Chinese military power all provide specific language about the region, its threats, and prospects for the future. The problem is that there is little consistency among the documents and in many places there are deep disagreements about worldviews and ultimate aspirations. These contradictions raise confusion, and the absence of a seminal or authoritative presidential statement or document about overarching US policy priorities in Asia is seen as a missing piece in the Bush administration's declarations of policy.

Despite some of the shortcomings listed above, the United States still enjoys enormous influence in the region and the Bush team has handled many diplomatic issues with dispatch. There is, however, a profound paradox associated with American power. America's "hard power" in terms of military capacity and resolve has never been greater; yet America's "soft power," in terms of the appreciation for its values and ideology, has never come under such duress. It is this enormous gap between our precision-strike munitions and the perceived adherence (or lack thereof) to our own political values that has led to near historic levels of anti-Americanism throughout much of Asia. These trends, if unaddressed, threaten to undermine general goodwill towards the United States and its citizens in the long run in ways that are bound to be inimical to larger American interests.

This growing gap has led to some complex coping and hedging strategies throughout Asia. There are worries about a preoccupied American colossus, a militarizing Japan (old worries die hard), growing instability in Southeast Asia, and most importantly, the rise of a confident, economically dynamic, and more subtle China. Every country in Asia today seeks closer ties with China and each secretly hopes that the kinder, gentler China we have seen on display in recent years is the one we will continue to see. And yet, the greatest uncertainties currently in the region are not over what China will do but how the United States will conduct its policy now and in the future. The enormity of American power coupled with the unpredictability of its policy decisions is unnerving to many in Asia and further reinforces efforts to seek greater certainty and stability through other measures, either alone or in combinations with other states.

US alliances with Japan and South Korea, respectively, remain the linchpins for larger American pursuits in Asia, and it is difficult to imagine how the United States could manage effectively without close partnerships in Tokyo and Seoul. Yet, just as US relations with Japan are probably stronger than at any time in modern history, US ties with South Korea are weaker and under greater tension. This imbalance puts a strain on both Japan and South Korea, but each in different ways. For Japan, the alienation between Washington and Seoul raises the prospect that someday soon Japan will "bear the burden" of hosting the US military presence alone in Asia and serve as the lone security "entry point" for the Americans into the region. For South Korea, the newfound closeness between Washington and Tokyo simply underscores the distance that now exists in the US-ROK relationship. There are also persistent anxieties in South Korea surrounding Japan's new assertiveness in the security arena and concern over what that might mean for the future of the peninsula. It is this imbalance in the two bilateral relations—more than any single development with either ally—that ultimately raises concerns about the future of US standing in Northeast Asia, a commanding position that America cannot afford to lose.

JAPAN

THE JAPAN-US ALLIANCE IN EVOLUTION[1]

Kuriyama Takakazu

The fifty-year-old Japan-US alliance[2] is going through a serious testing, the outcome of which is by no means certain. At issue is the dispatch of some one thousand troops of Japan's Self-Defense Force (SDF) to Iraq on noncombat missions. The necessary cabinet decision on the basic plan for the dispatch was made on December 9, 2004. The final go-ahead order for the ground troops has yet to be given as of this writing.

I. The War on Iraq

The issue has become increasingly contentious particularly since the loss of two Japanese diplomats on November 29. The tragedy caused a traumatic shock to the Japanese people. Public opinion is now overwhelmingly opposed to sending SDF troops to Iraq. The Japanese public seems willing to approve the dispatch of noncombat troops to engage in humanitarian and reconstruction aid. It is, however, extremely reluctant to support such a mission when there is considerable risk of troops being attacked by insurgents or terrorists and suffering casualties. Moreover, many Japanese are not convinced that the dispatch of troops under such circumstances is constitutional.[3] They are asking, Does the alliance with the US require Japan to take on an out-of-area security role?[4]

Prime Minister Koizumi, who stresses that Japan's interests are best served by making the Japan-US alliance and international (multilateral) cooperation compatible and mutually reinforcing, has stood firmly with President Bush on the war against terrorism and the war on Iraq. But now, faced with mounting public pressure, how he deals with the issue of sending troops to Iraq will affect Japan's standing as America's ally and also as a responsible member of the international community.

II. The Original Treaty

The Japan-US alliance has always been the mainstay of the regional security structure in East Asia, which has served the strategic interests of both the United States and Japan.

The original security treaty, concluded in the midst of the Korean War, reflected the reality of the postwar bilateral relationship at the time: Japan's total dependence on the US for its own security as well as regional security in East Asia, or, to use the treaty term, the Far East. John Foster Dulles, who negotiated the treaty, refused to give Japan a written defense commitment on the grounds that Japan lacked the capability to make its own contribution to collective defense.[5] Under the terms of the treaty, the US was granted an unrestricted right to use its military bases in Japan. In addition, the peace treaty gave the US the exclusive right to administer Okinawa, which was considered of great strategic value.

The Yoshida government of Japan, after some resistance, finally yielded to the US demand to rearm and established the Self-Defense Force at a modest size (180,000 troops) in 1954. This was of course a complete reversal of US policy during the occupation to demilitarize Japan, which was reflected in the new postwar Japanese constitution.[6] The reversal was necessitated by the Cold War. In retrospect, had it been possible for the Japanese government to amend the constitution to expressly allow the maintenance of the SDF, it would have avoided the need for the government to make tortuous interpretations of what the constitution actually meant. Amending the constitution, however, was not politically possible in light of the strong pacifism of the people, for whom World War II was a living experience. It would have also given rise to serious objections from Japan's neighbors which had been victims of its aggression.

III. 1960 and the New Treaty

1960 represented an important milestone in the history of the Japan-US alliance. It was the year the new security treaty replaced the original one. The conclusion of the new treaty marked the beginning of the long process of evolution of the alliance from a one-sided relationship of dependence toward a more balanced and mature relationship of shared responsibility.

What the Japanese side (the Kishi government) wanted to achieve by negotiating the new treaty was:

- first, to obtain a written US commitment to defend Japan against armed attack; and
- second, to place certain restrictions on the use of US military bases in Japan through a prior consultation mechanism.[7]

The US side (the Eisenhower administration) agreed to accommodate the Japanese position. Thus the new treaty represented for Japan a remarkable diplomatic success while what the US got in return was a better prospect of a stronger and more stable alliance relationship.

Yet Japan was rocked by large-scale anti-treaty demonstrations, which led to the last-minute cancellation of President Eisenhower's state visit and to Prime Minister Kishi's resignation.[8] The main reason for such strong domestic opposition was that many Japanese perceived that the treaty with its regional security role would draw Japan into an "American war" against its will. Thus the alliance faced a major crisis.

Few Japanese, however, recognized at the time the true significance of the new treaty, which was almost completely overlooked in the national debate: the prior consultation mechanism as provided for in the treaty marked the first step toward responsibility sharing between the two alliance partners. This should have been obvious from the fact that whether the Japanese government would consent, for example, to the launching of US combat operations from bases in Japan would be a crucial factor in America's ability to carry out its defense commitments to South Korea or Taiwan. Unlike the old treaty, which permitted the US to act unilaterally, the new treaty depended on the ability of the US and Japan to form a common position in order to deal with regional security in East Asia.

IV. The 1969 Joint Communiqué and the Reversion of Okinawa

The issue of responsibility sharing became the focus of negotiations in 1969 between the Nixon administration and the Sato government on the reversion of Okinawa.

Prime Minister Sato committed himself to the basic position that post-reversion Okinawa should be free of nuclear weapons[9] and that the security treaty including the prior consultation mechanism as applied to mainland Japan should also apply to Okinawa without modification. The Nixon administration, while sympathetic to Japan's legitimate wish to see Okinawa revert to Japan, was nevertheless concerned lest the reversion under Japan's terms (more specifically, the prior consultation mechanism) seriously undermine the US ability to maintain regional security in East Asia.

The Sato government correctly understood that if the reversion negotiation was to succeed, it must accommodate the US concern without compromising its Japan's basic position.[10]

The creative wisdom of the negotiators on both sides finally produced the Japan-US joint communiqué issued in November 1969 during the prime minister's visit to Washington for a bilateral summit. Paragraph 7 of the joint communiqué stated:

The President and the Prime Minister agreed that, upon return of the administrative rights, the Treaty of Mutual Cooperation and Security and its related arrangements would apply to Okinawa without modification thereof. In this connection, *the Prime Minister affirmed the recognition of his government that security of Japan could not be adequately maintained without international peace and security in the Far East and, therefore, the security of countries in the Far East was a matter of serious concern for Japan.*[11] The Prime Minister was of the view that, in the light of such recognition on the part of the Japanese government, the return of the administrative rights over Okinawa in the manner agreed above should not hinder the effective discharge of the international obligation by the

United States for the defense of countries in the Far East including Japan. The President replied that he shared the Prime Minister's view. [12]

In the author's view, the 1969 joint communiqué is a historic document concerning the Japan-US alliance since it was the first clear-cut statement by a Japanese prime minister that Japan was prepared to share the responsibility with the United States for the maintenance of regional security in East Asia within the framework of the security treaty and the bounds of its constitution. What is stated in the communiqué as the recognition of the Japanese government of the close relationship between the regional security of East Asia and Japan's own security is of course still very much relevant today, particularly in light of the uncertainty on the Korean peninsula.[13]

V. The Post–Cold War World and the Gulf War

The end of the Cold War brought about a tectonic change in the post–World War II international order with its East-West bipolar structure. The rapidly receding ideological and military threat of the Soviet Union and the emergence of new democracies in Central and Eastern Europe fundamentally altered the outlook of the West. The central theme of the political declaration of the Houston G7 summit (July 1990) was "Securing Democracy," which stated:

> As we enter the final decade of this century, which we intend should be a Decade of Democracy, we reiterate our commitment to support the strengthening of democracy, human rights, and economic reconstruction and development through market-oriented economies.

The governments of the G7, however, were not oblivious to the diffusion of various threats (both traditional and nontraditional), which would be new challenges of the post–Cold War world. The summit issued a "Statement on Transnational Issues," which focused on terrorism and nonproliferation as two major challenges. Its "Chairman's Statement" expressed the concern that "the Asia and Pacific region has yet to see the same process of conciliation, military disengagement, and reduction of tensions that has characterized East-West relations in Europe" and referred in particular to the Korean peninsula as "an area of sharp concern."

A serious threat to international order, however, arose suddenly from a different direction: the Middle East. Less than a month after the Houston G7 summit, Iraq invaded Kuwait. And the ensuing Gulf War became a major challenge to the post–Cold War Japan-US alliance.

In the context of the Japan-US security treaty, the Gulf War was an out-of-area regional conflict, which did not involve any legal obligation on the part of Japan of responsibility sharing with the US.[14] Nevertheless, the Kaifu government recognized the crucial importance of supporting the US efforts by diplomatic and military means to organize a broad international coalition of like-minded countries to repel the Iraqi aggression under the authority of the United Nations. That Japan's vital interest was at stake seemed beyond doubt. Not only was the Iraqi action a clear violation of the UN Charter, but it threatened the peace of the region on which Japan depended heavily for the supply of oil.

Hence Japan was among the first to implement the economic sanctions that were demanded by the Security Council. More importantly, it contributed 11 billion dollars to the US-led coalition forces[15] and extended 2 billion dollars of emergency assistance to three key front-line countries (Egypt, Turkey, and Jordan) whose economies were severely affected by the economic sanctions because of their heavy dependence on trade with Iraq.

The Kaifu government, however, recognized that even billions of dollars in financial contributions was not considered commensurate with a country of Japan's international standing without any human participation in the efforts of the coalition forces. Considering the constitutional constraint against sending SDF troops overseas for combat purposes, the government submitted to the Diet a bill that would authorize the dispatch of a noncombat corps to engage in logistic operations in support of the coalition forces. But the bill had to be withdrawn in the face of strong opposition in the Diet. The government, despite its serious efforts, still could not convince the opposition parties in the Diet and the public in general that sending troops strictly on noncombat missions in support of the international community to defend peace was constitutional. The only human participation by Japan in the Gulf War was a fleet of minesweepers that were dispatched to the Gulf after the cease-fire.

The Gulf War was a trying experience for Japan as it forced the Japanese to reexamine the meaning of their post–World War II pacifism. Foreign media (particularly American) showed little appreciation of Japan's large financial contribution: "too little, too late" was their favorite characterization.[16] They caricatured Japan's policy as "checkbook diplomacy." Many Japanese resented such criticisms. But it was by no means easy to justify to the critics why their pacifism was so self-centered and risk-averse. As a result, America's image of Japan as a dependable ally became negative as reflected in a number of opinion polls taken in the first half of the 1990s.[17]

The impact of the experience was such as to lead to a substantial change in Japan's security policy in the ensuing decade.

VI. From PKO to Japan-US Defense Cooperation

The first major change in Japan's policy toward a larger role in international peace and security was the enactment in 1992 of the law authorizing Japan's participation in United Nations peacekeeping operations (the so-called PKO Cooperation Law).[18] Under this law the Japanese government dispatched some 1,300 personnel including 1,200 SDF troops to Cambodia to support the activities of UNTAC. This was an epoch-making development, which led in the following years to participation in other PKO missions; e.g., in Mozambique, Rwanda, the Golan Heights, and East Timor.

It must be pointed out, however, that although the Japanese public has largely come to accept Japan's role in PKO missions, its security policy is still under the substantial constraints of the constitution as interpreted by the government and the pacifism of the public in general.

For example, when a civilian volunteer and a police officer were killed in an ambush by insurgents in Cambodia in 1993, there was a swell of public opinion in Japan calling for immediate withdrawal of Japanese personnel including the SDF troops. And it was only because of Prime Minister Miyazawa's personal decision at great political risk that the Japanese presence in Cambodia was maintained.

It should be noted also that the PKO Cooperation Law limits Japan's participation to traditional peacekeeping operations only (strict neutrality, no peace enforcement mission, and the consent of the governments concerned). It expressly prohibits the use of force and, therefore, permits the use of weapons for the sole purpose of protecting the safety of the Japanese personnel and those under their custody (e.g., refugees) when actually attacked.

Taking part in peacekeeping missions obviously does not fall within the scope of the Japan-US alliance within the narrow meaning of the term. If, however, one considers the alliance to mean a broad framework of global cooperation to strengthen international peace and security, Japan's active participation in such missions should be regarded as an important positive step in responsibility sharing with the United States.[19]

The next major development concerning the alliance was the agreement in 1997 on the "Guidelines for Japan-US Defense Cooperation," which set forth in specific terms the modalities of defense cooperation between the two governments under the security treaty:

- first, "under normal circumstances,"
- second, "in response to an armed attack against Japan"; and
- third, "in situations in areas surrounding Japan that will have an important influence on Japan's security (situations in areas surrounding Japan)."

What was noteworthy in particular was the third part of the guidelines regarding "situations in areas surrounding Japan" as defined above.[20] How the Japanese government viewed the relationship of the peace and security of the "areas surrounding Japan" (the Far East, or East Asia) to Japan's own peace and security was discussed in section 4 in the context of the reversion of Okinawa and the prior consultation mechanism of the security treaty. The guidelines agreed upon in 1978 meant to be the first attempt by the two governments to work out specific plans of defense cooperation, particularly between US forces and the SDF, to deal with such contingencies that would adversely affect Japan's security. The exercise, however, never went very far mainly because the Japanese government was reluctant to take the necessary political risk of facing negative public reaction.

The agreement on the new guidelines was prompted by the serious tension on the Korean peninsula that arose in 1993–94 over North Korea's covert nuclear activities and its declared intent to break out from the NPT regime. The US and Japanese governments, together with the South Korean government, engaged in intensive consultations with the common objective of preventing North Korea from becoming a nuclear weapon state, which would drastically change the security environment in Northeast Asia. The Clinton administration, faced with the possibility of military confrontation with North Korea, wanted to know in what way and to what extent Japan could support US military action under the security treaty if such need arose. The consultations revealed, however, that the Japanese government had practically no legal authority to ensure effective defense cooperation with the US either inside or outside Japanese territory. Although the tensions on the Korean peninsula eventually subsided, thanks to the so-called US-DPRK framework agreement concluded in 1994,[21] Tokyo and Washington both recognized the urgency of putting the alliance on a more solid basis capable of responding effectively to a future crisis.

With a view to translating the third part of the guidelines into domestic legislation, the Japanese government enacted in 1999, with the approval of the Diet, the Law Concerning Measures to Ensure the Peace and Security of Japan in Situations in Areas Surrounding Japan (in short, the Law Concerning Situations in Areas Surrounding Japan). The most notable feature of the law is that it authorizes the Self-Defense Force to engage in what is called "rear-area support" for US forces as well as in search and rescue operations in "rear areas." The term "rear areas" refers to Japanese territory and to those areas on the high seas and in international airspace surrounding Japan where no combat operation is, or is likely to be, conducted.

The reason the SDF's support for US forces is limited to noncombat missions and confined to "rear areas" (as distinguished from combat areas) is because, in the view of the Japanese government, the constitution does not allow the exercise of the right of collective self-defense[22] and also limits the use of force exclusively to the purpose of defending Japan.

It is clear from the foregoing that the 1997 guidelines and the 1999 law for Japan-US defense cooperation together mark a significant departure from Japan's passive posture of the past. But, in the author's view, the existing constitutional and political constraints make it difficult for the SDF to give full and effective noncombat support to US forces.[23]

VII. Out-of-Area Cooperation: Afghanistan and Iraq

The response of the Japanese government to September 11 and the subsequent war on terrorism was prompt and firm with strong support of the public in general. Prime Minister Koizumi immediately declared Japan's solidarity with America and the international community. And the government enacted, with the speedy approval of the Diet by overwhelming majority, the so-called law on special antiterrorism measures, authorizing the SDF to engage in rear-area support for the coalition forces in Afghanistan.[24]

Because of the constitutional constraints discussed in the preceding section, it was not possible to send ground troops to Afghanistan, where the rear areas (free of combat operations) could not be identified. Hence, a small fleet of the maritime SDF (MSDF), consisting of supply ships and escort frigates, was dispatched to the Indian Ocean to supply fuel to the US and other fleets of the coalition forces. As of today, the SDF fleet is still deployed there.[25]

What was significant in this connection was the muted reaction from Japan's Asian neighbors (e.g., China and South Korea) to its more active posture on security issues, which would have been unthinkable ten years before. This was partly a reflection of the strength of the international solidarity on antiterrorism, in which they all joined. But it also showed half a century after the end of World War II, Japan's neighbors have finally come to accept its larger international security role though they remain wary of its history. The change allowed Japan to assume larger responsibility and a wider role in the alliance even beyond the bounds of the security treaty.

Iraq presents a more difficult problem for Japan, both the government and the public. Several factors have made the sending of SDF troops a highly controversial and divisive issue:

- First, the legality of the war. Were the US and the UK justified in their use of force against Iraq without an explicit authorization by the UN Security Council?
- Second, the issue of WMD. Where are the weapons of mass destruction that Iraq was said to have been hiding?
- Third, Japan's national interests. What are those interests that are vital enough to justify sending the SDF to Iraq?
- And fourth, the definition of "combat." Given the highly unstable security conditions prevailing in Iraq, is there a "noncombat area" to which SDF troops may be lawfully dispatched?[26]

On these points, Prime Minister Koizumi and his government argued:

- Iraq repeatedly violated the 1991 Security Council resolution that set forth the conditions for the cease-fire and failed to comply fully with Resolution 1441, which gave Iraq its final opportunity to disarm.

- Even the UN inspectors (UNMOVIC) reported to the Security Council that there was a large quantity of chemical and biological weapons–related material which remained unaccounted for.
- Japan's dependence on the Middle East for energy makes political stability in the region its vital interest. Equally vital for Japan is to firmly maintain its alliance relationship with the US.
- The government would take every possible precautionary measure for the safety of the troops. A "noncombat area" was not meant to be the same as a "zero risk area." Unorganized hostile actions by non-state insurgents or terrorists were not considered "combat operations" under the law.

The government, however, is hard put to convince the public, which is constantly being exposed to reports in the media, both Japanese and international, of American unilateralism, indiscriminate suicide bombings, an increasing number of casualties of military and civilian personnel in Iraq, and the skeptical voices of some families of SDF members who may be sent to Iraq. It is an image problem that is difficult to overcome. No matter how hard Koizumi may stress that he is not sending the troops to engage in combat but in humanitarian relief and reconstruction operations, people still ask, 'If the troops are attacked and they use weapons to defend themselves, wouldn't you call that combat?' Under such circumstances, public reaction to SDF casualties could be politically explosive. (It must be noted, however, that recently there have been signs of an increase in the level of public support for the dispatch of SDF troops.)

The prime minister, therefore, is being extra careful in deciding the timing of his final order for the dispatch of the ground SDF troops.[27] Obviously for the prime minister the politically fatal scenario would be to find himself in a situation in which he would be forced to withdraw the troops.

VIII. Conclusion: Personal Observations

This paper has attempted to review, from a Japanese perspective, the evolution of the Japan-US alliance over the past fifty years. It focused on the issue of responsibility sharing particularly in the post–Cold War era. There are two aspects of this issue: one is defense cooperation under the security treaty and the other is out-of-area cooperation on some transnational issues such as terrorism and WMD. In this context, the author has tried to explain how far government policy as well as public opinion has come in accepting a larger Japanese role on the international scene. At the same time, he has also observed the legal (constitutional) and political constraints that place substantial restrictions on the extent to which Japan can assume an even larger security role, whether regional or global.

What follow now are my personal observations on the future of the Japan-US alliance.

• There are two factors that may affect the future of the alliance in unexpected but decisive ways: Iraq and North Korea. If the SDF troops in Iraq suffer serious casualties, which are likely to give rise to a highly emotional public reaction, Japan's security policy may regress to the time of the Gulf War. What is more unpredictable is the way the failure of diplomacy to resolve the North Korean nuclear issue will affect the threat perception of the Japanese people regarding the Korean peninsula. It all depends on how much credibility the alliance has, or is perceived by the Japanese to have, to cope with a major crisis.

• The major remaining hurdle that stands in the way of further evolution of the alliance seems to be constitutional. Recent polls indicate that public opinion in Japan is gradually moving toward amending Article 9 of the constitution.[28] The author, however, does not think that a broad-based public consensus is likely to emerge in the near future on how it should be amended.[29] What seems to be the best way under such circumstances is to free Article 9 by a political decision from the excessively narrow and legalistic interpretation of the government that denies altogether the right of collective self-defense and also restricts the right of individual self-defense. Such a decision, however, involves considerable political risk, which no prime minister can easily take on.

• Japan's aversion to the use of force will remain strong. And Japan has always respected and appreciated America's post–World War II internationalism, from which it has enormously benefited. Japan (both the government and the public) will feel more comfortable with, and more supportive of, the alliance when the US is seen to be less committed to unilateralism and more restrained in the use of force. When the use of force becomes necessary to defend peace, Japan would like to see the US first seek a UN mandate, which will give the needed legitimacy to the US action.

• Finally, the author believes that the alliance is in need of a newly defined mission beyond Afghanistan, Iraq, and North Korea. This is not to deny the importance of the issues relating to the so-called rogue states or failed states. The author simply wishes to suggest that there is a more critical conceptual question: What does the Japan-US alliance stand for (not against)? With the end of the Cold War, the Western alliance, to which Japan belonged, seems to have been replaced by various coalitions of the willing, which are formed from time to time depending on the individual issues to be dealt with. This is a highly unstable international system, somewhat similar to the age of shifting alliances in nineteenth-century Europe. Although the need for such coalitions cannot be denied, the institutionalized alliances of democracies should continue to serve as the core of international order. In the absence of the East as an ideological and political concept, the West is now being used as a civilizational concept, to which Japan does not belong. Then, where does the Japan-US alliance conceptually belong?

NOTES

[1] Although the author holds the title of advisor to the Japanese foreign minister, the views expressed in this paper are not necessarily the official views of the Japanese government.

[2] The original Japan-US security treaty took effect in 1952 simultaneously with the San Francisco peace treaty. It was replaced by the present treaty in 1960. Unless specified otherwise, the term "the Japan-US security treaty" refers to the present treaty.

[3] According to the official interpretation, the constitution does not allow the SDF to engage in combat areas overseas. Hence, under the existing law, troops are allowed to be sent only to noncombat areas. In carrying out a noncombat mission overseas (e.g., PKO), weapons may be used strictly to defend individual troops under attack.

[4] The expressed purpose of the Japan-US security treaty is to defend Japan and to maintain international peace and security in the Far East including Japan. The term "the Far East" is understood to refer to the area in East Asia that covers Japan, the Republic of Korea (South Korea), Taiwan, and the Philippines.

[5] Dulles cited the so-called Vandenberg resolution of the US Senate which stated that the US government should enter into "such regional and other collective arrangements as are based on continuous and effective self-help and mutual aid, and as affect its national security." Dulles' argument was that Japan, with no defense capability, could not meet such congressional requirement.

[6] Article 9 of the constitution, drafted by the occupation authority, bans possession of "army, navy, air force, and other war potential."

[7] It was agreed that the following three categories of US action should be the subject of prior consultation between the two governments (meaning a Japanese veto):

1. introduction of nuclear weapons;
2. launching combat operations from bases in Japan; and
3. substantial increase in the size of US forces deployed in Japan (above a divisional strength).

[8] The aftereffect of the crisis was such that the first US presidential visit to Japan had to wait until 1974 (President Ford's visit).

[9] It was widely known then that IRBMs with nuclear warheads were deployed in Okinawa.

[10] What the US side needed was some kind of credible (if not legal) assurance by the Japanese government that it would not veto US combat operations from bases in Japan when a contingency arose. On the other hand, the Japanese side did not think it possible to give any assurance that would be considered tantamount to issuing a blank check to unilateral action by the US.

[11] Emphasis added.

[12] The communiqué also included the prime minister's statements that "the security of the Republic of Korea is essential to Japan's own security" and that "the maintenance of peace and security in the Taiwan area is also a most important factor for the security of Japan." These statements were intended to reinforce the basic recognition of the Japanese government as stated by Prime Minister Sato above.

[13] As regards Taiwan, the situation has changed somewhat since 1979. Both Japan and the US recognize the People's Republic of China and have committed themselves to the principle of "one China." The US no longer assumes a formal defense commitment to

Taiwan. Japan and the US are both opposed to Taiwan's independence. At the same time, both maintain the position that the Taiwan issue should be resolved by peaceful means. And peace and security in the Taiwan area is still a matter of serious concern for Japan.

[14] Obligations under the UN Charter to comply with legally binding Security Council resolutions under Chapter 7 were a different matter.

[15] Japan's financial contribution was by far the largest among the donors except Saudi Arabia and Kuwait. In order to secure the necessary budgetary measures, the government had to raise taxes, which required the approval of the Diet.

[16] This characterization was not entirely fair because in the early phase of the war (both Desert Shield and Desert Storm) the US administration itself did not know how large its cost would be and how the expense should be shared among America's friends and allies.

[17] It should be noted that the unfavorable image of Japan was partly the result of the trade frictions in the early 1990s. The opinion polls turned positive in the second half of the decade.

[18] The law also authorized Japan's participation in internationally organized humanitarian relief operations other than PKO.

[19] This is why the Japan-US Joint Declaration on Security, issued jointly in 1996 by Prime Minister Hashimoto and President Clinton, states under the subtitle of Global Cooperation that the security treaty is "the core of the Japan-US alliance, and underlines the mutual confidence that constitutes the foundation for bilateral cooperation on global issues" and that "the two governments will strengthen their cooperation in support of the United Nations and other international organizations through activities such as peacekeeping and humanitarian relief operations."

[20] The guidelines were the product of the joint exercise of the two governments under the mandate given by the Japan-US Joint Declaration on Security of 1996, in which the prime minister and the president agreed to initiate a review of the 1978 guidelines and "to promote bilateral policy coordination, including studies on *bilateral cooperation in dealing with situations that may emerge in the areas surrounding Japan and which will have an important influence on the peace and security of Japan*" (emphasis added).

[21] Under the framework agreement, North Korea agreed to freeze its nuclear development program and the US promised to supply two light-water reactors, the construction of which would be financed primarily by South Korea and Japan.

[22] Such a view leads to the interpretation that the constitution also prohibits any noncombat action if such action is deemed inseparable from the use of force by a third party (say, US forces).

[23] For example, circumstances may arise in the event of an armed conflict under which it will be difficult to distinguish a "rear area" from a combat area where SDF troops cannot engage in support activities.

[24] At an early stage of policymaking, the possibility of using the 1999 law on defense cooperation (mentioned in the preceding section) for such a purpose was discussed with a view to saving time. The idea was soon discarded, however, because even with an imaginative interpretation of the law it would be difficult to consider Afghanistan part of "the areas surrounding Japan."

[25] Since December 2001, the MSDF fleet has engaged in over 300 operations supplying fuel to the navies of the United States and nine other members of the coalition forces deployed in the Indian Ocean.

[26] According to the newly enacted special measures law on humanitarian and reconstruction assistance to Iraq, SDF troops are authorized to be sent only to areas where no combat operation is, or is likely to be, undertaken—the same condition present in the 1999 law on defense cooperation and the 2001 law on anti-terrorism.

[27] The government currently plans to deploy 550 ground SDF troops in an area in southern Iraq called Samawah. They will engage mainly in humanitarian relief activities

(e.g., water supply and medical assistance). Three air SDF transport aircraft are also planned to be sent to transport goods for similar purposes.

[28] According to an NHK poll in December, for example, 37 percent favored amending Article 9 while 44 percent opposed it.

[29] Many among those who favor amending the constitution do not necessarily support a more active security role for Japan but simply feel the need to remove certain ambiguities in the language of Article 9 (e.g., can Japan possess armed forces?).

THE CHANGING AMERICAN GOVERNMENT PERSPECTIVES ON THE MISSIONS AND STRATEGIC FOCUS OF THE US-JAPAN ALLIANCE

Rust M. Deming

Since the 1950s, the US government's strategic objectives with respect to Japan have been remarkably consistent. These objectives include:

- Prevent Japan from once again emerging as a military threat to the United States (This objective receded quickly into the background as it became evident that postwar Japanese society had firmly rejected militarism);
- Support Japan's development as a democracy aligned with the free world;
- Ensure that Japan's industrial and human resources do not become aligned with major powers or alliances hostile to the United States;
- Maintain use of US military facilities in Japan;
- Harness Japan's political and economic power and influence, along with its military potential, in support of US interests, particularly in East Asia;
- Prevent Japan's exports from disrupting US domestic markets, undermining US industries, or threatening US technological dominance in key areas;
- Gain equitable American access to Japan's markets, including direct investment and, later, Japanese technology.

The relative emphasis on these objectives has varied, primarily as a function of shifts in the global strategic setting and the regional security environment; the economic power relationship between the two countries; the state of the US economy; the fluctuating influence of American departments and agencies, including the Congress, involved in policy toward Japan; and, importantly, the political and bureaucratic personalities on the American side. The interplay of these forces has sometimes produced internal tensions and contradictions in the development and execution of US policy, occasionally resulting in abrupt shifts in tactics and emphasis in the US approach to Japan. Nevertheless, the overall thrust of American policy has remained consistent: to build a closer, more collaborative, and better balanced relationship, with Japan playing a more active role in support of shared interests. The US has largely achieved these objectives, representing one of the major success stories of postwar American foreign policy.

The success of the US-Japan alliance was achieved because American leaders, along with their Japanese counterparts, made adjustments as circumstances changed. These adjustments have not always been smooth, but they have incrementally transformed the alliance from a patron-client relationship to partnership approaching true equality. The key transition points in the alliance have been:

- The 1960 Security Treaty Revision, which conceded to Japan the right of "prior consultation" on the use of American bases for combat operations, thereby removing a major irritant and putting the security relationship on a more equal and sustainable foundation;
- The agreement in the Nixon-Sato communiqué of 1969 to return Okinawa to Japanese sovereignty, removing the last vestige of the Occupation, in return for Japan's formal recognition of its shared responsibility for security in the Far East;
- The "Nixon shocks" of 1971–72, which shook the foundation of the relationship but helped push Japan into a more assertive international political role within the context of strategic cooperation with the US;
- The conclusion in 1978 of the Guidelines for Defense Cooperation, authorizing joint military planning for the defense of Japan and the allocation of roles and missions;
- The use of the term "alliance" for the first time in the 1981 Reagan-Suzuki communiqué to characterize the nature of the bilateral relationship, an initiative that created controversy in Japan but set the stage for Prime Minister Nakasone's 1983 declaration of the "indivisibility" of the security of the West;
- The US pressure before and during the 1990–91 Gulf War for Japan to put "boots on the ground," which created bilateral tensions but helped induce Japan later to put in place the legal foundation for dispatching Self-Defense units abroad for noncombat activities, adding an important new dimension to Japan's international role and to the alliance;
- The 1996 Clinton-Hashimoto security declaration, which set forth a post–Cold War rationale for the alliance, restored a collaborative tone to the relationship after the "trade wars" of the early 1990s, and set the stage for the 1997 revision of the Guidelines for Defense Cooperation, which established the criteria for bilateral defense cooperation in response to a regional crisis.

The events of September 11 and the war on terrorism represent another transition that is still being played out. Japan has responded with unprecedented speed and assertiveness, including dispatching naval vessels to the Indian Ocean to provide rear-area support for US forces in Afghanistan and sending SDF units to Iraq for reconstruction and humanitarian activities, despite strong domestic opposition. These initiatives represent the "globalization" of Japan's security perspective and, if successful, may open new avenues for the globalization of US-Japan defense cooperation.

The alliance has succeeded largely because:

- The US has continued to meet its explicit and implicit alliance obligations to ensure Japan's strategic defense and provide "public goods" in terms of a stable international political system, open trading regime, and Japanese access to the American market;
- Japan has stepped up its responsibility to play a greater international role within the context of a strategic alliance with the United States;
- Both sides have successfully made adjustments in alliance mechanisms and roles and missions as circumstances and power relationships have changed;
- The alliance has not been tested beyond its ability to respond by, for example, a renewed Korean war or a conflict in the Taiwan Strait.

The alliance has thus overcome many hurdles in evolving from a one-sided "post-Occupation" relationship to an increasingly equal partnership of great strategic benefit to both parties. However, the future is not assured. The uncertainties associated with the SDF mission to Iraq, the North Korean nuclear program, China's emerging power, conflicting views on the appropriate balance between unilateralism and multilateralism in response to security threats, and the ascendancy of a new generation to leadership positions in both societies are among the challenges the alliance will face.

This paper will review the evolution of American strategic thinking toward Japan, from the end of the Occupation through the war on terrorism, and discuss the challenges ahead.

I. Ending the Occupation and the Post-Occupation—1951–60

The US postwar strategic vision of Japan grew out of the objectives of American occupation policy: first, to reform Japanese institutions and policies to make the country into a vibrant democracy that would never again pose a threat to its neighbors; and, later, to help it rebuild so it could become a willing and vital partner in the containment of communism, both at home and in the region.

By 1950, there was agreement within the USG that further progress toward these objectives required the conclusion of a "nonpunitive" peace treaty at an early date. While the Joint Chiefs of Staff wished to delay ending the occupation until hostilities in Korea had been terminated,[1] the State Department and John

Foster Dulles, appointed by President Truman as the peace treaty negotiator, argued against delay on the basis that this would only create doubts in Japan about the wisdom of casting its lot with the United States. They suggested that the conclusion of a bilateral security treaty allowing the US to maintain forces in Japan could achieve the objectives of the JCS without the risks associated with extending the occupation.[2]

"Securing Japan's Adherence to the Free Nations of the World"

Truman supported Dulles and the State Department. In his letter of instructions to Dulles, the president spelled out that "the principal purpose of a settlement is to secure the adherence of Japan to the free nations of the world and to assure that it will play its full part in resisting the further expansion of communist imperialism."[3] In briefing the relevant congressional committees on the philosophy of a peace settlement, Dulles emphasized the danger of the industrial potential of Japan falling into the hands of the communists and the need to ensure the future security and economic stability of Japan.

Making Peace Conditional on a Military and Political "Alliance"

In Dulles' initial meeting with Prime Minister Yoshida to discuss the peace treaty, Dulles raised the need for a simultaneous bilateral security treaty, a concept Yoshida endorsed. Dulles also suggested the need for Japan to reconstruct its military, arguing, "The collective security burden must be shared by all in the free world."[4] Yoshida objected, citing Japan's constitutional constraints and the internal political dangers and economic risks, but finally agreed to the establishment of a limited "Self-Defense Force." Dulles also demanded that Japan follow the US lead on policy toward China, emphasizing to Yoshida that it would be difficult to obtain Senate ratification of the peace treaty if Japan did not make clear its intention to open diplomatic relations with the Chinese Nationalist Government in Taiwan rather than the regime in Beijing. US-Japan tension with respect to China policy would persist through the "Nixon shocks" of the 1970s and beyond.[5]

Broadening the Definition of Burden-Sharing

In the first statement of policy toward Japan after the end of the Occupation and the coming into effect of the bilateral Security Treaty, a National Security Council memo in late 1952 called for Japan to increase its army to ten divisions totaling 325,000 troops to deter a Soviet invasion of Hokkaido and encouraged Japan to join in the economic development of the free nations of the Pacific. The need for greater Japanese military and economic burden-sharing became a consistent theme of US policy over the next few years, with US policymakers voicing growing frustration with perceived Japanese foot-dragging. At the end of 1953 Dulles, who had become Eisenhower's secretary of state, wrote

Ambassador John Allison of his "exasperation with Japan's failure to get its economic and military act together." Allison responded that Japan was making progress, that overt pressure was counterproductive, and that "Japan need to be treated as an ally, not a satellite."[6]

By late 1954, however, a debate had opened within the USG on the wisdom of pushing Japan to rearm. Allison in Tokyo argued that the US should shift its emphasis to Japan's faltering economic recovery, citing the fertile ground that economic instability provided for internal communist forces and the lure of the Chinese market.[7] While the State Department agreed that "too much emphasis on defense could be self-defeating" and economic development needed higher priority, the military command in Tokyo and the JCS characterized Allison's approach as "defeatist" and argued that Japan should not only develop the military capability to handle its own defense but should help with regional security.[8]

President Eisenhower again sided with the State Department, and when Prime Minister Yoshida came to Washington in November of 1954 the focus was Japan's economic recovery and the need for Japan to play a more active role in assisting countries in Southeast Asia against communist influences. The issue of the Japan's defense efforts fell completely off the agenda. In April 1955 this policy was formalized in an NSC statement that stipulated that the US should avoid pressing the Japanese to increase their military forces to the prejudice of political and economic stability.

In the last half of the 1950s, the Japanese economy began to recover, Japan restored diplomatic relations with Moscow and entered the UN, the situation in East Asia stabilized, and US attention shifted to dealing with a series of Japanese demands for settling remaining postwar issues. These included renegotiating the 1952 Security Treaty to remove elements that were seen as impinging on Japanese sovereignty (e.g., lack of prior consultation); release of war criminals; and return of administrative rights over the Bonins and Ryukyus.

Renegotiating the Terms of the Relationship

In a May 25, 1957, letter to Secretary of State Dulles, the new American ambassador, Douglas MacArthur, recommended that the US take advantage of the strength and pro-American orientation of Japan's new prime minister Nobuo Kishi to revitalize the bilateral security arrangements by making them more equal.[9] MacArthur subsequently sent Washington a draft revised treaty. He also argued that the US needed to give Japan greater access to its markets to keep it from turning elsewhere and suggested that time was running out on the US ability to continue to administer Okinawa.[10]

In the spring of 1958 the NSC undertook a reappraisal of US policy toward Japan. The NSC listed five long-term objectives:

1. A militarily strong Japan able to defend its own territory and willing to use its forces abroad for defense of the free world;

2. Japan as a member of a regional security pact;
3. Continued US military presence in Japan;
4. The right to introduce nuclear weapons into Japan;
5. A strong Japanese economy, tied to economic growth in East Asia.

The study recognized, however, that while Japan was aligned with the US, there were serious tensions in the relationship, and the US needed to accommodate Japan on key issues. These included:

1. Agree to consult Japan on the disposition of US forces in Japan;
2. Eliminate discrimination on Japanese textile imports;
3. Reexamine the question of the Bonin Islands.[11]

Ambassador MacArthur endorsed the NSC study, adding that Japan had yet to become a dependable ally because of a feeling that it was being used in a one-sided manner for the US's own purposes and arguing that Japan wanted to be liberated from its "unequal status" and to gain control over the use of US bases on its soil.[12]

Over the next two years, the US and Japan focused on defining a new security relationship along the lines envisioned by MacArthur, with the JCS and to a lesser extent the civilian Defense Department leadership fighting a rear-guard action with respect to surrendering rights in the old treaty and delaying the implementation of the new.[13] President Eisenhower invariably sided with the State Department and MacArthur, supporting the JCS only on the issue of maintaining control over Okinawa, although with reservations on this as well.[14]

The new treaty was successfully negotiated and went into effect in mid-1960, but not without strong opposition to its ratification from the Japanese left which resulted in riots that forced the cancellation of President Eisenhower's scheduled June visit to Japan and the resignation of Prime Minister Kishi.

Broadening the Focus of the Alliance

In a statement of US policy as the new Security Treaty went into effect, the National Security Council declared that the fundamental goal of the US was to "assure that Japan continues to exercise its international role predominately in concert with free world interests," noting that militarily Japan was the key to the defense of the Western Pacific, economically it represented the second largest market for US agricultural products, and politically it was a voice of moderation among Afro-Asian nations. The NSC set forth specific objectives for US policy that differed in many respects from those (see above) laid out just two years before by placing greater emphasis on regional objectives:

1. Preserve Japan's territorial integrity against communist aggression and subversion;
2. Keep Japan allied with the US and the free world;

3. Support Japan's continued development as a stable democracy and prosperous country engaged with the free world;
4. Encourage Japan to contribute to international society by:
   a. Assisting the economic development of least developed countries in Asia and more broadly;
   b. Playing a moderating role among the Afro-Asian leadership;
   c. Strengthening its own defense capabilities to resist aggression;
   d. Continuing to provide bases to the US;
   e. Ultimately participating more freely in defending free-world interests.

With respect to the defense relations under the new Mutual Security Treaty, the NSC stated that the US should encourage Japan to develop its armed forces but avoid pressure.[15]

During this ten-year period, the focus of US policy had shifted from an emphasis on the rapid and heavy rearming of Japan while shoring up its economy to a more nuanced approach that recognized that Japan could contribute to US interests in the economic and political arenas as well as in the defense field. This reflected American appreciation of the changed circumstances in the region, including the stabilization of the situation on the Korean peninsula, the reduced risk of a Soviet invasion of Japan, the recovery of the Japanese economy, and Japan's firmer commitment to the Western camp under the Kishi government. It also reflected the strategic vision of American leaders, particularly Eisenhower and Dulles, who recognized that to secure Japan's support for the long term the United States needed to respond to legitimate Japanese grievances even if this meant conceding rights that the US military considered important.

II. Moving Beyond the Residue of Occupation—1960–1972

Consolidating the Relationship

The advent of the Kennedy administration in 1961 ushered in a period of relative tranquility in US-Japan relations. After the tumult over the security treaty in 1960 there was fatigue on both sides. President Kennedy was preoccupied with Berlin, Cuba, and Laos and left Japan policy largely to the experts, including Ambassador Edwin Reischauer. When Prime Minister Ikeda came to Washington in June of 1961, Kennedy responded favorably to Ikeda's suggestion that new mechanisms for bilateral consultations be established, and the Cabinet Economic Committee and the Security Subcommittee were inaugurated. An October 1961 NSC policy paper endorsed the basic themes set down the year before (see above) but recommended that security aspects of the relationship be downplayed in light of the 1960 disturbances. The NSC also established an interagency process to consider the question of Okinawa, beginning the process that would lead to the return of the Ryukyus in 1972.[16] Reischauer for his part focused on repairing the "broken dialogue" with the Japanese intellectual community and increasing cultural and human exchanges between the two countries.

By the end of 1962, defense issues were back on the agenda, with Secretary of State Rusk pushing Japan on defense spending but this time targeting host-nation support with a proposal that Japan pay all the local costs of US forces stationed there.[17] The Kennedy administration, increasingly concerned about the US's deteriorating balance of payment situation, focused on the economic implications of defense issues, and even considered cutting US forces in Japan to save foreign exchange.[18]

A Vietnamese Lens

With the exception of the issue of Okinawa, which became the subject of increasingly intense US-Japan interchanges and interagency debate, the Johnson administration saw Japan almost exclusively through a Vietnamese lens. The summit meeting between President Johnson and Prime Minister Sato focused on Asian issues, with the US calling on Japan to assume greater regional responsibility, including increasing its official development assistance to Southeast Asia to help stabilize those countries in the face of communist pressure.[19]

By the 1967 Johnson-Sato summit, Vietnam had become an issue in bilateral relations because of strong criticism by the Japanese press and public of the US bombing of North Vietnam and Johnson administration dissatisfaction with Japan's "passive" position. Sato, however, agreed to publicly support the US policy on Vietnam in return for US agreement in principal to return the Bonin Islands and greater Japanese involvement in Okinawa.

In a final meeting with Foreign Minister Miki in the fall of 1968, Rusk described US priorities in its relations with Japan as (1) greater Japanese leadership in Asian regionalism; (2) assumption of greater responsibility for its own defense; (3) close consultations on developments in China; and (4) greater economic and technical assistance to the nations of Southeast Asia,[20] demonstrating that greater Japanese regional leadership had reached the top of the US agenda.

Shocking Japan into a More Activist Role

The Nixon administration policy toward Japan gave the appearance of being fundamentally contradictory. One the one hand President Nixon recognized the need to remove the major irritant in the alliance by agreeing at the 1969 summit with Prime Minister Sato to return Okinawa to Japan in exchange for Sato's recognition of Japan's shared responsibility for the security of the Far East; on the other, President Nixon's decisions to open relations with China, to devalue the dollar without consultation with Japan, and to invoke the "Trading with the Enemy Act" to impose unilateral textile quotas were seen by the Japanese as breaking basic postwar bargains.

Consistent with his "Guam Doctrine," which asked Asian states to take more responsibility for their own defense, both Nixon and Henry Kissinger believed that Japan needed to be "shocked" out of its postwar habit of relying almost exclusively on the United States for security while pursuing a single-minded mercantilist policy. They also hoped to prod Tokyo to do more to use its economic and political strength in support of common interests.[21] After the "shocks" wore off, the Nixon administration established a constructive relationship with Japan, encouraging its normalization with Beijing ahead of the US's and expressing understanding of the need for Japan to break with the US on policy toward the Middle East in the wake of the 1973 oil embargo.[22] Nixon also became the first American president to voice support for a permanent UN Security Council seat for Japan.

The end of this period marked the formal close of the postwar era with the return of Okinawa, the reintroduction of China into the strategic equation in East Asia, detente with the Soviet Union, and the ascendancy of trade issues to the top of the bilateral agenda. The change in the strategic environment took US pressure off Japan on defense issues and gave both the US and Japan more diplomatic room to maneuver. In addition, the rise of Japan's economy introduced a new power balance, and new tensions, into the relationship. Military, political, and economic cooperation with Japan remained a strategic imperative for the United States, but the terms of this cooperation were in transition.

III. Building an Alliance—1973–1989

The mid-1970s was a period of steady consolidation of the security relationship. The United States reduced its military presence in the Tokyo urban area, removing daily irritants, while forward deploying the aircraft carrier *Midway* to Yokosuka, thereby demonstrating US resolve to remain engaged in East Asia after its withdrawal from Vietnam. President Ford's 1974 visit to Tokyo, the first ever by an American president, was largely ceremonial, as was Emperor Hirohito's 1975 three-week tour of the United States, but both served to demonstrate publicly the friendly relations between the two countries. Various corporate scandals (Lockheed, Toshiba) and trade issues (color television, steel), along with revelations about possible nuclear weapons on American naval vessels in Japanese ports, ruffled the relationship without fundamentally disturbing close political and military cooperation.

Korean Troop Withdrawals and Nuclear Nonproliferation

The advent of the Carter administration in 1977 introduced two disruptive elements into the bilateral relationship: President Carter's proposal to remove US forces from Korea and his efforts to prevent the operation of Japan's nuclear fuel reprocessing plant at Tokai Mura as part of the president's nonproliferation campaign to keep separated plutonium out of the nuclear fuel cycle. The Japanese regarded the first proposal as destabilizing and the second as threatening its nuclear power program, which was seen as essential to its energy security and economic survival. Although Carter eventually backed away from the Korean troop withdrawal idea and compromised on Tokai Mura, the two issues raised doubts in Japan about the reliability of the US as an ally.

Strengthening Defense and Political Cooperation

On bilateral defense issues, the Carter administration took a low-key approach, focusing on:

- Helping Japan to make qualitative improvements in its defense forces through acquisition of P-3Cs and F-15s;
- Increasing Japanese host-nation support through labor cost sharing;
- Negotiating the Guidelines for Defense Cooperation that authorized joint planning on the defense of Japan between the uniformed Japanese and American services;
- Opening discussion on the respective roles and missions of US and Japanese defense forces in carrying out the security treaty, which later led to Japan assuming responsibility for protecting specific sea-lanes.[23]

With respect to political cooperation, the administration encouraged Prime Minister Fukuda's active diplomacy in East Asia and the Middle East and sought to channel Japan's economic assistance in support of the Camp David process and other shared interests. This was the first step toward a "strategic dialogue" between deputy foreign ministers that was formalized in the 1980s.

Combating the "Evil Empire"

In 1979, the Soviet invasion of Afghanistan, coupled with the ongoing buildup of Russian forces in the Far East, altered fundamentally the global strategic atmosphere and strongly influenced the tone of US-Japan security relations. Tokyo joined Washington in boycotting the Moscow Olympics, and the Japanese public became more receptive to US-Japan defense cooperation.

The Reagan administration saw Japan as a key player in the struggle against the "evil empire" and embraced Tokyo as a "global partner" that needed to take more responsibility for maintaining the international security and economic systems from which it benefited. Specific policy objectives included:

- Induce Japan to break the 1 percent limit on defense spending so that it could improve its naval and air defense capabilities and increase host-nation support for US forces;
- Persuade Japan to share military technology with the US;

- Expand the discussion on the respective roles and missions of US and Japanese forces in defense of Japan;
- Explore possible cooperation on missile defense;
- Station F-16s at Misawa Air Base in northern Japan as part of the maritime strategy of horizontal escalation in the event of Soviet aggression in Europe;
- Make Japan face up to economic issues, including rectifying the trade imbalance, controlling exports in sensitive sectors, and opening markets to US products.

Reagan brought in a strong team of like-minded officials on Asian policy[24] who took key State Department, Pentagon, and NSC positions, which ensured good interagency coordination on political and security issues related to Japan. When George Shultz became secretary of state in May 1982, he brought with him considerable knowledge and understanding of Japan and his later appointment of Michael H. Armacost as under secretary of state further strengthened the State Department role on Japan.

Bringing the Alliance Out of the Closet

The tone of the new relationship was set when Prime Minister Zenko Suzuki came to Washington in May of 1981. The joint communiqué used the word "alliance" for the first time to characterize the relationship, and Japan agreed to join in the protection of two sea-lanes. These developments were marred by Suzuki's subsequent refutation of "alliance" as implying a military relationship and the resignation of his foreign minister, but they opened the door to expanded defense cooperation.

In late 1982 Suzuki was replaced by Yasuhiro Nakasone, a long-time nationalist and defense hawk who was eager to develop Japan's strategic relationship with the United States, referring to Japan as "an unsinkable aircraft carrier" in the Cold War. During his first visit to Washington in January of 1983, Nakasone and Reagan hit it off and launched the "Ron-Yasu" relationship. Nakasone had announced a significant increase in Japan's defense budget and made clear that he was ready to move Japan more directly into the global Western security framework. This was solidified at the Williamsburg summit in May 1983 when Nakasone declared that the defense of the West was indivisible, a position motivated as much by concern that NATO-Soviet negotiations on SS-20s would not include the Soviet Far East as out of a desire to strengthen Japan's identification with the US and Europe. The US insistence on a global "zero based" solution was critical in demonstrating to the Japanese that it would not sacrifice their security interests for those of its European allies.

While security issues dominated the Reagan administration approach to Japan, trade issues were not absent. The Reagan team continued the Carter administration efforts to induce Japan to take macroeconomic steps to rectify the trade imbalance, without notable success. Despite its free trade orientation, the Reagan administration could not resist congressional, industry, and labor pressure to negotiate "voluntary restraints" on Japan's exports of steel and autos. The administration broke new ground in undertaking sector-specific negotiations to try to open Japanese markets to US exports, a process that proved frustrating for both sides but which did produce some results.[25]

Trade and Defense Intersect

This period also saw the first clear crossover between the US defense and trade agendas in the form of the FSX issue. The Japanese had for some time been intent on developing indigenously their next-generation ground-attack aircraft. US defense officials had sought to persuade their Japanese counterparts that from the perspective of interoperability and efficient use of scarce defense resources it would be much better for Japan to buy an off-the-shelf American aircraft or to engage in joint development and production. "Techno-nationalists" in Congress and trade agencies saw the program as the Defense and State departments naively providing Japan with technology that it could use to develop commercial aircraft. The Japanese reluctantly agreed to a joint program to develop and produce a plane based on the F-16, but the heretofore sacrosanct barrier between defense cooperation and trade disputes had been broken.

Contributing to the End of the Cold War

As the Cold War came to a triumphant close, the United States could be very satisfied with the contribution made by the US-Japan alliance. The alliance had played a critical role in maintaining relative stability in East Asia, not only by providing the platform for the US military presence but by allowing Japan to develop its economy and become the engine of growth for the region. Particularly in the later days of the Cold War, Japan's solidarity with the West had put increased pressure on the Soviet Union and perhaps hastened its demise.

For Japan, however, the collapse of the Soviet Union represented less of a clear-cut triumph. Remnants of the Cold war remained in East Asia in the form of a divided Korean peninsula and Russian occupation of Japan's Northern Territories, and Japanese leaders were worried that the US and Western Europe would forget about the Asian angle as they rushed to embrace Yeltsin and provide assistance to a struggling Russia.

Both countries faced the challenge of redefining their relationship in a world without the unifying force of a powerful and aggressive Soviet Union.

IV. Adjusting to the Post–Cold War World—1989–2001

When President Bush went to Japan for the funeral of Emperor Hirohito, two weeks after the president's inauguration, the only issue of substance taken up in side meetings was the FSX arrangement, with the new administration demanding that the agreement be reopened to increase US work-share at the production stage. This signaled that economic factors were not only intruding into security issues but were becoming dominant. American concern about Japanese economic penetration of the US, symbolized by its purchase of Rockefeller Center and Pebble Beach, and Japanese technological domination of certain fields (e.g., semiconductors) had combined with "revisionist" arguments that the US "free ride" to Japan on defense and access to the US market had allowed Japan to threaten the US economically.

Managing Trade Differences in the Context of a Global Partnership

While trade issues had risen to the top of the agenda, the Bush administration was very mindful of the importance of strategic cooperation with Japan, coining the term "global partnership" to characterize an effort to harness Japan's economic and political power to achieve agreed international objectives. To keep differences on trade issues from poisoning the overall relationship, the administration sought to find joint projects, such as assistance programs in Eastern Europe and Central America and projects to address transnational issues on the environment and scientific research, that would help demonstrate to the publics in both countries the benefits of US-Japan cooperation.

The Bush administration also intensified coordination with Japan with respect to foreign policy issues, particularly Russia, China, Cambodia, and Korea, generally to good effect. Tensions did develop, however, with respect to Malaysian prime minister Mahathir's proposal for an "East Asian Economic Caucus," excluding the United States, as a counterweight to NAFTA. The US publicly and privately insisted that the more inclusive APEC should be the forum for regional economic discussions, while Japan was reluctant to reject the idea outright.

The Gulf War

An issue that neither the US nor Japan had anticipated proved to be the one that most shaped the relationship—Iraq's invasion of Kuwait and the Gulf War.[26] The Bush administration was not unmindful of the constitutional, legal, political, and psychological constraints on Japan's ability to participate directly in the international coalition, but American officials were deeply disappointed by Japan's perceived passive response, particularly given Japan's stake in the UN, the rule of law, and stability in the Middle East. The American public more broadly, already in a "Japan-bashing" mood because of trade issues, saw Japan's absence as another example of a "free ride" on the back of the United States.

Under American pressure, the Japanese government made an effort to pass legislation that would have allowed Japan to send noncombatants, but when this failed the GOJ fell back on financial contributions. The US complicated the process by sending mixed messages on what was expected, but in the end Japan produced a very generous total of $13 billion. Unfortunately the protracted process and subsequent disputes about exchange rates kept the GOJ from getting due recognition abroad for its contribution.

With the success of the Gulf War, US-Japan relations soon returned to normal, but the lessons were not lost on either side. The two governments recognized that if a crisis developed closer to home, e.g. Korea, and Japan responded in the same passive way, the alliance would be strained to the breaking point. Japan quickly passed the Peacekeeping Law, which allowed it to send forces abroad (with tight restrictions) for UN peacekeeping operations (the first contingent went to Cambodia) and reorganized its crisis management procedures. The Bush administration, however, facing a faltering American economy with an election approaching, turned its attention to trade issues, leading to the ill-conceived and ill-fated January 1992 "Auto Summit" in Tokyo and setting a tone of mutual recrimination that carried over into the Clinton administration.

"It's the Economy, Stupid"

Even before the inauguration, the new administration launched a review of policy toward Japan, led by the incoming trade and economic team, many of whom had had business or academic experience with Japan. The premise of this review was that while the security alliance and political partnership were in good shape, the economic relationship was not. Japan's economic might and predatory trade and industrial practices posed a serious threat to American interests and needed to be attacked aggressively and comprehensively. The team also shared a conviction that during the Cold War the US had "pulled its punches" on trade issues out of deference to the alliance. Now, the US was free to bring much more pressure to bear on Japan with respect to the economic agenda with less worry about the implications for the security relationship.

Three years of acrimonious negotiations ensued, reaching a climax with an accord on autos in May 1995. For all the effort and political capital expended, the results were modest, and, in the words of one close observer, "the framework negotiations that had begun with a bang ended with a whimper."[27]

Reanchoring a Drifting Alliance

During the first three years of the Clinton administration, the security agenda had been allowed to drift. There was no senior official in the Defense Department who "took charge" of the US-Japan security relationship the way figures like Richard Armitage had in the Reagan and Bush administrations. Professionals in the Defense and State Departments and in the embassy in Tokyo continued to push the agenda forward with agreements to pursue joint research on theater missile defense and to fully fund host-nation support in the face of GOJ budget pressure, but the Clinton administration approach to Japan lacked an overall strategic framework.

The appointment of Joseph Nye in late 1994 as assistant secretary for international security affairs at the Pentagon represented a turning point. Nye recognized that even with the end of the Cold War, the US-Japan alliance remained essential to US interests in terms of dealing with the tensions on the Korean peninsula, managing the rise of Chinese power, and maintaining American influence in East Asia. The North Korean nuclear crisis that had erupted earlier that year (see below) was a wake-up call to both US and Japanese officials because the crisis made it clear that the GOJ did not have in place the legal framework or the political consensus necessary to support the US in the event of a military contingency on the peninsula.

Nye also recognized that with the collapse of the Soviet threat, a new rationale needed to be articulated for the US-Japan alliance and the US military presence in East Asia that was not based on containing a specific enemy. The result was the East Asian Strategic Review (EASR), better known as the Nye Initiative, issued in early 1995, which described the US-Japan alliance and the US's other security arrangements in East Asia region as the "oxygen" that allowed the region to flourish by maintaining stability and avoiding a power vacuum. The study also reaffirmed the US intention to maintain about 100,000 forward deployed forces in the Western Pacific, reassuring Japan about the administration's fundamental commitment to remain engaged in the region.

With the EASR study as a basis, American and Japanese officials set about drafting a "US-Japan Security Declaration," to be issued when President Clinton was to visit Japan for the APEC summit in November 1995. The purpose of the declaration was to celebrate the success of the alliance, reaffirm the shared values and interests on which it was based, and revitalize the security relationship by providing a post–Cold War rationale for the continued presence of American forces in Japan and our bilateral defense cooperation. The declaration was also designed to lay out an agenda for strengthening the alliance by revising the Guidelines for Defense Cooperation to promote cooperation in dealing with situations that "may emerge in areas surrounding Japan" (e.g., the Korean peninsula), putting in place a cross-servicing agreement, and addressing issues associated with US bases in Japan.

The concept of a security declaration took on new urgency with the gang rape of a twelve-year-old Okinawan girl by three US servicemen, a crime that produced an explosion of outrage throughout Japan and sparked a national debate on the need for a US military presence in Japan after the end of the Cold War. The US moved quickly to deal with the crisis with public apologies by President Clinton and Ambassador Mondale and agreed to set up a "Special Action Committee on Okinawa" (SACO) to examine the consolidation of US facilities in Okinawa and other measures to improve relations between the US military and local community.

Fortuitously, a domestic budget crisis in the US forced President Clinton to cancel his participation in the November APEC summit, and release of the declaration was delayed until April when the president was to visit Japan and Korea. The intervening five months allowed the debate in Japan on the alliance to play out, with a consensus developing that the security relationship remained necessary, a conclusion helped by the Chinese missile tests in March that landed near Taiwan. In addition during this period SACO produced a report that contained a number of significant steps, including the return of Futenma Marine Corps Air Station, and Prime Minister Hashimoto replaced the figurehead socialist Prime Minister Tomiichi Murayama, putting in place someone supportive of and conversant with the US-Japan alliance.

The April summit was a major success and went far in restoring vitality to the alliance. In 1997 the revised Guidelines for Defense Cooperation were issued, which shifted the focus of the alliance from defense of Japan to cooperation in responding to regional contingencies. The guidelines spelled out in detail the kind of assistance that Japan could provide in such situations, including rear-area support and such noncombat operational activity as minesweeping, surveillance, and intelligence gathering, and authorized detailed bilateral planning. At the same time the guidelines reaffirmed that Japan would conduct all its actions within the limitations of its constitution and in accordance with its exclusively defense-oriented policy, thereby attempting to reassure both the Japanese public and Japan's neighbors.[28]

Cooperation on Korea and Other Regional Issues

Beyond addressing economic imbalances and revitalizing the security relationship, the Clinton administration attached importance to enlisting Japanese support on foreign policy issues, particularly with respect to Korea, China, Russia, and Asia-Pacific cooperation.

North Korea reemerged as a major issue in 1994 when it left the nuclear Non-Proliferation Treaty, broke IAEA safeguards, and began separating plutonium from spent nuclear fuel. The intervention of former president Carter defused the crisis. The administration proceeded to negotiate an "Agreed Framework" with Pyongyang by which North Korea promised to freeze its nuclear activities in exchange for US agreement to provide North Korea with two light water reactors to replace the proliferation-prone heavy water reactors. Washington, however, intended to have Seoul and Tokyo pay for the $4 billion project but had not consulted with either in advance.

The Japanese were furious, and there was strong resistance in the Diet to any such deal, but after months of a combination of strokes and threats the GOJ got on board. The tripartite Korean Energy Development Organization (KEDO) was set up to administer the project, and the US organized the Trilateral Consultative Group (TCOG) to coordinate policy toward North Korea among the three countries. The process worked surprisingly well given the different perspectives and politics on North Korea in Tokyo, Seoul, and Washington, and the perceived success in dealing with the North Korean problem became a positive factor in US-Japan relations.

Coordination on policy toward China was much more problematic, with Tokyo and Washington often out of sync, as they had been on many occasions in the past. At the beginning of the administration, US China policy was dominated by human rights considerations fed by Tiananmen Square, concerns that did not figure prominently in Japan's approach to China. Subsequently US-China relations warmed up to such an extent that Clinton characterized the relationship as a "strategic partnership," creating anxiety in Tokyo that Japan-bashing was being replaced with "Japan passing." Then US-China relations cooled sharply with the Chinese missile tests near Taiwan in 1996 and the dispatch of US carriers to the strait, followed by the accidental bombing of the PRC embassy in Belgrade in 1999.

Meanwhile Japan was expanding its economic engagement with China while worrying about the PRC's growing military power and regional influence. A new generation of Japanese was growing increasingly resistant to China's continued use of the "history card" to exact economic benefits from Tokyo, symbolized by Jiang Zemin's failed visit to Japan in 1998. Both Tokyo and Washington were in accord that a containment policy in response to China's growing power was not an option, but different historical and domestic political circumstances and competing economic interests made it very difficult for the two to coordinate their terms of engagement with Beijing.

The Clinton administration approached cooperation with Japan on Asian regional issues with a certain ambivalence. On the one hand Washington and Tokyo shared an interest in strengthening the role of such organizations as APEC and the Asian Regional Forum (ARF), even if there was a degree of competition for leadership and differences with respect to agenda priorities. On the other, the Clinton administration continued the Bush/Baker concern about Japanese support for or involvement in Asian regional forums that excluded the United States. Despite these concerns, Mahathir's EAEC was in fact reborn as the "Ten Plus Three" (ASEAN plus Japan, China, and the ROK), evolving from a luncheon during the ASEAN Postministerial Conference to a regular meeting at the leaders level.

The US took much greater exception to Tokyo's suggestion of the establishment of an "Asian Monetary Fund" in response to the 1997 Asian financial crisis, with Treasury Secretary Rubin calling it a threat to the IMF. The Japanese backed down, but saw it as American sour grapes after Washington's failure to come to the aid of Thailand and Indonesia while Japan provided substantial financial support.

Another Clinton administration strategic priority with respect to Japan that met with greater success was enlisting GOJ support for the new Russia. Through steady quiet diplomacy, led by Strobe Talbott, the administration was able to persuade Japan that it was in its interest to help stabilize and reform the former Soviet Union by providing financial assistance and permitting it to join the G-7, even in the absence of dramatic Russian concessions on the territorial issue. In turn, the US assured Japan that it would continue to support Japan's position on the four northern islands and ensure that this issue was not neglected in the G-7/G-8 process.

The Second Bush Administration

The George W. Bush administration approach to Japan was foreshadowed in the "Armitage Report" of October 2000,[29] produced by a nominally bipartisan study group, seven of whom subsequently took important policy positions in the new administration.[30] With the premise that the US-Japan alliance was more important than ever in view of all the potential flash points in the region, the report alleged that both sides had allowed the bilateral relationship to drift in the period after the 1996 Security Declaration, in part because of Washington's exaggerated concerns about Beijing's hostile reaction to the reinvigoration of the US-Japan security partnership. The authors saw the US-UK "special relationship" as a model and suggested the following elements in a revitalized alliance:

- A reaffirmed US defense commitment to Japan;
- Diligent implementation of the revised Guidelines for Defense Cooperation and Japanese implementation of crisis management legislation;
- Increased cooperation between the US armed services and their Japanese counterparts, including greater joint use of facilities, integration of training activities, and a review of the division of roles and missions agreed upon in 1981;
- Removal of Japan's self-imposed restraints on full participation in peacekeeping and humanitarian relief operations;[31]
- Adjustments in the American force structure in Japan to make them more mobile and to take advantage of developments in technology and changes in the region;
- Full and rapid implementation of the SACO agreement to consolidate the US presence in Okinawa and reduce friction with local communities;
- Increase in the flow of US defense technology to Japan and encouragement of the American defense industry to form strategic alliances with Japanese companies to facilitate a greater two-way flow.
- Broadening of the scope of bilateral missile defense cooperation;
- Expansion of intelligence cooperation.

The Bush administration has in fact pursued an approach to Japan very much along the lines of the Armitage Report and has shown progress in achieving many of these objectives, particularly after the events of September 11.

V. The War on Terrorism and Beyond—2001–2003

Following the attacks on New York and Washington, cooperation on the war on terrorism joined the more traditional strategic objectives of the US-Japan alliance. Tokyo did not wait to be prodded by the US before shifting its focus in this direction.

Koizumi Steps Up to the Plate

Having learned the lessons of the Gulf War and with new crisis management tools and more dynamic leadership in place, Prime Minister Koizumi immediately voiced strong and unequivocal support for the US war on terrorism and moved quickly to provide concrete support in terms of passing a counterterrorism law that allowed the Japanese military to protect US bases in Japan and authorized the Japan Maritime Defense Force to provide supply, transportation, and communication support to US forces operating in Afghanistan.

Japan followed up by dispatching Aegis class destroyers to the Indian Ocean to provide such support. Japan was also very active in the nonmilitary area, joining Washington as co-chair of the November 2001 Washington meeting on reconstruction assistance to Afghanistan, and Tokyo hosted the ministerial-level meeting of this group in January 2002. Washington encouraged and supported these Japanese initiatives, but the Koizumi government undertook these steps without the traditional overt pressure from the US, reflecting a new decisive top-down leadership style made possible by the evolution in Japanese politics, psychology, and governmental structure since the Gulf War.

Koizumi used the opportunity presented by the US invasion of Iraq to further strengthen the alliance by quickly announcing his understanding and support of the American action, despite strong public and political opposition to the war. Again Koizumi followed up with concrete action by obtaining Diet agreement to legislation allowing the Self-Defense Force to undertake noncombat reconstruction activities in Iraq, and the GOJ is now undertaking preparative steps to send some six hundred ground Self-Defense Force troops to the country, despite the recent deaths of two Japanese diplomats there and continued domestic opposition. In addition the GOJ has announced $5 billion in reconstruction assistance.

The Japanese government also moved forward with cooperation with the US on missile defense and pushed through the first phase of long-stalled "emergency legislation" giving the GOJ authority to take special measures in the event of a crisis, legislation that is crucial to Japan's ability to provide rear-area support to US forces in Japan in the event of a Korean crisis.

Besides the war on terrorism, the other issue that has been at the center of Bush administration policy toward Japan is North Korea's nuclear program. Policy coordination got off to a rocky start with the administration distancing itself from the Agreed Framework and President Kim Dae-jung's engagement policy, leaving Tokyo in an awkward middle ground between Seoul and Washington. Koizumi's September 2002 visit to Pyongyang was not coordinated with Washington, and it appeared that US and Japanese policies toward Korea were going in fundamentally different directions. However, Japanese disillusionment with the results of the North Korean summit and Washington's decision to engage with the North in the context of the six-party talks have narrowed differences between the two capitals.

China policy, on the other hand, has not been an issue in US-Japan relations, at least since the administration shifted back toward engagement after September 11. At the strategic level, the US and Japan both enjoy good relations with China, a rare occurrence in the postwar (or prewar) period. Moreover, the preoccupation of the US trade community and Congress with the flood of Chinese imports took the heat for Japan on economic issues.

Why Has the Alliance Succeeded?

Looking back on the last fifty years, there is a remarkable consistency in the US strategic perspective of Japan and the policies that have flowed from this perspective. There have been moments of crisis – the 1960 Security Treaty riots, the early 1970s Nixon shocks, the Gulf War, and the trade conflicts of the early 1990s – when it appeared that the postwar strategic bargain might come apart, but each time the two countries have recognized the stake they have in continued strategic cooperation and worked to contain centrifugal forces. What has been the glue that has held it together? Let me suggest four key factors.

- The United States has continued to meet its formal and implied obligations of:
    - o Ensuring Japan's security and regional stability through extended deterrence (the "nuclear umbrella") and by maintaining conventional military forces in East Asia;
    - o Providing "public goods" in terms of a stable, rule-based international political and economic system and an open American market for Japanese goods and investment;
    - o Supporting Japan's full participation in the international community (e.g., UN, GATT, OECD, G-7).
- Japan, often responding to US pressure, has steadily assumed more international political, economic, and military responsibility within the context of continued strategic dependence upon the United States;
- Both sides have successfully adjusted alliance mechanisms and roles and missions to new power realities, albeit with some stumbles along the way;
- The alliance has had the good fortune not to be tested beyond its capacity to respond, e.g. by a renewed Korean war or a conflict in the Taiwan Strait, although there have been periods when such a crisis has been narrowly averted.

What Lies Ahead

Can this success continue? Some scholars have noted that it is unprecedented for the world's second economic power to entrust its strategic security to the world's leading power. They have suggested that for this reason the US-Japan alliance is unsustainable over the long term and that at some point Japan will feel compelled to take on the enormous domestic political and economic costs, as well as the regional and international opprobrium, of seeking strategic independence. Thus far there is no indication that Japan is moving in this direction, but below I suggest four issues that bear watching.

For the United States, Japan remains central to the achievement of its strategic objectives in East Asia, even as these objectives have shifted from deterring Soviet aggression and containing communism to dealing with regional instability and such emerging threats as terrorism and proliferation. In the defense area, there is little talk of Japan having a "free ride." US-Japan military cooperation promises to break new ground as Japan overcomes postwar taboos with respect to sending forces abroad, cooperating on missile defense, and engaging in collective security.

While the leaders in both countries are likely to continue to see strategic cooperation as critical to the achievement of their respective regional and global objectives, there are developments that could take US and Japanese policies on key issues in different directions. These include:

- **Iraq:** While both governments now characterizes the alliance as never having been stronger and advancing rapidly toward a true "equal partnership" on a global scale, some Japanese and American observers caution that Koizumi's decision to send SDF units to Iraq, by being substantially out in front of the consensus in Japan, runs the risk of a backlash against his government and by extension the United States should, for example, Japanese forces in Iraq incur substantial casualties. The leaders of the Democratic Party of Japan have come out strongly against the deployment, arguing that the Koizumi government is "blindly" following the US and calling for a more independent Japanese policy giving equal weight to relations with Asia, the United Nations, and the United States. In the unlikely event that Iraq policy leads to the fall of the Koizumi government and brings the DJP to power, there could be an abrupt shift in Japanese policy that would strain the alliance.
- **Korea:** Despite the present close collaboration, Korea still has the potential to be a divisive factor in the alliance. Failure to reverse, or at a minimum cap, the North Korean nuclear program could stimulate debate in Japan about its own nuclear options, creating tensions in the region and with the US Moreover, Washington and Tokyo, with different geographic and domestic political circumstances with respect to the Korean peninsula, may find it difficult to agree upon the appropriate response to a crisis. At the other end

of the spectrum, the termination of the nuclear crisis in the DPRK, along with North-South détente or unification, could be seen by elements in both the US and Japan as removing the rationale for forward deployed forces in Japan while setting in motion a new and perhaps destabilizing dynamic among Washington, Tokyo, Seoul, and Beijing.

• **China:** US-China and Japan-China relations could once again go in different directions, creating major tensions between Washington and Tokyo. In particular, a Taiwan Strait crisis would likely produce different reactions in the US and Japan, with Tokyo less prepared to support a military response. More broadly, if China's economy continues its pace of growth and Japan falls back into stagnation, the strategic equilibrium in East Asia could shift. If accompanied by political liberalization and foreign-policy moderation in Beijing, there may be those in the US who would see China as a more attractive strategic partner than Japan. If, on the other hand, China's increasing economic power is accompanied by a more aggressive foreign policy, there will be pressures in the US to move toward a containment policy. Either eventuality would likely produce great strains in the US-Japan alliance unless managed carefully.

• **Multilateralism:** The current perception of US policy as downplaying the role of the United Nations in conflict resolution, distancing the US from international agreements that impinge on sovereignty, and giving less weight to the views of traditional allies in formulating and carrying out its objectives, has not produced in Japan thus far the kind of backlash that has occurred in Canada and Europe. Nevertheless, many Japanese regard this more unilateral American approach as being in conflict with the importance that Japan has traditionally attached to the United Nations and international law. Moreover a younger, more nationalistic generation is emerging on the political scene in Japan in both the ruling Liberal Democratic Party and the opposition DPJ who call for a more assertive Japanese foreign policy. Most of these new leaders appear to see this new activism in the broad context of the alliance with the United States. However, if the US is perceived as pursuing policies that do not adequately take into account Japan's interests, there could be demands from this generation for a more independent Japanese stance.

Final Thoughts

Over the fifty-plus year life of the alliance, there have been several points of crisis when it appeared that the US and Japan might be on the way to strategic separation. Each time, a recognition of shared interests and wise leadership on both sides prevailed, and the relationship moved forward. At this juncture in history, with postwar systems and institutions facing unprecedented challenges, it is difficult to envision how either the United States or Japan could achieve its foreign policy objectives without continued close cooperation with the other.

History demonstrates, however, that a rational calculation of one's interest is not always the determining factor, and committed leadership in both countries will be required to ensure that the alliance survives and prospers. Without leaders who are able to articulate the benefits of partnership, develop a common approach to critical issues, and manage their internal policy processes, the alliance will have great difficulty in moving forward and may be subject to centrifugal forces.

With both countries seeing the weakening of bureaucracies that have been the traditional alliance managers and the increasing intrusion of domestic politics into foreign policy, the old patterns may be hard to replicate. It is necessary but not sufficient for experts like those gathered here to meet to try to develop a forward-looking strategy based on the 1996 Security Declaration, the 2000 Armitage Report, and other efforts. We need to move beyond this "club" to broaden the base to include a new generation of politicians and private-sector leaders, as well as academics and bureaucrats, in order to create the broad support necessary for the alliance to endure.

* * *

This paper was informed by the discussion at the January 14–15, 2004, roundtable on "America's Alliances" hosted by the Asia-Pacific Research Center, Stanford Institute for International Studies. The views expressed in this article are those of the author and do not reflect the official policy or position of the National Defense University, the Department of Defense, or the US Government.

NOTES

[1] JCS Memo to Secstate contained in *Foreign Relations of the United States*, vol. VI, 1951–52, p. 778.

[2] Dulles memo to Secstate, January 4, 1951, ibid., p. 782.

[3] Ibid., p. 789.

[4] Rusk memo to S/P, November 9, 1951, ibid., p. 1432.

[5] Yoshida later provided a letter to Dulles setting forth Japan's intention to open relations with Taiwan after its sovereignty was restored, a policy it followed until 1972. The UK, which had recognized the communist government in Beijing, objected strongly to this US pressure on Japan.

[6] Ibid., vol. XIV, 1952–54, p. 1572.

[7] September 9, 1954, Embassy Tokyo cable no. 798, ibid., p. 1718.

[8] Embassy and CCFE cables, ibid., p. 1732.

[9] Ibid., vol. XXIII, 1955–57 p. 328.

[10] Ibid., vol. XVIII, 1958–60, p. 3.

[11] Ibid., pp. 12–14.

[12] MacArthur letter to Asst. Sec. Robinson, April 18, 1959, ibid., p. 67.

[13] In a May 1960 National Security Council meeting, JCS chairman Twining complained that the US was being "too nice to Japan and that is why it is slipping away." President Eisenhower responded that 'we had to be nice to Japan since it was an independent nation.' Ibid., p. 264.

[14] Eisenhower expressed concern that Okinawa could become like Cyprus or Algeria and suggested the US establish an enclave of minimum size. Ibid., p. 189.

[15] Ibid., p. 337.

[16] Ibid., vol. XXII, 1961–63, p. 235.

[17] Ibid., p. 365.

[18] Ibid., p. 382.

[19] Priscilla Clapp and Mort Halperin, *US-Japan Relations in the 1990s* (Cambridge: Harvard, 1974), p. 130.

[20] SECTO 36, dated October 6, 1968.

[21] Henry Kissinger, *Years of Upheaval* (New York: Little, Brown & Co., 1982), p. 6.

[22] See pp. 735–745 in Kissinger's *Years of Upheaval* for a detailed discussion of dealings with Japan on the energy crisis.

[23] National Security Council memo from Michael Armacost to Zbigniew Brzezinski, September 13, 1977.

[24.]E.g., Paul Wolfowitz, Richard Armitage, James Kelly, Gaston Sigur.

[24] George Shultz, *Turmoil and Triumph* (New York: Charles Scribner's Sons, 1993), p. 185.

[25] In addition to my own recollections I have drawn heavily on Michael H. Armacost's chapter on the Gulf War (pp. 98–128) in Armacost, *Friends or Rivals?* (New York: Columbia University Press, 1996).

[26] *Friends or Rivals?* p. 188.

[27] For an excellent review of the Nye Initiative see Michael Green's chapter "The Search for an Active Security Partnership: Lessons from the 1980s" in *Partnership—The United States and Japan 1951–2001*, edited by Akira Iriye and Robert Wampler (Tokyo: Kodansha International, 2001).

[28] "The United States and Japan: Advancing Toward a Mature Partnership," an INSS Special Report published by the Institute for National Strategic Studies at the National Defense University, October 11, 2000, Washington, DC.

[29] Richard Armitage, deputy secretary of state; Michael Green, assistant to the president for Asian affairs; James Kelly, assistant secretary of state for East Asian affairs; Torkel Patterson, assistant to the president and then special advisor to Ambassador Howard Baker in Tokyo; Robin Sakoda, special assistant to Mr. Armitage; Robert Manning, State Department policy planning staff, and Paul Wolfowitz, deputy secretary of defense.

[30] After passage of the 1992 Peacekeeping Law, the GOJ had "frozen" certain provisions relating to the right to bear arms and operate in dangerous areas because of domestic sensitivities. These provisions were in fact "unfrozen" in 2003 as part of Japan's response to the war on terrorism.

Japanese Adjustments to the Security Alliance with the United States: Evolution of Policy on the Roles of the Self-Defense Force

Yamaguchi Noboru

Since the end of the Cold War, the Government of Japan (GOJ) has taken a number of new approaches to adjust its security policy to match the new security environment. These measures were extremely sensitive or even unthinkable during the Cold War. Japan, for the first time in its post–World War II history, dispatched Self-Defense Force (SDF) minesweepers to the Gulf in 1991, then participated in the United Nations peacekeeping operation in Cambodia in 1992. In the latter half of the 1990s, the GOJ took further steps toward a new national security posture focusing on measures to enhance the Japan-US alliance. These included a revision of the Guidelines for Japan-US Defense Cooperation in 1997 and an enactment of laws in 1999 to implement the particulars of the revised Guidelines. This series of efforts was even accelerated after 9/11. In October 2001, by enacting the Anti-Terrorism Special Measures Law and revising the SDF Law, the GOJ tasked the SDF to perform missions to assist the international efforts to combat terrorism in Afghanistan and to protect US bases in Japan against terrorist attacks. At the end of February 2004, Maritime Self-Defense Force (MSDF) vessels were in the Indian Ocean to support the international fleet combating terrorism in Afghanistan, and SDF contingents were operating in the Golan Heights and East Timor for UN peacekeeping missions. SDF soldiers, sailors, and airmen were also starting humanitarian and reconstruction operations in Samawah, Iraq, based on the Law Concerning the Special Measures on Humanitarian and Reconstruction Assistance in Iraq, enacted in 2003.

This paper will examine what the United States and Japan have done to manage their alliance in recent years and address Japan's tasks in particular. The paper will cover the following points.

1) During the Gulf crisis and the Gulf War, the implications of the end of the Cold War became clear for Japan and encouraged the GOJ to look for new approaches to Japan's security policy.
2) In the mid-1990s, the governments of the United States and Japan made efforts to reaffirm and adjust the alliance, resulting in the US-Japan Joint

Declaration on Security in 1996 and the revised Guidelines for US Japan Defense Cooperation in 1997.

3) Japan took slow but steady steps to implement what the two governments concluded to be the necessary approach toward the future alliance.

4) There are remaining tasks for the future.

Turning Point: Learning from the Gulf War

During the crisis and the war in the Persian Gulf in 1990 and 1991, Japan made financial contributions of thirteen billion dollars, which accounted for nearly 20 percent of the financial support for the war that the United States received from allies and friends.[1] Japan was in fact the third largest contributor after Saudi Arabia and Kuwait. This contribution, however, was not accompanied by human contributions such as sending troops, and attracted little appreciation from the international community.[2] In March 1991, when the Kuwaiti government—in major US papers and magazines such as the *Washington Post* and the *New York Times*—thanked those who made efforts to liberate Kuwait, Japan was not named in the list of contributors.

Through this experience, policymakers and military planners in Tokyo realized that "checkbook diplomacy" did not work. They started making serious efforts to look for policies that would allow Japan to contribute to international efforts for peace and stability in the world, even as they scrutinized the post–Cold War security environment. Right after the Gulf War, the GOJ decided to dispatch minesweepers to the Gulf for postwar reconstruction. Meanwhile, the Diet passed laws enabling the SDF to participate in UN peacekeeping operations (PKOs) and international disaster relief operations in 1992. Since then, the SDF has participated in UN PKOs and international humanitarian relief operations (HROs) such as those in Cambodia (1992–93), Mozambique (1993–95), Zaire (1994), the Golan Heights (1996–), Honduras (1998) and East Timor (2002–).

Behind these policies, there was a notion of the characteristics of the post–Cold War world. Security specialists identified fundamental security requirements for Japan's post–Cold War security policy, particularly during the process of developing the new National Defense Program Outline (NDPO) of 1995. In February 1994, the administration asked a group of scholars, business people, former government officials, and a former military officer for proposals on Japan's security policy in the post–Cold War strategic environment. After a series of intensive discussions, the prime minister's Advisory Group on Defense Issues concluded its report, "The Modality of the Security and Defense Capability of Japan," in August 1994, known as the Higuchi Report (named after the chairman of the panel, Kotaro Higuchi).[3] Many of the ideas recommended in this report were finally reflected in the new NDPO, which set forth the guidance for Japan's future defense policy and force structure of the SDF.

The report clearly pointed out the fundamental differences between the Cold War and post–Cold War roles of Japan's defense capabilities as follows:

> The defense capability of Japan in the Cold War period was built up and maintained for the primary purpose of preparing for attacks on Japanese territory by hostile forces ... [and] Japan's mission was to defend the country based strictly on the right of self defense. In light of its geographical position, however, Japan naturally played an important role in the anti-Soviet strategy of the Western bloc.[4]

While NATO established the western front against the East's massive ground forces in Europe, Japan was directly facing the Soviet Far East forces across the maritime border. Defense of Japan itself was a significant contribution to the Western allies since Japan's three key straits happened to be the critical exits for the Soviet Pacific Fleet from the Japan Sea to the East China Sea and the Pacific Ocean. Then the Cold War ended. Japan's previously vital contribution to the West—its defense capability— suddenly ceased to be critically important because its geostrategic significance drastically decreased in terms of anti-Soviet strategy.

The advisory group also raised a serious question about how Japan should deal with new threats in the new environment.

> While clearly visible threats have disappeared and moves toward arms control and disarmament have made some progress centering on the US, Russia, and Europe, we found ourselves in an opaque and uncertain situation. In other words, there exist dangers of various qualities which are dispersed and difficult to identify, and it is hard to predict in what forms such dangers would threaten our security.[5]

From a military point of view, the future will require Japan not only to respond to a direct military invasion but also to deal with a variety of unpredictable threats, such as the proliferation of weapons of mass destruction and missiles and spillover of regional conflicts. There may also be new types of lower-intensity military and paramilitary threats, including violation of territorial water and air space, illegal occupation of territories, interruption of sea lines of communication, terrorism, armed refugees, and sabotage by commando type units. These concerns were validated by events such as the crisis over North Korea's nuclear program in 1993 and 1994, the NoDong missile launch in 1993, and the sarin gas attack on the Tokyo subway system in 1995.

Meanwhile, Japan has inherent vulnerabilities that should be taken into account when one thinks of its national security. As Japan's economy grew rapidly throughout the 1950s to the 1980s, cities became more complex, population and industry bases became denser, and domestic lines of communication grew more congested. Vulnerabilities have been increasing in international terms as well. Japan's dependence on imported energy is widely known. As the economic activities abroad are dispersed throughout the world, Japan is heavily dependent on the safety of its market, sea lanes of communication, and countries and areas supplying natural resources including energy. The peace and stability of the world as a whole continue to be of essential importance for Japan even as mere buildup of the SDF becomes less relevant to international interests in a post–Cold War world. Professor Akihiko Tanaka of Tokyo University states that "While Japan did not have to get involved in international conflicts in the world during the Cold War period, since the Cold War ended, even contingencies in remote areas became relevant to Japan's security."[6]

Redefining the Alliance: The Path to the Japan-US Joint Declaration

The above-quoted findings laid out in the Higuchi Report had a significant influence on Japan's post–Cold War security policy, particularly on the new National Defense Program Outline (NDPO) adopted in 1995. The report emphasized active and constructive security policy, noting that "Japan should extricate itself from its security policy of the past that was, if anything, passive, and henceforth play an active role in shaping a new order." Based on this idea, the NDPO pointed out the importance of the SDF's capability for "contribution to creation of a more stable security environment," and listed this as one of SDF's three major functions, as well as the capability for national defense and for response to large-scale disasters and various situations.[7] International PKOs, international disaster-relief operations, security dialogue, defense exchanges, and cooperation with arms control efforts are included as specific areas for such international contribution.

On the other hand, the Higuchi Report provoked concerns among security experts in Washington, who believed in the importance of the US-Japan alliance. Although the report recommended that Japan should enhance the alliance's functions, this recommendation came after the multilateral security cooperation in the report.[8] Patrick Cronin and Michael Green, in their paper "Redefining the US-Japan Alliance," stated that "momentum and energy in Japanese policy planning are flowing away from the alliance," and concluded that "decisive action is now necessary to redefine the alliance."[9] They further recommended that the Department of Defense (DoD) start "a comprehensive dialogue with Japan on new bilateral roles and missions."[10] Based on this recommendation, intensive policy coordination between the two countries began at the end of 1994, aimed at clarifying the significance of the alliance and developing policies to enhance it. Three major policy documents were issued during this process—the "US Security Strategy for the East Asia-Pacific Region" released in February 1995, the "National Defense Program Outline in and after FY 1996" adopted November 1995, and the "Japan-US Joint Declaration on Security: Alliance for the 21st Century" issued in April 1996.

The US side took the first step in this bilateral policy coordination. Joseph Nye, as assistant secretary of defense for international affairs, issued the "United States Security Strategy for the East Asia-Pacific Region," widely known as the East Asia Strategy Report (EASR of 1995) or the Nye Report. The EASR of 1995 emphasized Asia's new significance by quoting the fact that "United States trade with the Asia-Pacific region in 1993 totaled over $374 billion and accounted for 2.8 million United States jobs." [11] It also reconfirmed the US military commitment to the region with "a force structure that requires approximately 100,000 personnel." [12] The significance of the US-Japan alliance was specifically described:

> There is no more important bilateral relationship than the one we have with Japan. It is fundamental to both our Pacific security policy and our global strategic objectives. Our security alliance with Japan is the linchpin of United States security policy in Asia. It is seen not just by the United States and Japan, but throughout the region, as a major factor for securing stability in Asia. [13]

In 1995, policy planners in Japan were in the final stages of revising the National Defense Program Outline, which the GOJ had first adopted in 1976. In November 1995, the National Security Council of Japan and the cabinet announced the new NDPO. As mentioned earlier, the new NDPO took many of ideas raised by the Higuchi Report and emphasized wider defense capabilities. In addition, the new NDPO answered to the concerns of Cronin and Green stated earlier, and reflected the voices calling for a stronger alliance with the United States on both sides of the Pacific. The new NDPO states that "the security arrangements with the United States are indispensable to Japan's security and will also continue to play a key role in achieving peace and stability in the surrounding region of Japan and establishing a more stable security environment." [14] It identified four important areas for bilateral cooperation: (1) information exchange and policy consultation; (2) operational cooperation including joint studies, exercises, and training as well as mutual support in those areas; (3) exchange in the areas of equipment and technology; and (4) measures to facilitate smooth and effective stationing of US forces in Japan. When it was released, security specialists in the United States welcomed this document and pointed out that "the new NDPO mentioned Japan-US security arrangements thirteen times while the old one referred to them only once." [15] The new NDPO also elaborates a newly introduced dimension of the alliance that stipulates, in short, Japan's role in regional contingencies close to but outside Japan. It states:

> Should a situation arise in the areas surrounding Japan which will have an important influence on national peace and security, take appropriate response in accordance with the Constitution and relevant laws and

regulations, for example, by properly supporting UN activities when needed, and by ensuring the smooth and effective implementation of the Japan-US Security Arrangements.[16]

This point on how Japan should deal with contingencies in the surrounding region was thoroughly reviewed during and after the revision of the Guidelines for Japan-US Defense Cooperation.

In 1995, the alliance was reconfirmed by the two countries through the EASR in the United States and the new NDPO in Japan. These efforts to redefine the alliance were followed by the next step—joint endorsement at the highest political level. In April 1996, Prime Minister Hashimoto and President Clinton issued the Japan-US Joint Declaration on Security: Alliance for the 21st Century, in Tokyo. They specifically stated:

> For more than a year, the two governments conducted an intensive review of the evolving political and security environment of the Asia-Pacific region and of various aspects of the Japan-US security relationship. On the basis of this review, the Prime Minister and the President reaffirmed their commitment to the profound common values that guide our national policies: the maintenance of freedom, the pursuit of democracy, and respect for human rights. They agreed that the foundation for our cooperation remains firm, and that this partnership will remain vital in the 21st century.[17]

This joint declaration was significant for three reasons. First, as mentioned above, the political leaders of both countries affirmed that Japan-US cooperation in security areas was vital in a post–Cold War environment. The Japanese prime minister and the American president formally declared this belief to both domestic and overseas audiences. Second, the declaration set a widened agenda for the two countries by mentioning three areas for cooperation: (a) bilateral cooperation under the Japan-US security relationship, (b) regional cooperation, and (c) global cooperation. During the Cold War period, the alliance was narrowly defined and focused only on the bilateral context, such as the US commitment to Japan's defense, Japan's support for US stationing in Japan, and bilateral cooperation in military technologies and equipment. The two leaders made clear that Japan and the United States would cooperate on regional and global issues. Regional cooperation would include, for example, joint efforts for stability on the Korean peninsula and regional security dialogue. Strengthened cooperation in support of international peacekeeping and humanitarian relief operations and coordination between the two countries for arms control and disarmament were examples of global cooperation. The scope of the bilateral cooperation for security became wider than during the Cold War period. Finally, the third key component of the joint declaration was the proposal to revise the Guidelines for Defense Cooperation.

Revision of the Defense Guidelines

Following the guidance given by the two leaders, the two governments launched efforts to revise the Guidelines for Japan-US Defense Cooperation (Defense Guidelines). The first Defense Guidelines were authorized by the Japan-US Security Consultative Committee (SCC) and adopted by the National Defense Council and the Cabinet of Japan in 1978.[18] They were the result of intensive work by defense officials in both countries, and aimed for smoother, more effective implementation of the Japan-US Security Arrangements begun by the initiative of Minister of Defense Sakata and Secretary of Defense Schlesinger in 1976. While the first Defense Guidelines were important in enhancing operational cooperation between the two militaries through the late 1970s and the 1980s, they were designed to deal with a Cold War strategic environment.[19] As Japan and the United States entered the post–Cold War environment, it became crucial to review the Guidelines, and in August 1996 government officials and military planners of the two countries started working on revisions. After intensive discussions, including four case studies on various contingency scenarios, the revised Defense Guidelines were reported to the SSC in September 1997 in Washington, DC.[20]

The revised Defense Guidelines consist of three major elements: (a) cooperation under normal circumstances, (b) actions in response to an armed attack against Japan, and (c) cooperation in situations in areas surrounding Japan that will have an important influence on Japan's peace and security (Situations in Areas Surrounding Japan). In short, the revised Guidelines seamlessly addressed the full spectrum of Japan's national security, from peacetime to adjacent regional contingencies to Japanese defense and Japan-US security cooperation. Peacetime cooperation includes bilateral cooperation and coordination for peacetime activities such as PKOs, humanitarian relief operations, security dialogue, and defense exchanges as well as information sharing, policy coordination, and defense planning between the two governments. The second point of the guidelines, Japan's defense, made clear that "Japan will have primary responsibility immediately to take action and to repel an armed attack" while the United States "will provide appropriate support varying according the scale, type, phase, and other factors of the armed attack."[21] The revised Defense Guidelines particularly introduced specific kinds of bilateral cooperation for new types of threats, such as ballistic missile attacks and guerrilla-commando type attacks.[22]

Issues related to the third key point, cooperation in situations occurring in areas surrounding Japan, drew the most intensive debates among lawmakers and the public. The revised Defense Guidelines allocated the same amount of space for this section as for the section on defense of Japan. This contrasted sharply to the old guidelines, in which the chapter on contingencies in the Far East occupied only one-tenth the space devoted to the chapter on Japan's defense. Indeed, this point was so focal that the Japan-US Joint Declaration on Security noted that "the two leaders agreed on the necessity to promote bilateral policy coordination, including studies on bilateral cooperation in dealing with situations that may emerge in the areas surrounding Japan and which will have an important influence on the peace and security of Japan."[23]

The revised Defense Guidelines divided bilateral cooperation components into three categories. The first category is cooperation in activities initiated by either government, such as relief activities, measures to deal with refugees, search and rescue operations, noncombatant evacuation operations, and activities for international sanctions including UN-endorsed ship inspections. The second category specifies Japan's support for US forces' activities, such as US use of facilities in Japan and Japan's rear-area support for US forces. The third category includes operational cooperation, such as Japan's activities for intelligence gathering, surveillance and minesweeping operations, and US operations to restore peace and security in the areas surrounding Japan. Forty specific items for cooperation in total were listed in the appendix of the revised Defense Guidelines. Representing the US notion of Japan's support in "situations in areas surrounding Japan," the EASR 1998 states:

> ...the revised Guidelines outline Japanese rear-area support to US forces responding to a regional contingency. This support may include providing access to airfields, ports, transportation, logistics, and medical support. Japan would also be able, as applicable, to cooperate and coordinate with US forces to conduct such missions and functions as minesweeping, search and rescue, surveillance, and inspection of ships to enforce UN sanctions. By enhancing the alliance's capability to respond to crises, the revised Guidelines are an excellent example of preventive diplomacy: they contribute to shaping the environment by improving deterrence and stability in the region.[24]

Post-Guidelines Efforts: Situations in Areas surrounding Japan

Because the Guidelines are not a formal and legally binding agreement, "the Guidelines and programs under the Guidelines will not obligate either Government to take legislative, budgetary or administrative measures." However, "the two Governments are expected to reflect in an appropriate way the results of these efforts, based on their own judgment, in their specific policies and measures."[25] Based on this agreement, the Government of Japan undertook a series of measures to implement the revised Guidelines. On September 24, 1997, the day after the Defense Guidelines were released, the GOJ adopted a cabinet decision to initiate work to ensure the effectiveness of the revised Defense Guidelines. It was stipulated that the work should be done by the government as a whole, rather than only JDA or SDF, and should include legal issues. In April 1998, the administration submitted bills related to Japan's action in "situations surrounding Japan" to the Diet. In May 1999, the Diet passed the bills for the "Law Concerning Measures to Enhance the Peace and Security of Japan in Situations in Areas Surrounding Japan." In the meantime, minor amendments were made on the SDF Law and the Acquisition and Cross-Servicing Agreement between Japan and the United States (ACSA) to support the Law on Situations in Areas Surrounding Japan. During the process of deliberation on these bills, the Diet decided to take separate legislation measures for ship-inspection operations. The bill concerning ship-inspection operations was submitted to the Diet in October 2000, and enacted in November 2000.

This series of legislative actions enabled Japan to cooperate with US forces in Situations in Areas Surrounding Japan by conducting rear-area support and rear area search and rescue activities for US forces, and participating in ship-inspection operations for international sanctions. Under this legal framework, relevant government agencies as well as JDA and SDF are tasked to implement measures according to their respective jurisdictions. Heads of such agencies are authorized to require the cooperation of local governments and to request cooperation from nongovernmental bodies. This legislation set several conditions to avoid political and constitutional controversy over Japan's activities, including the SDF. First, these activities must not constitute the threat or use of force. Second, these activities must be conducted in areas where there is currently no combat action and where it is deemed that no combat action will take place during the term of the activities. Third, the prime minister must obtain prior Diet approval for activities carried out by the SDF except in cases where implementation of such activities is deemed urgent.[26]

Since this legislation was aimed at situations in areas surrounding Japan, the SDF's activities were inherently limited in purpose and in geographical area. There are, however, significant implications in the fact that concrete examples of activities are listed within the Constitution. In his book *The Japan-US Strategic Dialogue*, former vice minister for defense Masahiro Akiyama states that "what Japan can do and what Japan cannot do under the Constitution was made clear," and "the laws enabled Japan to offer as much cooperation as possible for the United States under the conditions that did not allow the exercise of right of collective defense."[27] In other words, a nearly maximum scope of the constitutional limitation was made clear. This later facilitated the GOJ's efforts to legislate the Anti-Terrorism Special Measures Law in 2001 and the Special Measures Law for Reconstruction and Humanitarian Assistance in Iraq in 2003. When the bills were drafted, the GOJ no longer had to scrutinize whether the activities proposed by these bills were constitutional, since they were the same as those listed in the laws concerning Situations in Areas Surrounding Japan.

Post-Guidelines Efforts: Widened Role of the SDF in International Missions

Since 1992, when the International Peace Cooperation Law was enacted, the SDF have dispatched troops for UN PKOs. For the first nine years, however, participation was limited to those in support of peacekeeping forces (PKF). The core assignments of PKF undertaken by SDF contingents—such as disarmament monitoring and stationing and patrol in a buffer zone—had been suspended until another law, the International Peace Cooperation Bill, was considered and approved by the Diet. In November 2001, the suspension was lifted after nine years, during which time the SDF had participated in six different UN peacekeeping missions. Part of the law was also amended to expand the scope of use of weapons, as well as the range of subjects to be defended.

After the terrorist attacks on 9/11, the role of the SDF in international missions expanded still further. On October 5, 2001, the GOJ submitted the draft of the Anti-Terrorism Special Measures Law to the Diet. The law passed the Diet on October 29, and took effect on November 2. At the same time, the SDF Law was amended to introduce a new category of SDF operations, called Guarding Operations. This amendment enabled the SDF to provide the US forces with support to protect their facilities and areas in Japan without issuing public security orders. The purposes of the Anti-Terrorism Special Measures Law are as follows:

> Recalling that UN Security Council Resolution 1368 regards the September 11 terrorist attacks that took place in the US as a threat to international peace and security, and also noting that UN Security Council Resolutions 1267, 1269, 1333 and other relevant resolutions condemn acts of international terrorism and call on all member states to take appropriate measures for the prevention of such acts, the purpose of the Law is to specify the following measures in order to enable Japan to contribute actively and on its own initiative to the efforts of the international community for the prevention and eradication of international terrorism, thereby ensuring the peace and security of the international community including Japan: (i) The measures Japan implements in support of the activities of the Armed Forces of the US and other countries which aim to eradicate the threat of the terrorist attacks, thereby contributing to the achievement of the purposes of the UN Chapter; and (ii) The measures Japan implements with the humanitarian spirit based on relevant resolutions or requests made by the UN and others.[28]

The law states that Japan's activities are for: (a) cooperation and support activities for foreign forces, such as provision of goods and services by the SDF including supply, transportation, repair and maintenance, medical service, communications, airport and port services, utilities for bases, lodging and disinfection; (b) search and rescue activities for personnel in distress; and (c) assistance to affected people including transportation of necessities, medical services, and other humanitarian activities. Most of these activities are included in the revised Defense Guidelines and many are the same as those listed in the law on Situations in Areas Surrounding Japan. While geographic areas for such activities are expanded to include high seas and foreign territory (when consent from the territorial countries is obtained), the conditions for such activities were the same as in the law on Situations in Areas Surrounding Japan. The law dictates that Japan's activities must not constitute the threat or use of force, and these activities are to be implemented in areas where combat is not taking place or not expected to take place while such activities are being carried out. Based on the law mentioned above, Japan has dispatched MSDF vessels and ASDF cargo aircraft for operations in support of foreign forces combating terrorism, and for humanitarian relief purposes in Southwest Asia. As of December 2003, three MSDF vessels were operating in the Indian Ocean, having supplied 327,000 kiloliters of fuel for the navies of ten countries including Canada, Germany, Italy, and the United States.

There has been an important implication in enacting the Anti-Terrorism Special Measures Law and the SDF activities that accompany it. The rhetoric for international PKO and for operations in the event of Situations in Areas Surrounding Japan merged, and became a template. SDF participation in international PKO had been initiated by the International Peace Cooperation Law, which was enacted in 1992 right after the Gulf War. The Anti-Terrorism Special Measures Law of 2001 has the same goals as its 1992 predecessor—to legislate Japan's participation in PKO and international humanitarian relief operations, and to involve Japan actively in international efforts to promote world peace and security. At the same time, the 2001 law employed the same rhetoric introduced by the laws related to Situations in Areas Surrounding Japan (especially with respect to particular activities of the SDF such as rear-area support, search and rescue operations and support for refugees). It can be said that individual parts of the revised Defense Guidelines and the laws to ensure their effectiveness were applied in legislation to expand Japan's contribution to international PKO. Therefore, the time dedicated to legislation of the Anti-Terrorism Special Measures Law was significantly shorter than before. For example, it took two years to enact the International Peace Cooperation Law since its predecessor, the UN Peace Cooperation Bill, was submitted in October 1990 and died in the next month. The laws concerning Situations in Areas Surrounding Japan, including the Ship Inspection Law, took two-and-a-half years from the time the bills were submitted in April 1998. By contrast, the bills concerning Japan's anti-terrorism activities were put into effect November 2, 2000, just one month after the GOJ submitted them to the Diet on October 5.

This acceleration technique was again applied in August 2003, when the GOJ enacted the Law Concerning the Special Measures on Humanitarian and Reconstruction Assistance in Iraq. As before, the GOJ utilized templates developed through legislative initiatives for the International Peace Cooperation Law, the laws related to Situations in Areas Surrounding Japan, and the Anti-Terrorism Special Measures Law. The major areas of SDF's activities are "humanitarian assistance activities," which involve such actions as distributing necessary goods to displaced persons, and "security assistance activities," which entail helping US (and other foreign) forces to maintain public order.[29] The new law set the same conditions on the SDF's activities as previous laws; it stipulated, for example, that such activities must not constitute the threat or use of force, and that they must be conducted in areas where there is currently no combat action and where it is deemed that no combat action will take place during the term of the activities. On December 9, 2003, Prime Minister Koizumi announced the Basic Plan to dispatch the Japanese contingents including those of the Ground, Maritime, and Air Self-Defense Forces to Iraq.[30] The basic plan tasks the SDF troops to conduct missions such as medical services, water supply, and rehabilitation and maintenance of schools and other public facilities in southeastern Iraq, centered on the Governorate of Al Muthanna.[31] This plan was approved by the Diet on February 9, 2004, a mere two months later. By the end of February, the main body of the SDF contingent—consisting of about 600 GSDF troops with about 200 vehicles and about 200 ASDF airmen with three C-130 cargo aircraft—was in Iraq and Kuwait. Meanwhile, the MSDF is supporting this contingent with the LST "Ohsumi" and the destroyer "Murasame" by transporting heavy equipment such as armored vehicles.

Post-Guidelines Efforts: Defense of Japan

Legal and political measures outlined in the previous section of this paper are for peacetime and for Situations in Areas Surrounding Japan in the context of the revised Defense Guidelines. Another element of the Defense Guidelines is Japan-US cooperation in case of direct attack against Japan. In this area as well, the GOJ has taken significant steps in recent years, first by enacting three laws concerning responses to armed attack, and second, by enhancing SDF capabilities to deal with newly emerging threats such as missile attacks and unconventional threats including guerilla-commando type attacks and terrorist attacks.

The revised Defense Guidelines state that "the two Governments will be mindful that bilateral defense planning and mutual cooperation planning must be consistent so that appropriate responses will be ensured when a Situation in Areas Surrounding Japan threatens to develop into an Armed Attack against Japan or when such a situation and an Armed Attack against Japan occur simultaneously." This suggests that the SDF might have to protect Japan while providing support for US forces operating to deal with Situations in Areas Surrounding Japan. The legal basis for countering Situations in Areas Surrounding Japan was made in the late 1990s. On the other hand, for more than a quarter-century, legal preparation for SDF operations in case of an armed attack lagged behind, and the JDA had been making efforts to establish just such a legal basis.[32] It is questionable to see Japan supporting others while having difficulty protecting itself, and US forces, a supported entity, may well have trouble depending solely upon the support provided by such a country. The legal basis for the defense of Japan was a must for the GOJ. In April 2002, the GOJ submitted three bills on responses to armed attack: (1) the Bill to Respond to Armed Attack, (2) the Bill to Amend the SDF Law, and (3) the Bill to Amend the Law on Establishment of the Security Council of Japan. While these three bills do not mean that legislative work for Japan's defense is complete, they may significantly improve Japan's defense posture on the following legal grounds.

1) The first bill will: a) set a general idea on how Japan responds to an armed attack; b) provide the GOJ with the guidelines for enacting necessary laws to ensure protection of people's lives, smooth and effective operations of the SDF, and smooth and effective operations of US forces in Japan. More importantly, the bill will c) set a two-year deadline to enact such laws.

2) The second bill is intended to amend the "SDF Law" in order to make partial improvements for the SDF's smooth operation in case of an armed attack against Japan. For example, this bill adds a series of special provisions on relevant laws such as the Road Traffic Law, Medical Service Law, Building Standards Law, and others.

3) The third bill is intended to clarify and strengthen the Security Council, which is the core element of Japan's decision-making in case of an armed attack against the country.[33]

In June 2003, the Diet passed these three bills with a nearly unanimous vote. As the first bill dictates, the GOJ will have to complete the work to enact laws for protection of people's lives and for smooth operations of both the SDF and US forces.

Another key component for the defense of Japan is the SDF's capacity to deal with newly emerging threats such as missile and unconventional attacks. With respect to missile defense, the Nodong launch in 1993 and Taepodong launch in 1998 drew the keen attention of the Japanese public as well as military planners and policymakers. Following approval of the Japan Security Council in 1998, the GOJ and the United States began a joint technical research program in 1999 on elements of a Navy Theater Wide Defense (NTWD) system. Nose cones, kinetic warheads, infrared seekers, and stage-two rocket engines have been the focus of the research. In May 2003, Prime Minister Koizumi observed to President Bush that "missile defense is essential for Japan's defense and joint programs on this issue will facilitate promotion of the credibility of the alliance. Japan will accelerate its efforts for deliberation on missile defense." The Defense White Paper of 2003, which particularly notes the technical feasibility of the US PAC 3 system and Aegis-mounted ballistic missile defense system, says that the GOJ will conduct intensive study on (a) the technical feasibility, including capabilities and timelines of various systems; (b) the operational concept and system architecture best suited for Japan based on thorough consideration (including finances); (c) the operational and legal issues related to missile defense; (d) the relation between missile defense programs and the Three Principles on Arms Exports, which virtually ban exports of weapons and related technologies; (e) the impact on neighboring countries; and (f) Japan-US cooperation on the programs.[34] In August 2003, the JDA proposed some ¥142 billion for the FTY 2004 procurements of Patriot missiles (PAC-3s) and Aegis-mounted Standard missiles (SM-3) and the funding for programs related to those systems.[35] On December 19, 2003, the GOJ issued a cabinet decision on "Introduction of Ballistic Missile Defense and Other Issues" and announced that the GOJ would build up a BMD system by upgrading Aegis destroyers and Patriot missiles and integrating them.[36]

In recent years, the SDF has also been making efforts to improve its posture to deal with unconventional threats such as attacks by terrorists and commando-type enemies. The MSDF, following the suspicious boat incident off the Noto Peninsula of 1999, activated the Special Boarding Unit in March 2001, and enhanced its capability for boarding inspections. The GSDF, likewise, is planning to activate a Special Operations Group by the end of FY2003 (March 2004) so that it can better cope with unconventional threats. The GOJ has made additional progress in terms of the legal basis for such operations. As mentioned above, in 2001, a new concept of Guarding Operations was introduced into the SDF Law, in addition to the existing, and more traditional types, including defense, pubic security, and disaster relief. Through this amendment, SDF units are authorized to conduct operations to protect the facilities of the SDF and of US forces in Japan whenever the prime minister sees the possibility of sabotage against such facilities.

When the SDF units conduct antiterrorism or anticommando operations, it is essential to have close coordination and cooperation with law enforcement authorities, such as police forces. In this context, there have also been significant improvements. The 1954 agreement on the procedures of coordination between the SDF and the police in case of public security operations was amended in December 2000, in order to make the agreement workable in incidents such as illicit activities by armed spy agents. Previously, the agreement had only presupposed riot suppression. In recent years, more and more SDF units have started training regularly with local police authorities in order to be prepared to deal with unconventional threats.

Conclusions: Remaining and Urgent Tasks

This paper has discussed the policies undertaken by the GOJ in recent years for bilateral cooperation with the United States on security issues. These political and legal measures can be categorized into three groups according to geographical proximity to Japan: (1) measures for defense of Japan, (2) measures for bilateral cooperation in case of Situations in Areas Surrounding Japan, and (3) measures for expanding the role of the SDF in international PKO. While remarkable progress has been made in each area, urgent tasks remain.

First, with respect to bilateral cooperation for Japan's defense, a general legal architecture has been established by enacting three laws related to dealing with armed attacks against Japan. The SDF has started to improve its capabilities to deal with newly emerging threats, but it has more to do. On the one hand, in June 2003, the SDF Law was amended to streamline SDF operations for the defense of Japan. On the other hand, the GOJ is likewise tasked with enacting laws to ensure that US forces operate smoothly and effectively, and to safeguard people's lives in the event of armed attack against Japan within the next two years. When these tasks are accomplished, a legal framework for national contingencies will have been established, and the JDA's thirty-year-long dream will come true. The posture for missile defense and anti-terrorism operations requires a comprehensive approach, involving cooperation among various agencies of national and local governments, the private sector, and the SDF and US forces. It is essential to deepen the nationwide discussions on these issues.

Second, the enactment of the law on Situations in Areas Surrounding Japan in May 1999 and the Ship Inspection Law in October 2001 provided a legal basis for bilateral cooperation in such situations. The revised Defense Guidelines stipulate mechanisms for planning and execution on coordination and cooperation between the two countries. As former vice defense minister Akiyama states, "these mechanisms do not seem to perform as efficiently as the Defense Guidelines expected." [37] It is important to develop bilateral contingency plans with relevant agencies and ministries in the two countries, so that the SDF and US forces can operate and cooperate with each other. In addition, it is necessary for all the players to develop their experience in such cooperation through bilateral exercises and simulations. Such exercises will be beneficial to evaluate the contingency plans and to verify the effectiveness of the mechanisms for coordination dictated by the Defense Guidelines.

Third, the role of the SDF in international PKO has been expanded in recent years. Thus the scope of Japan's bilateral cooperation with the United States is much wider than before in terms of activities dealing with global issues, such as peace and security in Iraq. As noted above, the revised Defense Guidelines, the law on Situations in Areas Surrounding Japan, the Anti-Terrorism Special Measures Law, and others have identified a nearly maximum scope for what Japan or the SDF can do under the conditions that did not allow the exercise of the right of collective defense. Meanwhile, Japan has continued to enact "special measures laws" to provide an ad hoc legal basis for specific missions, such as anti-terrorism activities after 9/11 and humanitarian and reconstruction assistance in Iraq. These special laws have arisen because Japan lacks a permanent legal basis that provides an overall concept for its contribution to international efforts for world peace and security, with the exception of UN PKO and humanitarian relief operations. The SDF has continued to organize provisional units for the latter missions based upon relevant special measures laws or specific UN requests. This is partly because international PKO are not treated as major missions as described by Article Three of the SDF Law; rather, these include defense, public order, and disaster-relief operations. PKO and humanitarian missions are listed in Article 100, which dictates the SDF's miscellaneous roles. Many believe that this situation requires adjustment. For example, the ruling Liberal Democratic Party, in its 2003 general election manifesto, argued that peace cooperation should be based on permanent, rather than special measure laws. [38] The Defense

White Paper of 2003 quotes the Report of the Advisory Group on International Cooperation for Peace recommending that the government "amend the SDF Law to establish international peace cooperation as a regular duty of the SDF, and prepare units within the SDF with a high level of readiness to ensure timely and appropriate dispatch."[39] Japan must continue discussions on these points.

In 2004, the GOJ has already begun to discuss defense policy aimed at revision of the National Defense Program Outline. The issues raised throughout this paper will be examined during this process. The United States is reviewing its own national security posture focusing on forward deployment to better deal with the post–9/11 security environment. Both US forces and the SDF are pursuing their transformation based on rapidly advancing information technology. Since the two countries are standing at a pivotal point in their respective security policies, it is vitally important for us to have comprehensive, strategic dialogue. The two governments made continuous efforts in the mid-1990s to exchange views on Japan's NDPO and the US–East Asia Strategy Report, which resulted in the Japan-US Joint Declaration on Security and the revised Defense Guidelines. The two governments also devoted tremendous energy to discussing the base issues, centering on those located in Okinawa. Such dialogues involved participation from people at all levels, from national leaders and cabinet members to policymakers and military planners. The expertise and flexibility of those from outside the governments, such as academics and business people, facilitated the exchange. Such Japan-US dialogue is particularly crucial in the post–Cold War period. Today's agenda is wide-ranging, from policy consultation on global issues to operational coordination for specific crises, from strategic concepts to base issues, and from day-to-day business to long-term objectives. Experts across professional levels and fields should be mobilized in order to revitalize the strategic dialogue that the United States and Japan enjoyed in the mid-1990s.

NOTES

[1] According to a DoD report, out of $61 billion of US expenditure for the crisis and the war, some $54 billion (88 percent) was from the international community, of which $11.2 billion came specifically from Japan.

[2] The Diet rejected Prime Minister Kaifu's proposal on the Law on UN Peacekeeping Operations in November 1990, which was designed to authorize participation in UN activities for peace, such as UN PKO and coalition operations under the UN auspices.

[3] Prime Minister Hosokawa first summoned the Advisory Group on Defense Issues on February 28, 1994. The group submitted the report, "The Modality of the Security and Defense Capability of Japan: The Outlook for the 21st Century," to Prime Minister Murayama on August 12, 1994.

[4] See Advisory Group on Defense Issues.

[5] See Advisory Group on Defense Issues.

[6] Akihiko Tanaka, *Anzenhosho: Sengo 50 nen no Mosaku* (National Security: Fifty Years after World War II), Yomiuri-shinbunsha (1997: Tokyo).

[7] National Defense Program Outline In and After FY 1996 (NDPO 1995), decided by the Security Council of Japan and the Cabinet on November 28, 1995.

[8] The report indeed pointed out three core policies in the following order: (1) promotion of multilateral security cooperation on a global and regional scale; (2) enhancement of the functions of the Japan-US security relationship; and (3) possession of a highly reliable and efficient defense capability based on a strengthened information capability and a prompt crisis-management capability.

[9] Patrick M. Cronin and Michael J. Green, "Redefining the US-Japan Alliance: Tokyo's National Defense Program" (McNair Paper 31), Washington, DC: National Defense University, November 1994, pp. 2–3.

[10] Cronin and Green, p. 15.

[11] Office of International Security Affairs, "United States Security Strategy for the East Asia-Pacific Region, (EASR of 95)," February 1995.

[12] The US commitment of 100,000 personnel along with the same number for Europe was first declared by the "Report on the Bottom-Up Review," issued by Secretary of Defense Les Aspin in October 1993.

[13] EASR of 1995, p.10.

[14] NDPO 1995.

[15] Masaru Honda, "Reisengo no Doumei Hyoryu (Drift of the Alliance after the Cold War)," *Nichibei Domei Hanseiki* (Japan-US Alliance in a Half-Century), Tokyo: Asahi-Shimbunsha, 2001, p. 502.

[16] NDPO 1995.

[17] *Japan-US Joint Declaration on Security: Alliance for the 21st Century*, issued by Prime Minister Hashimoto and President Clinton on April 17, 1996.

[18] The Security Consultative Committee was established in 1960. The SCC started with the membership of ministers for foreign affairs and defense from the Japanese side, the US ambassador to Japan, and the commander of the Pacific Command (U.S). In 1990, the level of US membership was raised to secretaries of defense and state.

[19] Tanaka, pp. 382–84.

[20] Honda, p. 502.

[21] "The Guidelines for US-Japan Defense Cooperation," reported by the Subcommittee for Defense Cooperation to and authorized by the Security Consultative Committee on September 23, 1997 (hereafter Revised Defense Guidelines).

[22] See Revised Defense Guidelines.

[23] Japan-US Joint Declaration on Security.

[24] Department of Defense, The United States Security Strategy for the Asia-Pacific Region (East Asian Strategy Report 1998), released on November 1998.

[25] See Revised Defense Guidelines.

[26] The *Defense of Japan* (Defense White Paper) of recent years contain detailed explanations of the laws. See also the English version of *Defense of Japan 2002*, Tokyo: Urban Connection, 2002, pp. 189–93.

[27] Masahiro Akiyama, "*Nichibei no Senryaku-taiwa ga Hajimatta* (The Japan-US Strategic Dialogue)," Tokyo: Aki-Shobo, 2002, p. 270.

[28] The Anti-Terrorism Special Measures Law, cited in *Defense of Japan 2002*, p. 112.

[29] Foreign Press Center/Japan, "Diet Enacts Iraq Reconstruction Law; Self-Defense Forces to be Dispatched to Provide Assistance," July 29, 2003.

[30] Statement by Prime Minister Junichiro Koizumi on the Basic Plan regarding the measures based on the Law Concerning the Special Measures on Humanitarian and Reconstruction Assistance in Iraq, *http://www.lkantei/foreign/policy/2003/031209danwa_e/html*.

[31] See the outline of the Basic Plan regarding Response Measures Based on the Law Concerning the Special Measures on Humanitarian and Reconstruction Assistance in Iraq, *http://www.lkantei/foreign/policy/2003/031209housin_e/html.*

[32] Since the late 1970s, the JDA has been studying necessary legal measures to ensure smooth operations in the event of an armed attack against Japan. While interim reports were submitted in 1981 and 1984, few efforts to enact necessary laws were made until recently.

[33] The "General Outline of Legislation Regarding Responses to Armed Attack" is explained in detail in the *Defense of Japan 2002,* pp. 146–59.

[34] *Defense of Japan 2003* (Defense White Paper, Japanese Version), pp. 308–10.

[35] Japan Defense Agency, *Focal Points of Defense Buildup and Budget Request for FY 2004.*

[36] "On Introduction of Ballistic Missile Defense System and Other Issues," Decisions of the National Security Council and the Cabinet of Japan, December 19, 2003.

[37] Akiyama, pp. 270–71.

[38] Policy Research Council of the Liberal Democratic Party, *Jimin-to Juuten Shisaku 2004* (Policies with Priority for 2004), p. 51.

[39] *Defense of Japan 2003,* pp. 212–13.

US-JAPAN DEFENSE COOPERATION: CAN JAPAN BECOME THE GREAT BRITAIN OF ASIA? SHOULD IT?

Ralph A. Cossa

The depth and breadth of defense cooperation between Washington and Tokyo since September 11, 2001 have been unprecedented; the only thing that has risen faster than the level of cooperation has been Washington's expectations regarding the creation of an even more "normal" defense relationship with its long-standing ally in East Asia. While Japan may not yet be the "UK of Asia," as once envisioned by Deputy Secretary of State Richard Armitage, it is not a stretch to call Japanese prime minister Koizumi Junichiro Asia's answer to Tony Blair.

Prime Minister Koizumi is one of a small, select group of Asia-Pacific leaders—Australian prime minister John Howard is another—who have won President Bush's utmost trust, confidence, and sincere gratitude. Koizumi has unyieldingly supported the US war on terrorism in all its manifestations and has willingly bucked domestic public opinion to provide support to the two major campaigns in Washington's ongoing war: Afghanistan and Iraq. This has paid handsome dividends in helping to achieve what both sides generally agree are the "best relations ever." However, it may also raise hopes in Washington (and in certain quarters in Tokyo) that will not be easily fulfilled as both sides strive to create a more equal partnership.

Prime Minister Koizumi's recent, unprecedented decision to send Japanese Ground Self-Defense Force (JGSDF) troops to Iraq—which remains militarily unstable, despite the declared end to major combat operations—to help in that country's pacification and reconstruction is just the most recent in a series of adjustments that have occurred in the operational arrangements underpinning US-Japan defense cooperation. And, while 9/11 and the resulting war on terrorism are pivotal in understanding and justifying the expanded defense relationship, it is important to look back to the mid-1990s, when examining the current evolution of the alliance. Looking at this recent history is crucial not only because it puts today's changes into perspective, but also because the current trend toward developing a "more equal" partnership dates back to an earlier turning point in the relationship: the *US-Japan Joint Declaration on Security Alliance for the 21st Century* issued by then-president Bill Clinton and his Japanese counterpart, Prime Minister Hashimoto Ryutaro, during their April 1996 summit meeting in Tokyo.

The 1996 Clinton-Hashimoto summit, which signaled an official end to the "Japan-bashing" era (and predated the subsequent Clinton "Japan-passing" era), set the stage for the revised 1997 Defense Guidelines, which in turn ushered in the dramatic changes we have witnessed since 9/11. It is interesting to note that the Joint Declaration and revised Guidelines were provoked by several events that are strangely reminiscent of more recent occurrences: a US-led military campaign against Iraq and a Korean peninsula nuclear crisis.

One need only compare and contrast Japan's response to the previous Iraq/DPRK crises with the current ones to realize that, thankfully, it is not déjà vu all over again. Despite justifiable criticism of President Clinton's tendency to ignore the alliance during the closing (Japan-passing) years of his administration, his Joint Declaration with Prime Minister Hashimoto laid the groundwork that their successors would subsequently build upon. This is especially true given that 9/11 provided the political cover to move the relationship forward much faster than anyone drafting the Joint Statement or revised Defense Guidelines would have then imagined.

Pre–9/11 Developments

1991 Gulf War

In 1991, when a global "coalition of the willing" was forming to drive Iraqi forces out of Kuwait, Japan opted out of active participation, electing instead to write a very large check (US$13 billion) to help cover Desert Storm expenses. Despite this generosity (which required a tax increase to finance and accounted for some 20 percent of all the outside financial support the United States received for the war), many in Washington criticized Tokyo for not doing more, particularly in light of Japan's heavy dependence on Persian Gulf oil. The (George H.W.) Bush administration understood the political and constitutional constraints under which Japan was operating, but many senior officials still privately expressed frustration that even noncombat logistic lift support seemed a bridge too far for Tokyo to even attempt to cross.

On the positive side, Washington was grateful for Tokyo's assistance (even though it occasioned much soul-searching and heated debate) in clearing mines in the Persian Gulf and its associated sea lanes once hostilities ended. This minesweeping effort can be seen as one of the first major examples of a new operational arrangement between Tokyo and Washington: it helped to set the stage for greater Japanese involvement in subsequent peacekeeping operations (PKO) both within and beyond the Asia-Pacific region. The public acceptance of this mission within Japan—where it generated considerable national pride—and the broad support for Japan's involvement in this military activity demonstrated that nonthreatening Japanese security contributions to international efforts were acceptable. (Participation in Cambodian PKO was another example.)

This opened the door for greater involvement in PKO efforts, in Timor and elsewhere, even prior to 9/11. Nonetheless, after-the-fact support during the first Gulf War did not fully blunt skepticism about Japan's reliability as an ally once the shooting starts.

1993–94 Korean Crisis

Of perhaps greater concern to military planners, and those concerned about alliance maintenance,was the 1993–94 crisis that emerged on the Korean peninsula after Pyongyang threatened to withdraw from the nuclear Non-Proliferation Treaty (NPT). The Clinton administration initially took a hard line, building up defenses on the peninsula and initiating a move toward imposing UN sanctions against North Korea if it carried through with its threat to withdraw from the NPT and deny International Atomic Energy Administration (IAEA) inspection and safeguards at its nuclear facilities. Questions were raised about what Japan could or would do to support a UN sanctions effort and the answer seemed to be "not much." Given that North Korea was also stating that the implementation of sanctions meant war, prudent US military planners also started asking what Japan could or would do in the event that happened. Disturbingly, the answer was assumed to be, "even less."

What was even worse was Japan's reluctance even to discuss possible or desirable types of military cooperation in the event of a crisis or war. A timely intervention by former president Jimmy Carter and the subsequent 1994 US-DPRK Agreed Framework allowed both sides to step back from the brink and let Tokyo off the hook. However, the practical limitations of the alliance once again became all too apparent, this time not in some remote location but in Japan's own backyard.

This, more than anything else, sounded warning bells in Washington and Tokyo, especially when combined with the understandable outrage that followed the tragic rape of an Okinawan schoolgirl, which further called the alliance's viability into question. Had a crisis that threatened US and Japanese interests erupted in the region—conflict on the Korean peninsula being the most obvious example—and Japan had refused adequately to support US efforts, this could have torn at the fabric of the alliance. Defining "adequately support" to the satisfaction of both nations, and in a manner not threatening to Japan's neighbors, was the challenge. As former US assistant secretary of defense (and current deputy secretary of state) Richard Armitage noted in early 1996, "The most important issue in the current relationship is not 'how many forces?' or 'what weapons systems?' but rather 'What are the US and Japan going to do as security partners should the need arise?'"

Largely unspoken but clearly recognized was concern not just over a Korean contingency but also a potential crisis across the Taiwan Strait. This worry became more prominent in the run-up to the March 1996 Taiwan presidential elections, when Beijing used a series of missile tests to underscore its warnings against potential independence movements. The move largely backfired, especially after Washington deployed two aircraft carrier battle groups to the region to demonstrate its commitment to a "peaceful resolution" of the issue. This also bears traces of *déjà vu* all over again, given the even more provocative—at least in Beijing's eyes—Taiwan presidential campaign of 2003. However, Beijing seems to have learned the lesson of 1996 and has, at least as of this writing, taken a more measured, nuanced approach—with help from Washington—in discouraging pro-independence forces in Taiwan.

1996 Joint Declaration

The April 1996 Clinton-Hashimoto Tokyo summit was a significant step forward in answering Armitage's provocative question. Building upon the Defense Department's 1995 *East Asia Strategy Report (EASR)*—which stressed the centrality of the alliance to Washington's East Asia security strategy and the coincident US and Japanese security goals and objectives in Asia—the summit represented a major effort by both allies, and especially by Japan, to revitalize the bilateral security relationship in order to ensure its relevancy in the post–Cold War era. It also demonstrated Tokyo's increased willingness to take a more active leadership role in regional economic and security affairs.

The Joint Declaration signed by both leaders during the summit meeting committed both sides to the revitalization of the defense relationship. It recognized close bilateral defense cooperation as a "central element" in the security relationship and went on to say that "The two leaders agreed on the necessity to promote bilateral policy coordination, including studies on bilateral cooperation in dealing with situations that may emerge in the areas surrounding Japan and which will have an important influence on the peace and security of Japan." In short, the Joint Declaration recognized the need, in peacetime, to begin to define each country's respective role and, most importantly for Japan, to develop procedures for overcoming obstacles to performing them. Prior to this, contingency planning for any scenario short of invasion or other direct attack on Japan was difficult, if not politically impossible.

The signing of the Joint Declaration opened the door for greater defense planning and cooperation. This was formalized at the September 1996 "2+2" Security Consultative Committee (SCC) Meeting (which brought together the foreign and defense ministers of both nations), when Washington and Tokyo both professed their commitment to "reaffirming and strengthening" the alliance. The SCC Subcommittee for Defense Cooperation was then tasked to review and revise the 1978 Guidelines for US-Japan Defense Cooperation. This review was completed in September 1997.

Defense Guidelines Review

The revised 1997 Defense Guidelines represented a praiseworthy attempt by military planners in Japan and the United States to find common ground between the type of support that US planners desired from Japan and the level of support Japan was willing and felt constitutionally capable of providing. They address defense cooperation under three broad categories: cooperation under normal circumstances; actions in response to an armed attack against Japan; and cooperation in situations in areas surrounding Japan that will have an important influence on Japan's peace and security. The common goal was enhanced defense cooperation in order to maintain peace and stability.

It is useful to note that the Guidelines do not *obligate* Japan (or the United States) to do anything new. Nor do they guarantee that Japan will provide the envisioned support under any and every conceivable circumstance. The new Guidelines merely provide "a general framework and policy direction." To emphasize this point, a line in the most controversial section dealing with "situations in areas surrounding Japan" notes that "in responding to such situations, measures taken may differ depending on circumstances." In other words, there is no guarantee that steps outlined in the Defense Guidelines will ever be taken. The Guidelines clearly delineate what Japan should not be expected to do—in and of itself, an important factor for military planners—but provide no guarantees of Japanese support.

The Guidelines also specifically tie Japan's support in enforcing economic sanctions to United Nations Security Council (UNSC) resolutions, although one can interpret the text as not excluding other types of sanction-enforcement operations. However, in this, as in all other actions outlined by the new Defense Guidelines, nothing happens without a decision on the part of the Japanese government at the time of the crisis. The framework's boundaries were clearly delineated; only "defensive actions" were envisioned. Nonetheless, the 1997 Defense Guidelines represented an important step forward in Japan's quest to become a more "normal" nation and a more equal security partner with the United States.

Implementing Legislation

The next step, which took several years to accomplish and in some cases was still not complete when the 9/11 attacks occurred, was the development and enactment into law of the necessary implementing legislation. The three primary pieces of legislation—amendment of the Acquisition and Cross-Servicing Agreement (ACSA) to include regional contingencies; amendment of the Self Defense Forces Law to permit certain rear-area support missions for US forces during regional contingencies; and the creation of a Regional Contingency Law to permit nonmilitary rear-area support in Japan for US forces during regional contingencies—passed the Diet in May 1999.

As the Clinton administration was drawing to a close, its final "2+2" SCC meeting (in New York, ironically on September 11, 2000) featured the establishment of a Bilateral Coordination Mechanism to link Japanese government agencies with the US Embassy and US forces in Japan in times of war. This coordination mechanism was critical to implementing the revised Defense Guidelines, since the United States and Japan lacked a joint and combined command of the sort that manages military responses in NATO or the US-ROK alliance. In late November, the Diet also passed a watered-down Maritime Interdiction Operations Law that gave the Japanese Maritime Self Defense Forces (JMSDF) the authority to stop and search nonmilitary vessels (but only when acting in support of UN-authorized sanctions or with the consent of the ship being boarded).

Armitage/Nye Report

Just prior to the November 2000 US presidential election, the Institute for National Strategic Studies at the National Defense University in Washington published a report (October 11, 2000) that outlines what a more activist US security policy with Japan might look like. While the report was drafted by a bipartisan team of specialists led by Republican Richard Armitage and Democrat Joseph Nye (another former assistant secretary of defense), it was generally interpreted in Tokyo as a "Republican" plan (and, to this day, is often referred to merely as "The Armitage Report"). The report called for "excellence without arrogance" from the United States—a theme used by candidate Bush—while suggesting a more open door in Washington for Japanese ideas and initiatives. It also encouraged Tokyo to expand its security and diplomatic responsibilities in Asia.

The most controversial aspect of the report was the observation that Japan's decision not to exercise the right of collective defense is an obstacle to alliance cooperation. Many in Tokyo interpreted this as an endorsement of constitutional revision. However, the report was careful to emphasize that decisions on the Constitution must be thoroughly considered by the Japanese people themselves. For the most part, the report was well received in Japan, though many questioned whether the Japanese political system, especially under a very weak and ineffective Prime Minister Mori Yoshiro, was up to the task. This question was quickly laid to rest following the surprise election of Prime Minister Koizumi in April 2001.

The Bush-Koizumi Era

Pre-9/11

US-Japan defense cooperation has clearly been taken to a higher level under President George W. Bush and Prime Minister Koizumi. While much of the progress has been attributed to 9/11—and, as previously argued, the terrorist attacks on that day provided both the impetus and the political cover to accelerate the defense relationship—both sides had already clearly signaled their intention to create a broader, deeper security relationship. In fact, even before Koizumi's election, President Bush had issued a joint statement with his predecessor during Prime Minister Mori's visit to Washington that seemed to go beyond the 1996 Clinton-Hashimoto Joint Communiqué in pledging "a dynamic approach to bilateral defense consultation and planning." Included also was a pledge to "strengthen joint efforts to address the transnational challenges of the twenty-first century." (The ability of both sides to handle effectively the tragic accidental sinking of a Japanese training ship by a US submarine also demonstrated that the defense and broader bilateral relationship were on solid ground.)

The selection of Koizumi Junichiro as prime minister dramatically increased the prospects for still deeper cooperation. Fears that Japan would prove a reluctant partner largely vanished amid Koizumi's talk of leading his nation toward a more "normal" role in international affairs. Seemingly taking a page from the Armitage/Nye Report, Koizumi stated that it was desirable for Japan to be allowed to participate in collective defense activities and to help defend its allies (read: the United States) in the event of regional crisis. He also noted that Article 9 of the Japanese constitution—which stipulates that Japan shall never maintain land, sea, or air forces—"fails to reflect reality." Koizumi's view seems to dovetail nicely with calls for a more equal relationship coming from Washington.

Deputy Secretary Armitage seemed to echo Mr. Koizumi's remarks during his May 2001 visit to Tokyo when he noted that "the lack of an ability to participate in collective self-defense, although they are signatories to a defense treaty, is an obstacle. I think it is a healthy thing for the Japanese to look at some of these things and see what is reasonable and what is not." But, while the Bush administration clearly supports an increased Japanese security role, even if this requires constitutional reinterpretation or revision, Armitage and other administration spokesmen have been careful not to call directly for revision, again stressing that this is a domestic Japanese decision.

The Bush administration continues to reinforce this message. Secretary Armitage, as recently as early February 2004, told a Japan National Press Club audience in Tokyo: "I believe that we can say that this debate [about changing the constitution] has never been more serious than it is today in discussing how to deal with collective self-defense, which many of us in the global community, and apparently increasingly in Japan, view as common sense, though clearly these are decisions that only the people of Japan can make."

Washington had other good reasons to applaud the new prime minister. Shortly after taking office, Koizumi said that definitions of "rear areas" were flexible, implying that Japan might be able to provide more support for US forces in a contingency than had previously been thought. His chief cabinet secretary, Fukuda Yasuo, also ordered studies on ways to lift restraints on Japanese soldiers participating in UN PKO. Koizumi also expressed support for missile defense (telling the Diet in early June that the project deserves further study). In short, the trend toward enhanced defense cooperation had been set in motion well before the tragic events of 9/11.

Response to 9/11

Immediately after the attack, Prime Minister Koizumi went on record stating that Japan would "spare no effort in providing assistance and cooperation" in support of America's war on terrorism. He followed this up with even stronger commitments to provide intelligence and military logistical support during his late September 2001 visit to New York and Washington. During his meeting with President Bush, Koizumi said (in English, for emphasis): "We Japanese firmly stand behind the United States to fight terrorism." He then added, much to Washington's amazement and delight, that "It will no longer hold that the Self-Defense Forces should not be sent to danger spots. There is no such thing as a safe place."

Backing up these assertions, Koizumi quickly put together a seven-point program to respond to the crisis. It included measures allowing the Self-Defense Forces to provide logistical support to the US military in the event of a retaliatory strike; strengthening security measures at important facilities in Japan; dispatching Japanese ships to gather information; strengthening international cooperation over immigration control; providing humanitarian and economic aid to affected countries; assisting refugees fleeing areas that might be hit by US retaliation; and cooperating with other countries to ensure stability in the international economic system. In addition, the Japanese government announced that it would send warships to collect intelligence in the Indian Ocean and would provide support for US vessels heading for battle stations.

At the same time, however, the prime minister made it clear that Japan would be bound by its constitutional limits and President Bush acknowledged the limits and restraints under which the Japanese operate. Bush applauded the Japanese contribution and noted "people contribute in different ways to this coalition . . . resources will be deployed in different ways—intelligence-gathering, diplomacy, humanitarian aid, as well as cutting off resources" to terrorists.

To almost everyone's amazement, Prime Minister Koizumi quickly delivered on his seven-point package, getting emergency legislation through both Houses of the Diet by the end of October 2001. As promised, the legislation enabled the Self-Defense Forces (SDF) to provide noncombat support to the US coalition and to protect US facilities in Japan. It also allowed Japanese forces to fire against territorial violators. In a concession to the opposition, the bill had a two-year time limit, and required that the Diet approve any deployment within twenty days of the dispatch of the SDF. To minimize chances of conflict with the Constitution, the transportation of ammunition and arms in foreign territory was not allowed.

RALPH A. COSSA

New Operational Arrangements After 9/11

Enduring Freedom

This emergency legislation allowed new operational arrangements to evolve quickly. In early November 2001, two Japanese destroyers and a supply ship left home port for the Indian Ocean to provide offshore, noncombat support for Operation Enduring Freedom. The only disappointment was Japan's failure, despite not-so-subtle US pressure, initially to include an Aegis destroyer in its Indian Ocean task force. The Japanese Cabinet has since routinely voted to extend SDF support for the war in Afghanistan and, in a significant step, finally decided in December 2002 to dispatch one of its high-tech Aegis-equipped vessels to the Indian Ocean as part of that effort. Critics had argued that the protection afforded by the Aegis radar, which can track two hundred enemy aircraft and missiles simultaneously and shoot down ten targets at the same time, would appear to constitute "collective self defense," which has been prohibited by the prevailing interpretation of the Japanese Constitution.

Immediately prior to and since the March 2003 Iraq invasion, Tokyo has stepped up its logistical support for the coalition forces operating in Afghanistan. In early March, JMSDF ships began refueling Italian, Spanish, French, German, New Zealand, and Dutch warships participating in Operation Enduring Freedom, in addition to the US and British vessels. This freed up US logistics forces to support Operation Iraqi Freedom. At the onset of hostilities in Iraq, the Japan Defense Agency (JDA) ordered additional air surveillance by AWACS over the Sea of Japan and stepped up air and sea monitoring of North Korea. (Similar US flights operate from Kadena Air Force Base in Okinawa.) The National Police Agency increased security at 174 US military bases and facilities and at 162 embassies and facilities of countries supporting the United States.

Operation Iraqi Freedom

Japan did not directly participate in Operation Iraqi Freedom, but the above measures—and especially the expanded Indian Ocean refueling operations—allowed the United States to shift more assets to the Iraqi campaign and thus constituted significant (yet still constitutional) indirect support to the war effort. It was sufficient to have Tokyo listed on the Iraqi Freedom coalition of the willing membership list.

Boots on the Ground

The remaining issue to be addressed was Deputy Secretary Armitage's repeated observation about the need for Tokyo to put "boots on the ground" in Iraq, despite continuing low- (and, at times, not-so-low-) level hostilities. This has now been accomplished with the December 2003 announcement that Prime Minister Koizumi had finally approved a troop deployment plan, submitted by

Defense Agency Minister Ishiba Shigeru, formalizing Japan's first military move into a war zone since 1945. Japan's air force sent an advance team of about forty airmen to Iraq, Kuwait, and Qatar in late December to prepare the way for an airlift operation by a larger contingent starting in early 2004. Ishiba also ordered the army and navy to get ready for deployment later, though without giving dates.

The army is to send about 550 medics and engineer troops to Samawah, south of Baghdad. The navy's job is to ferry in vehicles and heavy equipment for the troops. Starting in January, about 150 air force troops will provide transportation services for US and other coalition forces, flying a U-4 multipurpose plane and a Boeing 747 as well as C-130s, between Kuwait, Baghdad, Basra, Balad, and Mosul. The planes are not permitted to transport weapons and ammunition for other countries (although Ishiba said they are not going to open each crate). The deployment plan also said it was permissible to transport soldiers who are carrying weapons. This statement shows how far things have come but also how far they must still go, given that even seemingly simple and mundane matters like a soldier carrying his or her own personal weapon draws scrutiny. The current operating guidelines also stipulate that if combat breaks out near where they are, Japanese troops are to stop work, evacuate, report the circumstances to the Defense Agency minister in Tokyo, and await instructions on what to do.

Diplomatic and Financial Support

Tokyo's support for Afghanistan and Iraq has not been limited to military support. Tokyo has taken the lead role in Afghan reconstruction efforts, drawing high praise from Washington. In his landmark speech on Asia policy to the Asia Society in June 2002 (which remains the administration's most comprehensive review of Asia policy in general), Secretary of State Colin Powell praised Japanese support to Operation Enduring Freedom ("we could not have asked for a more resolute response") and underscored Tokyo's "superb leadership" in the Afghan reconstruction effort. He also praised Tokyo for collaborating closely with Washington in trying to take the war on terrorism to the international financial community.

Prime Minister Koizumi was also an outspoken supporter of Washington's efforts to obtain a stronger UNSC resolution against Iraq, making numerous phone calls to lobby Security Council members. More importantly, when the UNSC fig leaf was removed, Koizumi remained firmly behind President Bush and appeared delighted when Japan was named among the "coalition of the willing," even though no Japanese troops were committed to the war. Prime Minister Koizumi's actions, like those of counterparts Tony Blair in the UK and John Howard in Australia, required great political courage, given rising domestic opposition at the time to a war against Iraq, a fact not overlooked in Washington.

Korean Crisis

Japan's support to the United States has not been limited to Iraq and Afghanistan. Tokyo has steadfastly supported President Bush's multilateral approach toward the nuclear standoff on the Korean peninsula. Washington, in return, continues to argue that Japanese participation is "essential," despite complaints from Pyongyang and only lukewarm support from Seoul and Beijing for a Japanese seat at the table. Tokyo has also played an important role at the regular Trilateral Coordination and Oversight Group (TCOG) meetings with Washington and Seoul, urging US flexibility at times, but most importantly echoing Washington's insistence that nuclear weapons cannot be tolerated in North Korea. Japan's stance provides some much-needed backbone to Seoul, which seems to have a looser definition of "will not tolerate" than its other two TCOG partners.

Seldom have Washington and Tokyo been so close in their views of how best to deal with Pyongyang. Recall that in the closing months of the Clinton administration, there was great fear in Tokyo that Washington was going to get too far out in front of Tokyo on this issue. Following an exchange of high-level visits and amid preparations for a possible Clinton visit to Pyongyang, many were concerned that Japan would be pressured to speed up its normalization process with Pyongyang, perhaps beyond a point that was politically sustainable. Conversely, once the September 2002 Koizumi visit to Pyongyang was announced, concern was expressed that Japan might move ahead of a more cautious, tentative Bush administration, which seemed reluctant to engage in meaningful dialogue with a member of the so-called axis of evil.

Today, however, both Washington and Tokyo appear in lockstep, with both insisting on an immediate, verifiable halt to Pyongyang's nuclear weapons programs and ambitions, as well as an immediate full accounting and satisfactory resolution of the abductee issue. Japan's clear pronouncements about its right, under the principle of self-defense, to take preemptive action in the event of an imminent DPRK missile launch, while not too credible militarily, nonetheless provide political support to the US doctrine of preemption while also underscoring the need for close military-to-military cooperation between Washington and Tokyo. As a self-proclaimed member of the coalition of the willing, Japan's seemingly unqualified support for the US-led military campaign against Iraq also solidifies the alliance while sending North Korea a clear message that Tokyo would no doubt be equally, if not more, willing to support Washington in dealing with threats closer to home.

Proliferation Security Initiative

Crossing yet another threshold in military-to-military cooperation, Tokyo also became a charter member of the US-instigated Proliferation Security Initiative (PSI), aimed at stemming the flow of weapons of mass destruction. The PSI, first laid out by President Bush in May 2003 and formalized at an eleven-nation meeting (involving Australia, France, Germany, Italy, Japan, the Netherlands,

Poland, Portugal, Spain, the UK, and the United States) in Madrid in June, is "a global initiative with global reach," under which coalition members agreed, in Brisbane in July, "to move quickly on direct, practical measures to impede the trafficking in weapons of mass destruction (WMD), missiles, and related items." The Brisbane meeting focused on "defining actions necessary to collectively or individually interdict [WMD shipments] at sea, in the air, or on the land." A third meeting, in Paris in September "continued work on the modalities for interdiction, in particular effective information sharing and operational capabilities for interdiction." The eleven participants also agreed in Paris on a Statement of Interdiction Principles "to establish a more coordinated and effective basis through which to impede and stop [WMD] shipments . . . consistent with national legal authorities and relevant international law and frameworks, including the UN Security Council."

While participants have been quick to point out that the PSI is targeted at proliferation *per se* and not at any particular country, a State Department spokesman did note that Pyongyang "might find itself affected by this initiative" if it continued to "aggressively proliferate missiles and related technologies." "Unnamed Pentagon officials" were also quick to point out that the first major PSI exercise, dubbed Pacific Protector and held in the Coral Sea off the coast of Queensland on September 13, was aimed at sending "a sharp signal to North Korea." The Pentagon reportedly wanted to identify the target ship in this interdiction exercise as a North Korean vessel, but the Australian organizers, responding at least in part to Japanese concerns, elected instead to develop a scenario where a simulated Japanese freighter (played by a US destroyer) suspected of carrying contraband chemicals, was stopped and boarded by the Japanese Coast Guard backed up by Australian, US, and French navy and coast guard ships (with the other seven members sending observers). This was the first of a series of ten sea, air, and ground interdiction training exercises that will take place over the coming year. The long-term objective, according to Undersecretary of State for Arms Control and International Security John Bolton, is "to create a web of counterproliferation partnerships that will impede trade in WMD, delivery systems, and related materials." The idea of Japanese participation in such an effort would have been unthinkable a few short years ago.

Missile Defense Cooperation

From the onset, Prime Minister Koizumi has been a supporter of US-Japan missile defense joint research. A decision to develop and deploy such a system has been another issue, however, since the command and control coordination necessary for a broad-based system to be most effective would appear to cross the (ever-shifting) "collective defense" barrier. Nonetheless, in late December 2003, Tokyo announced that it would begin building a missile defense system, citing "a spread of missiles and a rise in weapons of mass destruction" as the primary reasons behind the decision. Chief Cabinet Secretary Fukuda said in a statement that "Ballistic missile defense is a purely defensive—and the sole—means of protecting the lives of our country's people and their property against a ballistic missile attack." Media reports said the plan initially calls for refitting four Aegis-equipped destroyers with sea-based anti-missile rockets and purchasing advanced Patriot anti-missile rocket batteries starting in 2004. The new system will be deployed from 2007 through 2011. The government will allocate $935 million for the program in the next fiscal year, beginning in April. The entire program was estimated at $4.67 billion. Joint research will also continue.

Chief Cabinet Secretary Fukuda also told reporters that the government may review its thiry-six-year-old ban on exporting weapons, their parts, and the technology to make them, with an eye to exempting the United States. Fukuda said it could be inconvenient if the continuing joint research moved on to joint development and manufacture of missiles or parts, but Japan couldn't sell them to the United States because of the policy. The ban on weapons exports was originally adopted in 1967 so that Tokyo could bar shipments to the communist bloc and countries on the UN sanctions list. The ban was extended in 1976 to cover all countries, but then eased in 1983 when the United States sought to buy high tech materials for its Stealth bomber fleet and for other uses. The changes now being contemplated open the door for still deeper military-to-military cooperation between Washington and Seoul.

More Like the UK . . . or Germany?

What does Washington wish that Tokyo would do now? The answer seems to be: more of the same. During his June 2002 Asia Society speech, Secretary Powell not only stressed Japan's positive contribution to regional stability—a familiar refrain—but also the alliance's role in providing "a framework within which Japan can contribute more to its own defense as well as to peace and security worldwide." Clearly, Washington supports, and wants to encourage, a greater regional (if not global) security role befitting a more "normal" Japan. As Secretary Armitage noted in February 2004, "I believe that Prime Minister Koizumi has set a new benchmark, not just in the dispatch of Japanese Self Defense Forces to Iraq, but also in redefining Japan's role in the world." But, with the decision to put boots on the ground in Iraq, it appears unlikely that Washington will be looking to Tokyo to move further forward, at least during the remainder of President Bush's first term in office.

Washington's greatest concern now will be to avoid backsliding, especially if (when) Japanese forces become targets, or worse yet casualties, once they arrive in Iraq. I for one have greater confidence in the resolve of Prime Minister Koizumi, the Japanese public, and the JDA than many of today's pundits. But, it is clear that Tokyo is more prepared militarily than it is politically or psychologically for what appears to be an inevitable first true test under fire, notwithstanding the fact that Japanese diplomats have already been killed in

Iraq and civilian peacekeepers were likewise killed in Cambodia. How Tokyo responds will determine the pace, but not the direction of, future, deeper defense cooperation.

Regardless of who wins the 2004 US presidential elections, but especially if President Bush returns for a second term, there will be continued—hopefully subtle and politically aware—pressure on Japan to continue to find new avenues of enhanced military cooperation and involvement in security matters in East Asia and beyond. "Japan can count on America, and increasingly, America can count on Japan," Secretary Armitage noted in Tokyo in February 2004. "Certainly a more self-confident Japan, with its own unique style of global leadership, can only add to that equation," he added, "both in the economic opportunities for our peoples and in advancing our shared global interests."

As long as Prime Minister Koizumi remains at the helm, such gentle pressure will be welcome and sufficient to see continued forward progress. The big issue is a purely Japanese one: constitutional revision or further reinterpretation to allow collective defense. Since many maintain that Japan, under the UN Charter, is already permitted to exercise collective self-defense but has merely chosen not to do so, it is possible that a political decision short of reinterpretation may be the vehicle Tokyo chooses to advance its quest to become a more normal nation. But given Prime Minister Koizumi's earlier comments on the subject, one can anticipate a move toward actual constitutional revision at some point in the not-too-distant future. Washington will be cheering on the sidelines, but is likely to continue its official hands-off policy.

Will Japan become the UK of Asia? Perhaps, but it will not happen overnight, even if constitutional reform does take place. The German model may—and I would argue, should—first apply. During the 1992 Gulf War, Germany increased its military operations in the Mediterranean and other NATO areas to free up more non-German NATO forces to participate in Operation Desert Storm, similar to what Japan did, and is continuing to do, in support of Operation Iraqi Freedom and its aftermath. By the time of the events in Kosovo, Germany had taken the next step in being a full partner in a wartime coalition and few blink an eye today at Germany's active involvement in Afghanistan—its reluctance to participate in Iraq is driven by other factors, and not by the lingering ghosts of World War II. Before Japan can become the UK of Asia in the twenty-first century, it must become the Germany of the last decade and finally put its own World War II ghosts to rest.

THE JAPAN-US ALLIANCE AND JAPANESE DOMESTIC POLITICS: SOURCES OF CHANGE, PROSPECTS FOR THE FUTURE

Hiroshi Nakanishi

As units of Japan's Self-Defense Force (SDF) head for Iraq in support of humanitarian and reconstruction efforts, there is little further need to emphasize the transformation Japanese security policy has undergone in the last decade or so. At the time of the Gulf War in 1990–91, Japan was the most hesitant among the Western allies, limiting its participation to a substantial 13 billion dollar financial contribution and a contingent of minesweepers sent to the Gulf after the conflict. Ten years later Japan has become the most faithful of America's allies along with Great Britain and Australia. The Koizumi cabinet hastily supported the war on terrorism by the United States after the September 11 attack, and sent a small fleet for logistical support in the Indian Ocean. Even in the Iraqi war, arguably the most divisive use of force by the West in the postwar era, the Koizumi cabinet staunchly showed its loyalty to the Bush administration. More surprisingly, there was no major turmoil at the political or public level, offering another clear contrast to the confusion in the Diet during the Gulf crisis or over the PKO legislation in 1991–92.

While government actions make this change apparent, it is not so easy to identify its sources. Most Japanese, including the author, could not have imagined ten years ago the form and scale of the shift. Attempts to discover a mastermind behind the scenes are futile. For example, not a few observers of Japan regarded Ichiro Ozawa as the country's most powerful politician in the early 1990s, but his political fate suggests that things did not go as he may have planned. As is often the case with affairs in Japan, things happen as a result of a combination of numerous factors and not conscious intent.

This paper tries to sort out the Japanese domestic factors that may have contributed to the transformation we are now observing. The paper discusses changes in the last decade in four areas: political leadership, public perception, regional security perception, and global security perception. In all four areas, substantial change can be identified and the general trend has been to reinforce rather than weaken the bilateral relationship with the United States. But this does not mean Japan is fully satisfied with the current state of the alliance. The last part of the paper will discuss some of the issues that may affect the future course of the Japan-US alliance.

I. Political Leadership: From the 1955 System to the Semi-Two-Party System

Japan experienced a dual shock at the beginning of the 1990s, namely the Gulf War and the end of the Cold War. The most lingering effect of the dual shock was the structural change in the Japanese political leadership.

Up until the early 1990s, the so-called 1955 regime constituted the basic framework of Japanese politics. In the late 1980s, the 1955 regime was characterized by the following elements: (1) the rightist Liberal Democratic Party (LDP) was the only viable political party that could rule Japan, (2) opposition parties led by the Japan Socialist Party (JSP) functioned as the veto power against the arbitrary use of power by the LDP, (3) the LDP supported the Japan-US alliance and the constitutionality of the SDF, but it located Japanese foreign policy primarily in economic pragmatism, staying away from international military affairs under the doctrine of non-use of the right of collective defense, (4) the opposition symbolized the postwar Japanese ideology of a reborn nation, especially in the form of the pacifist ideology defined by Article 9 of the Japanese constitution, originally drafted by MacArthur's occupying General Headquarters and adopted with some revisions in 1946.

By the late 1980s, the ending of the Cold War had already prompted the gradual decline of the 1955 system. The never-ending political scandals, the complete delegitimization of communist ideology, the virulent economic friction with other Western countries, especially with the United States, the psychological friction with its Asian neighbors, Korea (both South and North) and China in particular, all reinforced Japan's dissatisfaction with the 1955 regime. But it was the experience of the Gulf War, which was so humiliating in the eyes of the majority of Japanese, that dealt the most serious blow to the 1955 regime. The experience of not being appreciated for contributing 13 billion dollars of taxpayers' money and of being isolated in the West in the emerging new world order broke the postwar consensus of economic pragmatism and anti-military pacifism.

The upshot was the political realignment out of the 1955 regime. It occurred in several stages, and is still going on. The first break was the LDP's fall from power in the summer of 1993. The fall was caused by the departure of those in the party who were dissatisfied with the status quo. Ichiro Ozawa's group sought a more assertive foreign policy along the new conservative line, while the more liberal group led by Masayoshi Takemura formed the Sakigake party. They led to the anti-LDP coalition cabinets under Morihiro Hosokawa and Tsutomu Hata in 1993–1994. Though the two cabinets were short-lived because of divisions within the coalition and savvy political maneuvers by the remaining LDP members, the experience showed that the LDP may not be the only viable ruling political force in Japan.

The second break came as the JSP rose to power in 1994. The move was partly a result of the success of the attempt of the LDP to divide the anti-

LDP coalition and return to power. The prey in this attempt was the JSP itself. Once it had acceded to power the party had to forgo the ideological identity it embraced throughout the Cold War and wielded as veto power. The Tomiichi Murayama cabinet quickly admitted the utility of the alliance with the United States and the constitutionality of the SDF. In addition, the Murayama cabinet experienced arguably the biggest crises in postwar Japanese history: the Hanshin-Awaji (Kobe) earthquake in January 1995 and the sarin gas attack in the Tokyo subway by the religious cult group Aum Shinrikyo in March 1995. The Murayama cabinet was denounced by the public for the lack of security precautions and its failure to manage the crises. In early 1996 Murayama abruptly retired from premiership and handed power to Ryutaro Hashimoto. Hashimoto was the rising hope of the Keiseikai, the dominant faction within the LDP which had inherited the legacy of the Kakuei Tanaka faction in the early 1980s. From 1996 to 2000, Hashimoto and then Keizo Obuchi, both from Keiseikai, led the LDP-led coalition cabinets.

The third turning point came in 1996 when members of Sakigake and the JSP formed the Democratic Party (DP) at the time of the first general election under the new electoral system based on single-member districts. Later, a majority of the Japan Social Democratic Party (JSDP, formerly the JSP) and some Ozawa protégés joined the DP, to form the core of the anti-LDP group. In the meantime, Ozawa's group and his ally Komeito formed a coalition with the LDP to help strengthen the Japan-US alliance on the issue of the new security guidelines and related legislation as well as on the issue of the Okinawa base. But Ozawa, ever losing followers as he made moves, broke away from the coalition in 2000 and then joined the DP in 2003 as the third general election under the new system neared. From its inception, the DP has admitted the legitimacy of the SDF and the alliance with the United States. If anything, the DP has blamed the LDP for its ambiguous security policies including the apparent contradiction between the traditional constitutional interpretation and the response to newly emerging security measures such as the new guidelines in 1997 or the special laws on terrorism in 2001 and on Iraq reconstruction support in 2003. The LDP and the DP cooperated in legislating the Emergency against Armed Attack Law in 2003, showing that the DP in opposition would not oppose the LDP ideologically like the JSP in the 1955 system.

The fourth turning point was the launch of the Junichiro Koizumi cabinet in April 2001. When Obuchi became incapacitated by illness in April 2000, Yoshiro Mori from the Seiwakai faction was handed power by the LDP power brokers. But the whole process and his easy tongue made Mori extraordinarily unpopular among the public. He had to give up power in 2001. Koizumi was from Seiwakai, but a fairly maverick figure within the LDP. He won a surprising victory in the LDP leadership election against Hashimoto, advocating radical reform and targeting the LDP old guard as the major opponent, the "force of resistance," to reform. Koizumi became the most popular prime minister in Japanese constitutional history, scoring about 90 percent of public support at the beginning of the cabinet. His blunt and forceful style appealed to the public as international crises set the diplomatic agenda after September 11.

The 2003 general election showed clear signs that Japanese politics has moved from the breakup stage to the realignment stage. Three splinter parties, Hoshushinto (the New Conservative Party), the Japan Social Democratic Party, and the Japan Communist Party, lost greatly, while the LDP barely kept a majority and the DP increased its numbers. The wild card is Komeito, whose constituency is based on the loyal Buddhist group Sokagakkai. By agreeing to electoral cooperation with either of the two major parties, Komeito can keep its presence and the closer the competition between the LDP and the DP the greater the possibility that Komeito will cast the decisive vote.

All three major parties share the basic consensus that the Japan-US alliance is key to Japanese foreign and security policy. But none of them has come up with clear perspectives on the future course of Japanese foreign and security policy. Within both the LDP and the DP there is no small divergence on the issues of the constitution, Japan's security role, and its future relationship with the countries of Asia. Komeito also faces a big dilemma in terms of its pacifist-leaning constituency and the need to be pragmatic in order to form a coalition with either of the major parties. Much will hinge on the interaction between the political leadership and the perception of the general public, for as Koizumi has shown the popularity of the leader has become a key resource in Japanese politics. So it is now necessary to turn to an analysis of the Japanese public's perception.

II. Public Perception of the Japan-US Alliance: From Drift to Reaffirmation

According to opinion polls taken since the end of the Cold War, the general trend in the public's perception of the Japan-US alliance is clear (Charts 1 and 2). The United States has been the most familiar country in the eyes of the Japanese public throughout the decade. But from the late 1980s to the mid-1990s, the public increasingly saw problems in the relationship with the United States. According to the Yomiuri poll, the percentage of those who thought the bilateral relationship with the United States was good declined from 40 percent in the late 1980s to a little more than 20 percent in 1995. 1995 was the only year in the Yomiuri surveys when the percentage of those who thought the bilateral relationship bad was higher than the percentage who thought it good. As for the Japan-US alliance, the trend was generally the same. From the mid-1980s, positive views on the alliance slightly declined from a little more than 70 percent to 63 percent in 1991.

The trend was reversed in the latter half of the 1990s. The Yomiuri survey shows a steep rise in the percentage of those who thought the bilateral relationship good. In 1999, the figure reached more than 50 percent, while the number of those who thought the relationship bad declined to about 10 percent.

The positive view on the alliance also picked up, reaching more than 70 percent again. The surveys indicate Japanese public opinion moving from drift over the utility of the Japan-US alliance to reaffirmation of the alliance.

Several factors seem to have influenced this V-curve movement in the popularity of the Japan-US relationship. First, the fierce bilateral trade disputes harmed the overall relationship in the first half of the 1990s. The Bush Sr. administration started the Structural Impediment Initiative and Clinton followed his predecessor in terms of demanding from Japan numerical import targets of American-made goods. A series of confrontational trade talks boiled down to the showdown in the first half of 1995 when the Japanese yen rose steeply to an 80 yen/dollar rate and Japan threatened to sue the United States in the World Trade Organization (WTO) over the issue of autos and auto parts. Even though the notion of turning to Asia as an alternative to the West never became more than a minority view within official circles in Japan, Japan supported the cause of global multilateralism in the form of the WTO and regional multilateralism in the form of APEC in part in an attempt to sidestep and contain the American trade pressure.

As the Japanese economic slump became clear and the American economy boomed in the latter half of the 1990s, the trade pressure from the American government vanished. Instead the US became concerned with the prospect of Japan's depression becoming a brake on the world economy. The American irritation grew stronger after the financial crises hit Asian countries in 1997. On the other hand, there was dissatisfaction within the Japanese government with the Americans' blunt opposition to the Asian Monetary Fund scheme Japan proposed in autumn 1997. But as the financial crises showed signs of spreading globally in 1998, the two countries became more cooperative in containing the financial turmoil.

Second, in the first half of the 1990s there was a certain sense among the Japanese public that the costs of the alliance with the US were too dear compared with the benefits Japan enjoyed from the alliance. The so-called sympathy budget, the government's financial support of the American bases in Japan, was criticized even within the government. But the biggest issue was the social cost of the bases in Okinawa. The issue became more complex because of the delicate relationship between Okinawa and the rest of Japan. People in Okinawa were the only major population who experienced the land battle in the Pacific War, and the island was under American occupation until 1972. Even after the return to Japan of administrative rights over Okinawa in 1972, the high density of American bases in the central area of Okinawa caused strong irritation among the local residents. But the end of the Cold War made the social cost of the bases seem even more burdensome. In addition, the demise of the 1955 regime made it possible for the dissatisfaction of the populace to directly influence the political agenda.

The uproar against the American bases occurred when the rape of a schoolgirl by American marines became public in September 1995. Emotional accusations were prominent: the alliance was denounced for allowing American forces to enjoy the unfair privileges inherited from occupation days. But the two governments acted quickly to repair the damage. President Clinton apologized for the crime by the marines. The two governments set up the Special Action Committee on Okinawa (SACO) to discuss ways to reduce the burden American bases inflicted on the local population.

Emotional anger against the alliance with the United States gradually died down for several reasons. First, the SACO framework indeed moved to mitigate the social cost of the bases by reducing the base area, artillery live-firing training, noise levels, and so on. The symbolic issue was the Futenma Air Base used by the Marines. In February 1996 Prime Minister Hashimoto and US Ambassador to Japan Walter Mondale dramatically announced that the Futenma base would be returned in five to seven years.

Second, as emotion died down it soon became clear that the Okinawa base issue was not only an international issue but a complex domestic one. There was not enough mutual understanding between Okinawa and Tokyo. And opinion in Okinawa was torn between the social cost of the bases and the economic benefit they brought. There was also intra-island disagreement, as great economic disparities existed within Okinawa. Even though the Futenma base problem did not proceed smoothly because of the difficulty in finding an alternative helicopter base, attention to the Okinawa issue subsided in the late 1990s. In 1999, a special law was passed to keep certain private lands for base use by fiat of the central government.

The Okinawa incident functioned as an important lesson in managing the inevitable social friction surrounding the alliance. When the fishery high school training boat *Ehime-maru* sank after colliding with an American submarine near Hawaii in February 2001 and nine lives including those of students were lost, the two governments moved quickly and succeeded in preventing large political ramifications. Even though the treatment of American soldiers as criminal suspects is still an issue between the two governments, it became understood that crimes and accidents should not govern foreign and security policy.

Third, the level of foreign policy and security dialogue between the two countries stepped up. Based on the human connections formed in the 1970s and '80s, government officials and experts in both countries began to reaffirm and redefine the alliance in the mid-1990s. Because the pacifism of the left was greatly discredited within Japan by that time, there was no substantial opposition against this move. The so-called Nye Initiative was the result of consultation between officials in the two countries, which assured the Japanese. In November 1995 the Japanese government issued the New Defense Program Outline, which emphasized the close interdependence of the role and missions of the SDF and the Japan-US alliance. The high point of the redefinition of the alliance was the US-Japan Joint Declaration on Security issued at the time of President Clinton's visit to Japan in April 1996. The declaration clarified that the key role of the bilateral alliance was regional stability and reassurance.

The bilateral dialogue mechanism was further strengthened in 1996 when the Subcommittee on Defense Cooperation was enlarged to prepare new guidelines for defense cooperation, which were announced in September 1997. Diplomatic dialogue was also institutionalized as the North Korean issue loomed large at the end of the 1990s and the trilateral framework among Japan, the US, and South Korea increased in importance. Prime Minister Koizumi and President Bush agreed on the Japan-US Strategic Dialogue between high-level officials in 2001.

The political force that drove the movement to redefine the bilateral alliance and to enlarge the area of cooperation was the popular feeling among the public that the security of Japan both as state and a society was threatened. The Hanshin-Awaji (Kobe) earthquake and the Aum Shinrikyo sarin attack on the Tokyo subway were key incidents that changed people's mindset. *Kiki kanri* (translated as "crisis management," although the Japanese term includes matters related to emergency response) became the buzzword in the 1990s. Irritation over the lingering economic slump as well as anger against the existing political and bureaucratic system also underlined the security rationale. This popular sentiment also directed the general public mood to the right, blaming postwar Japan as overly naïve and pacifist. Cravings for radical reform among the public led to the election of celebrity local governors such as Shintaro Ishihara in Tokyo and Yasuo Tanaka in Nagano. The same sentiment seemed to support Junichiro Koizumi.

This heightened sense of insecurity appeared to be the driving force behind the passage of the emergency law in case of armed attack in 2003, which had been shelved for a quarter of a century. But, needless to say, the public's sudden obsession with security also derived from international factors. Changes in regional security perception played a particularly significant role.

III. Regional Security Perception: From Cooperative Security to Realist Outlook

Just after the end of the Cold War, it seemed that there was no longer any clear and present military threat in the traditional sense. Countries in general were thought to be cooperative in coping with the new types of threats such as international crimes, terrorism, environmental hazards, and refugee flows. The notion of "cooperative security" reflected this perception. Partly modeled after the Organization for Security and Cooperation in Europe (OSCE), it was believed that an inclusive and multilateral framework composed of the countries concerned would be better able to cope with these new types of threats than the traditional military alliances of the past. Although the alliances would not be broken up suddenly, they would be gradually replaced by the new multilateral framework.

This perception was widely held in this period. In a sense, the policy of "engagement and enlargement" advocated by the Clinton administration was one form of cooperative security. Japan too was optimistic about the prospect of regional security cooperation. It promoted the ASEAN Regional Forum (ARF) launched in 1994 as well as track one-and-a-half and track-two dialogues in the form of the Northeast Asia Cooperation Dialogue (NEACD) and the Conference on Security and Cooperation in the Asia Pacific (CSCAP).

The same logic was behind the report by the so-called Higuchi committee, a group of scholars and experts headed by business leader Kotaro Higuchi assembled by Prime Minister Hosokawa in early 1994. Its final report was presented six months later to Prime Minister Murayama. The report, while reaffirming the importance for Japan of the alliance with the United States, proposed enhancing the multilateral system in the Asia-Pacific region and slimming down the SDF.

But the optimism of the post–Cold War era soon waned. The North Korean nuclear crisis in 1993–94 heightened tension in the region. Even though Japan did not necessarily view North Korea as a military threat at this stage, it began to take the possibility of use of force on the Korean peninsula seriously and began to prepare for such a situation.

Then, in 1995–96, China loomed large in the eyes of the Japanese public as a political threat in the region. China repeated nuclear tests in 1995, which struck a nerve in the Japanese as the year was the fiftieth anniversary of Hiroshima and Nagasaki. Then the heavy-handed approach by China against the Taiwanese presidential election shocked the Japanese public. Beginning around this time the Japanese perception of China changed to one of wariness and rivalry. In the 1980s, nearly 80 percent of the Japanese public felt friendly toward China, much the same level as toward the United States. The number declined steeply in 1989 under the influence of the Tiananmen incident. Then, in 1995, those who felt friendly toward China and those who did not feel friendly became about the same percentage, around 50 percent. The situation has stayed the same since.

The sense of wariness was heightened further in 1997–98. China was eager to make sure that the new security guidelines would not be applied to the Taiwan Strait, but the Chinese attitude hardened the Japanese stance, as the latter decided to maintain ambiguity on whether the guideline covered the Taiwan Strait situation. Then in July 1998, Clinton visited China while bypassing Japan. This incident, labeled "Japan passing," wounded Japan's pride as the number one ally of the United States in Asia. When Jiang Zeming visited Japan late that year, he was received unexceptionally coldly for his continual demands for Japanese remorse over war guilt. As China increased its presence in the region, Japan opted to strengthen its ties with the US.

In the meantime the Japanese increasingly came to perceive North Korea as a security threat. The abduction issue came to be widely known by the public in 1998 and caused great emotional anger against the North. The North Korean spy ship found in Japanese territorial waters by the coast guard in 1999 increased the sense of threat within Japan.

But the sharpest turning point was the launch of the Taepodong missile in August 1998, which resulted in a furious uproar against North Korea. Not only did the Japanese government quickly resort to economic sanctions against the North, Japan also announced its intention to discontinue its financial contribution to the Korean Energy Development Organization (KEDO). Both the US and South Korea were shocked by this move and worked more seriously to contain the missile threat. This resulted in the so-called Perry process, in which Japan, the US, and South Korea tried to resolve the problem with North Korea comprehensively. The three countries formed a close consultation mechanism, the Trilateral Coordination and Oversight Group (TCOG). South Korean president Kim Dae-jung's decision to seek a future cooperative relationship with Japan rather than asking for a war-guilt apology certainly helped Japan to have a closer relationship with South Korea.

These experiences showed that a regional cooperative framework, though sometimes useful, cannot effectively cope with real security threats in the region such as the Taiwan Strait issue or the North Korean security threat. As a result Japanese thinking evidently became more realist, recognizing the role of power to secure the peace in the region.

In addition, the Taepodong shock pressed Japan to strengthen its military cooperation with the United States as well as to increase its efforts to gain a certain level of independence. The Japanese government decided to cooperate with the US on missile defense research. Later Japan decided to deploy a missile defense system. On the other hand, Japan opted for its own intelligence capability by deciding to launch a set of information satellites which can cover the region continuously.

The North Korean issue has dominated Japanese security discourse in the twenty-first century. But public pressure made Japan's priority on North Korea somewhat different from that of other countries in the region. The abduction issue gathers by far the most attention, followed by the missile launch and the spy ship or other forms of low-intensity attack. The nuclear issue, which reached a new stage of crisis when the North admitted to having a nuclear weapon program, is low in priority at least for the Japanese public.

Current Japanese thinking on North Korea holds that Japan needs to press the North by forming a concentric figure composed of the Japan-US bilateral alliance at the core, the trilateral framework of Japan, the US, and South Korea at the next level, and finally the regional framework including North Korea, China, and Russia. The Six-Party Talks begun in August 2003 provide such a framework. But Japan suffers from the divergence between the international priority on North Korea's nuclear program and domestic concerns about North Korea. Japan's dilemma is even more serious because two key regional players,

Japan and China, fail to communicate with each other closely. As China seems to increase its influence in the region, Japan seems to enlarge its role in the global arena, partly with a view to strengthening its position against China.

IV. Global Security Perception: From the New World Order to Cooperation against Rogue Threats

As is the case with its regional security perception, Japanese thinking on global security shifted from a liberal orientation to a more realist one in the last decade. In the early 1990s, Japan tried to adjust to the new world order which seemed to arise in the wake of the Gulf War. In this order the major countries of the world would cooperatively solve security questions, especially through the United Nations. The heightened interest in peacekeeping operations (PKO) by the UN formed one of the linchpins of this new world order.

In 1991–92, the ruling LDP took efforts to pass the so-called PKO law, which authorizes the dispatch of units of the SDF on relatively limited missions under the UN PKO framework. Since sending the SDF beyond Japanese territory was taboo during the Cold War, there was substantial opposition in both the Diet and the public. But successful missions in UN PKOs in Cambodia, Rwanda, Mozambique, the Golan Heights, and so on changed the public's perception. In this period the bilateral alliance with the US was thought to be closely linked to the PKO activity.

But as the weakness of the United Nations and the limits of peacekeeping operations became apparent in the 1990s, hope for the new world order waned. The American experience in Somalia as well as the never-ending conflict in the former Yugoslavia demonstrated that international institutions have limited power to cope with serious security threats.

Instead of a new world order, US military might increasingly became the decisive factor in world security situations. In the former Yugoslavia it was American air power that first brought about the Dayton Agreement and then stopped the Kosovo conflict. As Iraq defied UN weapons inspectors, American missile attacks put pressure on Saddam Hussein. And the US resorted to the retaliatory use of force against terrorist attacks in the late 1990s.

Increasingly Japan became one of the allies that was the most quickly sympathetic to American military actions. Characteristic of these cases was that the Japanese public did not show much interest. Affairs in Europe, the Middle East, or Africa seemed distant from Japan's interests. Even though there was a certain amount of skepticism voiced about the legitimacy of American military action, the general tendency was to follow the American decision. This was partly because of the traumatic experience of isolation during the Gulf War and partly because of the bandwagoning calculation.

The September 11 attack was the first opportunity for Japan to seriously consider post–Cold War global security. The vast majority of the public as well as the Diet supported Koizumi's offer of consolation and assistance to the United

States. The Koizumi cabinet hurriedly took counterterrorist measures and in October the Diet passed the Anti-Terrorism Special Measures Law, according to which SDF troops were sent to assist the war on terrorism conducted by the United States and other countries. Concretely, a contingent of the maritime SDF was dispatched in the Indian Ocean to supply fuel for the navies of the United States, Canada, France, the United Kingdom, and so on. The air SDF also provided aerial supply operations to the American forces both within and outside Japan.

In a more normal time this legislation might have caused serious constitutional and legal debate in the Diet. It could be argued that the operations by the SDF under this law violated the official constitutional interpretation banning the exercise of the right of collective self-defense. But in reality there was no serious opposition to the legislation. The shock caused by September 11 and the unity shown by international society in support of the United States made some form of Japanese participation in the war on terrorism necessary in the eyes of the public, overriding political concerns. The choice also seemed part of the natural evolution of Japan's security policy in the last decade, along with participation in PKO and the new Japan-US defense guidelines, which had gradually eroded the sanctity of the traditional interpretation of the constitution.

The Koizumi cabinet faced much harder opposition over its stance on the war in Iraq. Throughout 2002 the cabinet failed to clarify its stance as the debate became fierce among the major countries. Basically Koizumi took a line similar to that of the United Kingdom, apparently supporting the Bush administration but encouraging the US to take a more cooperative stance within the United Nations. But as the division within the UN Security Council became unbreachable in early 2003, the Koizumi cabinet began openly supporting the United States. The opposition parties led by the Democratic Party as well as public opinion in general were critical, but the opposition was divided between the pacifist stance, which was opposed to any use of force in Iraq, and the legalist stance, which demanded a specific authorization by the UN for the use of force. At any rate, the anti-war sentiment in Japan was weaker than in other countries in the West. There were no large-scale demonstrations against the government and the opposition in the Diet was also controlled.

The same can be said of the government's follow-up measures. The government passed in July 2003 another special law on assistance in the reconstruction of Iraq, intending to send the SDF including ground units to Iraq. The legislation was unpopular with the public but the opposition was generally spotty. After Koizumi won the LDP leadership election in September and kept his ruling majority in the general election in November, he made public his intention to send the SDF to Iraq. Again the majority of the public was opposed, but opposition was not strong enough to have a political impact.

This development suggests several things. First, despite the popular rhetoric in Japan depicting the United Nations as an ideal international society,

Japanese leaders realize that the UN is not capable of handling difficult security questions. The alliance with the United States is, for all the psychological difficulties it creates for Japan as a junior power, a far surer way to maintain Japanese security.

Second, Japan's security and foreign-policy concerns are still regional rather than global. People are far more interested in the Korean peninsula and the Taiwan Strait. Koizumi's explanation that Japan needed to support the US because it was the only country that would help protect Japan against the North Korean threat was crude but persuasive for the Japanese public.

Third, support for Koizumi's foreign policy comes from his popularity rather than his persuasiveness. Generally the public accepts Koizumi as someone who lifts the taboos of the past and leads Japan to be a more assertive and proud nation. His right-wing stance and his decisive and sometimes blunt style have so far won people's support. But popularity can evaporate quickly in the face of potential harm. Sending the SDF to Iraq is no doubt a big gamble for the Koizumi cabinet.

And in spite of the general acceptance of the alliance with the United States, there is criticism of American unilateralism. What was characteristic about the war in Iraq was that such criticism was voiced more from the rightists in Japan rather than the traditional pacifist left. Their intention was more to denounce what they perceive as the government's subordinate diplomacy to the United States *(Taibei Juzoku Gaiko)*, but it is possible that such criticism gains more political importance once it gains momentum.

V. Prospects of the Alliance from the Japanese Domestic Perspective

In the four areas the author has examined, political leadership, public opinion, regional security perception, and global security perception, the state of affairs in Japan has changed significantly in the last decade. And the changes as a whole have upheld the strong alliance with the United States as the linchpin of Japan's post–Cold War security policy.

But this does not mean that the current state is firmly institutionalized. It is no less a product of several accidents, and may change as the world situation changes.

First, the political realignment in Japan is not yet secure. Even though the trend toward a semi-two-party system seems irreversible, both of the major parties as well as Komeito have internal weaknesses resulting from the divergence of opinion on security policy. This weakness may lead to further political turmoil if, for example, the SDF in Iraq suffers causalities. Moreover, as constitutional reform nears reaching the real political agenda, there will be a fierce debate within Japan over Article 9 and its interpretation.

Second, the current cordiality between Japan and the US is to no small extent dependent on the personal relationship between Koizumi and Bush as well as the popularity of the former within Japan. If Koizumi loses his popularity, his cabinet will face serious difficulties. And once his government is gone, there is no guarantee that his policy line will be continued. Major policy changes especially in terms of the global fight against rogue threats have been impromptu, based on special laws with sunset clauses. This suggests the tentativeness of the current cordiality.

The stable mutual understanding among the officials in both countries supplements the ad hoc nature of alliance management. Officials have become adept at handling the emotions of the public, especially when unexpected social conflicts have occurred. But managing the public emotion is always a risky business. Even today the mishandling of a single accident or crime can have great repercussions for the alliance.

Third, most of the development in the alliance happened while economic problems were virtually neglected, which is extraordinary for the two major economies. They occurred during a time of evident Japanese economic sluggishness and American economic boom. This situation may change as the Japanese economy recovers and the American economy is beset with the twin deficits. We can already identify signs of economic friction over safeguards, American beef, and the exchange rate. In addition, the global economic system is moving toward regionally based free-trade agreements. There is no guarantee that the economic interests of the two countries won't diverge and lead to a new round of economic friction.

Fourth, as the Japanese place more importance on the alliance with the United States, concern over abandonment increases. For example, the current military transformation proposed by the Pentagon may have a complex psychological impact when implemented in East Asia. There is a certain level of hope in Japan that the military transformation will reduce the presence of American forces in Okinawa. On the other hand, however, a rapid reduction of the forces may shake the alliance's credibility in the eyes of the Japanese.

Another source of fear of abandonment is American policy toward the Korean peninsula and China. Japan is fearful of the American disengagement from the South and of the possibility of the US making a deal with the North on nuclear and related concerns that would neglect the abduction issue. Japan is also concerned that the US-China entente may replace the Japan-US alliance as the key bilateral relationship in East Asia.

Fifth, in spite of general trust on the part of the Japanese of American leadership, there is a certain level of fear and jealousy of the American "empire." The desire to have a more self-supportive security policy is growing. There is no realistic possibility of Japan having its own nuclear weapons, but it is notable that the matter has come to be openly debated in public journals, which is indicative of the desire by many for Japan to have a more assertive role in international society, including in its relations with the United States.

More directly, some opinion leaders have come to question the legitimacy of American predominance. They insist that aggressive American foreign policy is the root cause of global threats such as the Palestinian conflict, instability in the Gulf, or Islamic terrorism. So far this feeling has not acquired much political influence, but its potential influence is not to be ignored.

In general, the public mood in Japan has shifted toward the right. Koizumi has fanned debate within Japan by visiting the Yasukuni Shrine annually since he became prime minister, but generally this behavior has contributed to his popularity. Visiting Yasukuni is more popular among the young generation, not because the young have any emotional attachment to the shrine or the Second World War but because they are frustrated with other countries denouncing this behavior. So far Koizumi has failed to persuade neighboring countries, China in particular and to some extent South Korea, to accept the visits to Yasukuni as pure mourning for those who died in the war. The psychological divisions between Japan and its Asian neighbors may strengthen Japanese cordiality with the United States, but the United States may experience difficulty if the divisions lead to more serious conflict.

Thus many things are still in the midst of transformation, even though the Japan-US alliance may seem to be in good standing at the moment. It is not appropriate to be complacent about the current state of affairs, for the alliance still seems in search of an efficient and equitable division of labor in the post–Cold War security environment. Much of the future course of Japanese foreign and security policy will be dependent on developments both within Japan and outside it in the next few years.

KOREA

SHAPING CHANGE AND CULTIVATING IDEAS IN THE US-ROK ALLIANCE

Victor D. Cha

After half a century, the alliance between the United States and the Republic of Korea (ROK or South Korea) stands as one of the most successful political-military relationships forged out of the Cold War era. What started as a pact of mutual convenience—formed between two parties who knew little about each other and had little in common except a common threat—has emerged as a prosperous and militarily robust relationship between two market democracies. The alliance, from its humble origins to today, represents a model of success.

For fifty years, neither the governments nor their constituents on both sides of the Pacific questioned the alliance's rationale, its substance, or its purpose. However, a chain of events over the past fourteen months has shaken the foundations of the alliance. Growing anti-Americanism among a younger generation in South Korea, disparate perceptions of the threat posed by North Korea, and military transformation initiatives in the United States have created more forces for change in the last year than arguably existed in the previous forty-nine years.

The Past

The significance of the US-ROK alliance may not have been completely appreciated when it was first concluded. It certainly was not conceptualized as a centerpiece of the US security framework for Asia. It was once described as a "bribe" to persuade then-South Korean president Syngman Rhee to agree to the 1953 armistice ending Korean war hostilities.[1] Indeed, prior to the Korean War, the peninsula was not considered within Dean Acheson's famous "defense perimeter" of US postwar interests in Asia. Even after the Truman administration committed to defend the South after the North's invasion in June 1950, Korea remained a remote, unknown, and alien place that was strategically important to defend (i.e., keep out of communist hands), but intrinsically meaningless to Americans. Since those inauspicious beginnings, US-ROK relations have run the gamut from the fall of South Korean governments (e.g., Rhee in 1960), to military coups (by Park in 1961 and Chun in 1979), troop withdrawal plans (Nixon in 1969 and Carter in 1977), trade friction, radical anti-Americanism (1980s), democratization crises (1987), and financial crises (1997).[2] The alliance held despite these events, drawing its strength and cohesion from a clear combined mission and a commonly perceived threat.

The Present

For the United States today, a range of indicators determines the success of a military alliance. It (1) deters aggression; (2) facilitates US power accretion and projection; (3) shares risks and costs among the parties; (4) enables common tactics and doctrine through joint training; (5) promotes a division of security roles; (6) serves US security objectives in the broader regional context; (7) facilitates cooperation in production and development of military equipment; (8) facilitates a reasonable quality of life and hospitable environment for US forces stationed abroad; (9) reflects shared political values; and (10) elicits political support among domestic constituencies.[3] The alliance with Korea has generally met these expectations, despite a number of significant bumps in the road along the way.

No relationship is without its problems. For nearly fifty years since the formation of the alliance, the United States' role in inter-Korean relations was relatively uncontroversial. The animosity in Seoul-Pyongyang relations and the Cold War structure of regional security dictated one basic algorithm. The United States guaranteed successful deterrence against a North Korean attack on the South; moreover, US-ROK unity on a policy of diplomatic isolation and non-dialogue toward the North was indisputable. In recent years, this algorithm has been called into question. Despite arguments to the contrary by policy elites, the US role in inter-Korean relations is being contested, with the spectrum of views ranging from supporters of the Cold War template to dissenters who see the United States as a fundamental obstacle to improvement in inter-Korean relations. The controversial nature of the US role became increasingly evident in the aftermath of the June 2000 North–South Korea summit, when South Koreans perceived a relaxation in peninsular tensions. The Bush administration's designation of North Korea as part of an "axis of evil" did not help matters. Moreover, as the South Korean presidential elections of 2002 showed, for the general public, the distinction between the United States as security guarantor and ally against the North and as a spoiler of inter-Korean reconciliation has become at best muddled, and at worst destroyed.[4]

The Future

The events of the past two years provide a window on the emergence of a historically unique collection of forces around the peninsula that compel inevitable, if not imminent, changes to the alliance.

- **US strategy:** The US troop presence has been tailored successfully to deter North Korean aggression. However, because they are single-mindedly focused on the deterrence mission, these forces are currently positioned, trained, and equipped in a manner that does not fully contribute to overall American strategy in East Asia.

• **South Korean capabilities:** While US forces on the peninsula remain inflexibly tied to one mission, the ROK military has grown more robust and capable of bearing a larger defense burden, a far cry from the feeble force trained by the United States fifty years ago.

• **Demography and democracy:** As noted above, civil-military tensions over the US military footprint have grown immeasurably in the past year. This is not the radical anti-Americanism of the 1980s, but the showcasing of a younger, affluent, and educated generation of Koreans, bred on democracy, who see the United States less favorably than their elders.

• **Sunshine policy:** The Sunshine or engagement policy toward North Korea had the unintended consequence of worsening perceptions of US troops among the body politic. On the one hand, the policy's (exaggerated) success caused the public to be less welcoming to the US presence. On the other, the policy's failure led to the search for scapegoats, in which the US presence was a ready target.

• **Military transformation:** Larger trends in US security thinking also presage change. The Pentagon's 100,000 personnel benchmark in Asia is viewed by experts and the Department of Defense (DoD) as hindering transformational changes in regional military capabilities. The focus, they observe, should be on military capability and not a mere number. As the US military continues to transform itself into a more expeditionary (i.e., mobile) force increasingly equipped with precise weapons, fully networked command, information, and surveillance systems, and long-range striking ability, the US forces stationed in East Asia will of necessity be part of this transformation.

For years the belief predominated that the United States was too comfortably self-interested with its position on the peninsula to contemplate serious change, even in the face of anti-American demonstrations in Seoul at the end of 2002. Events have shown this belief to be an inaccurate. With no imperial aspirations, the United States would withdraw forces in the face of an unwelcoming host nation. The demonstrations at the end of 2002 might well have affected the timing of decisions about change to the alliance, but such change was in large part inevitable. The forces described above are inexorable, in this regard, compelling fundamental change to the alliance.

The US Presence

As the United States contemplates changes to its force presence on the Korean peninsula (USFK), it faces the difficult task of meeting four notional and sometimes contradictory criteria:

1) **The force must be flexible.** The presence must be large enough to be militarily significant, but with enough flexibility to handle a broad range of tasks.

2) **The force must be deployable.** Combined with other US capabilities in the region (especially those in Japan), the US presence in Korea must be able to react swiftly to regional developments and offer an integrated joint force with the full range of mobility, strike, maneuver, and sustainability that capitalizes on US technological advantages in long-range precision warfare;

3) **The force must be credible.** In spite of any transformations that the USFK might undergo, the resulting force must still represent and preserve USFK's traditional role as a credible manifestation of the American commitment to Korea's defense and security.

4) **The force must be unobtrusive.** As critical as it is for the USFK to be potent, deployable, and credible, a transformed USFK must also be perceived as unobtrusive. The new presence must be equivalent to the old as a symbol of the alliance, but possess a footprint that is not viewed as an obstacle to peace by the Korean people.

The first phase of the realignment of forces proposed by the Bush administration in mid-2003 makes useful steps toward achieving these criteria.

Table 1. US Rebalancing Elements for Korea (Phase 1)

• Base consolidation from 40 to 25, including 15 bases near the DMZ, to two major bases (Casey and Red Cloud)
• 14,000 2nd Infantry Division troops away from DMZ-Seoul to south of Han river (Phase I—Units north of the Han River will consolidate into bases in the Dongducheon and Uijongbu areas while facilities are prepared south of the Han River)
• Consolidate forces at major air hub in Osan-Pyongtaek, and major naval hub at Chinhae-Pusan
• Relocate 7,000 troops of 8th Army at Yongsan out of Seoul and further south by 2006

The notion of a tripwire deterrent that puts US soldiers in the direct path of any North Korean invasion has been an anachronism for a number of years. The idea that the United States requires the deaths of many young Americans in order to respond to a North Korean invasion has never been a sensible argument. It was presumably made to convince both North and South Koreans that keeping US troops proximate to the DMZ had contributed to deterrence when the US military was heavily engaged elsewhere in the world during the Cold War.[5] But this "proof of commitment" is now redundant and unnecessary. An equally lethal and more effective military deterrent could be fielded on the peninsula without the heavy ground-troop presence and the large military footprint in the capital city. Moreover, a presence in Korea that could move off the peninsula to other regional or global contingencies—akin to that in Japan—would enhance overall US contributions to regional stability.

Providing Assurances

The United States can do more to ensure that this rebalancing effort enhances rather than jeopardizes the alliance. Of the four criteria above, the weakest element may be credibility. Some argue that changes to the alliance appear ill-timed, given the heightened threat from North Korea. Accordingly, critics of the plan say that it has cast the United States as an abandoning ally that is less committed to the defense of South Korea. Other critics have gone further, arguing that the rebalancing plans cast the United States as an aggressive ally, in the sense that it is moving forces out of harm's way for a preemptive attack on North Korea.

The latter argument, in many ways, is a function of how much cost the United States is willing to bear in seeking nonproliferation objectives on the peninsula. The cost function, in turn, may be beyond US control, as it will ultimately be determined by the level of North Korean provocation. For example, if the Kim Jong-il regime carries through with threats made in April 2003 of transferring nuclear materials to other groups, then the cost of some punitive US military measure will pale in comparison with the imminent threat to homeland security posed by North Korea's facilitating such transfers to potential terrorists.

The former problem, the fear of US abandonment, however, is a potential negative externality, and one that Washington and Seoul can control. Dealing with this anxiety is important for two reasons. First, abandonment fears may reduce South Korean faith in the US commitment. Second, abandonment fears may embolden North Korea. Historically, neither outcome has had positive results. In the first case, the two occasions that the ROK contemplated its own secret nuclear weapons programs were also historically the times when US withdrawal plans created acute fears of abandonment among South Koreans.[6] In the second case, the last time North Korea was emboldened by a perceived absence of US commitment, the June 1950 invasion was the result. Assurances are now needed that assuage South Korean worries while making certain North Korea appreciates how deterrence is being increased. It is important that Pyongyang understand that rebalancing plans are being made from a position of strength.

The United States must provide both material and strategic evidence of its unflagging commitment to the alliance. This is particularly critical as subsequent phases of US realignment that raise the American base and troop profile in other parts of the region (e.g., Southeast Asia) might otherwise be misinterpreted by Koreans. Regarding material evidence, assurances can be provided by upgrading US defense capabilities even as forces and bases are rebalanced and eventually reduced. The US should continue to commit funds for the upgrading of US defense capabilities on the peninsula. The package of

$11 billion over four years announced at the second meeting of the Future of the US-ROK Alliance Initiative of over 150 enhancements to the combined defense, including antimissile systems and augmented Apache helicopters, is a useful step in this direction (see appendices). The US should maintain joint combined training with the ROK. This includes training north of Seoul and near the DMZ. The US should improve intelligence-sharing with the ROK, including supporting Korea's longer-term efforts to acquire an independent satellite intelligence capability.

An Alliance That Looks beyond North Korea

Perhaps the most important message that could be sent about the US commitment to the alliance is to locate any changes within a larger strategic vision that not only deters North Korea, but also looks beyond the North as the primary rationale for the US-ROK relationship. Fears of US abandonment or US preemption emerge because observers focus on changes to the alliance only as they relate to the North Korean threat. The rebalancing plans should be presented as an investment in the long-term future of the alliance, even after Korean unification. In other words, the consolidation of bases and the footprint are necessary steps not to abandon an ally, but to ensure a South Korean (or united Korean) public more welcoming of a continued US military presence on their peninsula. The pullback of forces and their eventual reduction should not be framed as preparing for an attack against the North, but as preempting American/congressional backlash against the dated concept of a tripwire deterrent (especially when the South Korean public is perceived as unappreciative of this deterrent). The transformation of US capabilities from a heavy ground-based presence to a more flexible and mobile air and naval one represents a longer-term investment in the Korean peninsula's continued utility for US strategy and power projection in East Asia. Therefore, rather than being ill-timed, these changes are forward-looking. Making radical decisions to improve the alliance is never easy, and many critics would argue that now is a poor time for such decisions. But realistically, there is never a good time to make changes on this scale.

Strategic Rationale after Unification

The "packaging" of revisions to the US-ROK alliance as necessary to preserve the alliance after unification still begs the question: What purpose does the alliance serve? One cannot overemphasize the importance of creating a clear, definable rationale for the alliance for the present moment. American alliance resiliency in Asia is deceptive. On the one hand, support today appears strong. However, American acceptance of alliances in Asia today contrasts with a strongly negative attitude only a few years earlier. In the late 1980s and early 1990s, trade frictions, economic nationalist arguments, and complaints about burden-sharing led many to envision the end of these Cold War relics. These complaints have largely disappeared among the public, media, and Congress but for reasons that have little to do with resiliency. The Asian financial crisis, security threats from North Korea, suspicions about China, and high levels of host nation support have ended them. The American alliances currently at work in Asia do not inspire domestic opposition. What we do not know is how much proactive support actually exists.

> The domestic politics of our Asian alliances is like the story of the dog that didn't bark. ... Asian alliance issues also have been on the back burner. The value of these alliances is rarely contested in our national politics. ... [T]here seems little reason to alter the status quo. So long as peace persists and host-nation support remains robust, the burdens of these alliances seem relatively light. Yet therein lies the rub. US public support for alliances with Japan and Korea may be deceptive—"a mile wide and an inch deep."[7]

Even if domestic support exists in principle, the type of commitment that might be politically acceptable to a US audience in a military contingency is not the type that most contingencies would require. For example, air power would be the most antiseptic manner in which the US could fulfill alliance commitments but contingencies in Korea, and perhaps Taiwan, would require ground forces.[8] The latter is a path the American public is unlikely to want to take again. In sum, the US-ROK alliance does not enjoy a resiliency equivalent to US alliances in Europe. While NATO could muddle through for an entire decade in search of a mission, the US-ROK alliance cannot afford to allow events to overtake a discussion of the future.

The most often-cited rationale for looking to the future is "regional stability," but this raises more questions than it answers.[9] Many have defined regional stability with regard to Korea as a code word for contingencies implying the quasi-containment of China—a politically unacceptable mission for the alliance from the Korean perspective. Others have defined regional missions for the US-ROK alliance more broadly to include nontraditional security activities like humanitarian intervention, peacekeeping and peacemaking operations, and counterterrorism operations.[10] In one of the more useful characterizations of the term, Jim Kelly and Mike McDevitt define regional missions in military terms as preventing power projection by others beyond the East Asian littoral.[11]

Yet these definitions still fail to get at the goal of the US-ROK alliance, beyond peninsular security. If regional stability includes peacekeeping and anti-power projection, then for what larger purpose are these missions pursued vis-à-vis the US-ROK alliance? How can the United States and South Korea define a rationale for their alliance that allows it to be more than ad hoc, reactive, and derivative of North Korea?

Answering such questions must begin with a frank assessment of the geostrategic landscape in Northeast Asia after Korean unification. This landscape is *unfavorable* to American interests. For reasons of geography, history, culture, power, economics, and demography, one could imagine the following post-unification trends in Asia:

1) the domestic politics of Korean unification push the United States military off the peninsula;
2) for reasons of geography and history, the new Korean entity seeks a continental accommodation with China;
3) Korea joins China in heightened tensions with Japan, as a combination of resurgent Korean nationalism and new military capabilities incite security dilemmas with its historical enemy;
4) a demographically old Japan is isolated from the rest of Asia but simultaneously uncomfortable as the last remaining US "outpost" in the region.

A variety of other nonlinear dynamics might flow from Korean unification, but given current and past geostrategic trends, this is only a best estimate of how events might play out.[12] What is striking about this picture is how heavily it weighs against US interests. If the United States has the will to remain an Asia-Pacific power after Korean unification, then it will not allow itself to be pushed out. Moreover, this picture is not in the region's interests because of its conflicting consequences. For example, an older, weaker, and isolated Japan that does not want to be labeled the last American "military colony" in Asia might finally choose greater self-reliance in security. This would set off balancing reactions in China and Korea such that the net assessment for the region's security could be substantially worse with higher levels of tension and armaments, and almost certain nuclear proliferation.

American strategic planners must not merely seek to avoid future war in Northeast Asia, but must also contemplate avoiding this kind of future peace. Geostrategic currents in Asia following unification therefore create a "preventive defense" rationale for the alliances in Asia—that is, prudent and premeditated actions that need to be taken by the United States and its allies not to deal with an imminent threat, but to prevent the emergence of potentially dangerous situations.[13] The imperative for the United States is to shape a direction away from these unfavorable geostrategic currents in Asia that could follow unification of the peninsula. A robust US-ROK relationship (tied tightly to Japan as well) would provide a strategic bulwark to ensure that post-unification events would neither expel the United States, isolate Japan, nor heighten tensions between Korea and its neighbors. In this regard, the alliance serves a nonproliferation function while also dampening security dilemmas and preventing the rise of regional hegemons.

Common Values

As critical as the alliance's post-unification vision is the infusion of the US-ROK and US-Japan alliances with meaning and identity beyond their Cold War roots. History shows that the most resilient alliances are those that share a common "ideational" grounding that runs deeper than the initial adversarial threats that brought the alliance into existence.[14] The Anglo-Japanese alliance, for example, never lasted beyond the threats that gave it coherence. Few would argue that the post-9/11 relationship between the United States and Pakistan is more than a utilitarian relationship. On the other hand, the US-Australia relationship stands for more than defending against a common threat. It is the embodiment of the two countries' new-world heritage, common language, and a history of fighting together in wars.

A key determinant of alliance resiliency is the degree to which shared identities underpin interaction. By identity, we mean the degree to which alliances are grounded in commonly held norms, values, beliefs, and conceptions of how security is best achieved.

> [W]hen an alliance either reflects or creates a sense of common identity ... [t]hen the entire notion of an individual national interest becomes less applicable. If elites and/or publics begin to view their own society as inextricably part of a larger political community, then members will find it difficult to conceive of themselves as separate and will see their interests as identical even if the external environment changes dramatically.[15]

Alliance identity can exist a priori based on similarities in regime type, religion, or ethnicity (e.g., the Anglo-American alliance). Common identities can also be constructed over time between unlike regimes through a wide range of economic and social interactions, development of elite networks, and high levels of communication.[16] In the latter case, alliances become institutions of socialization where constituencies in both countries develop common standards and expectations of conduct. Most important, the type of commitment that emerges from shared alliance identities is fundamentally different from those that lack this component. The decision to help the ally in the latter case is based on a cold calculation of the overlap in interests. In the former case, the decision may have as much to do with promoting certain commonly shared values (even if there is comparatively less overlap in interests). At the extreme end, shared identities may lead to an emotive attachment and loyalty to an ally irrespective of the issue at hand.[17]

For the US-Japan-ROK relationships, this means deliberate efforts at maturing the alliance beyond its narrow "anti-DPRK" rationale to encompass a broader definition.[18] Currently, this process has reached the level of "maintaining regional stability" as the alliance's future purpose, but there is room for further growth. Beyond regional stability, there are a host of extra-regional issues that define the relationship (i.e., liberal democracy, open economic markets, nonproliferation, universal human rights, anti-terrorism, peacekeeping, open society, free press, rule of law).[19] Moreover, the US-Japan-ROK alliances represent the "success stories" of these values in a region that does not yet readily accept them.

An Alliance That Stands for Something, Not against Something

Ideally, the US-ROK and US-Japan alliances should stand *for* something, rather than simply against a threat. The pressing task for the US-ROK alliance resiliency is therefore not only to deal with pragmatic, material alliance management issues, but also to lay the ideational foundation for the alliance in the post–Cold War era. As noted above, shared identities can be constructed even where they do not exist a priori. Deliberate efforts by US officials to frame the relationship in normative terms that resonate with the average—not specialist—American are helpful. In this vein, statements like those by former deputy assistant secretary of defense Kurt Campbell are a step in the right direction:

> ...the security alliance between the US and the Republic of Korea is more than treaty commitment: it is a close, mutually beneficial partnership built on a shared stake in democracy and free markets. Our alliance is an essential element of the strategy for achieving our long-standing security goal: a nonnuclear, democratic, and peacefully reunified Korean peninsula.[20]

Former ambassador Bosworth's statements offer similar attempts at reconstructing the alliance in ideational terms:

> The third element of our relationship is philosophical: our shared commitment to democratic values and democratic practice. As Korean democracy has developed strongly in recent years, democracy has become in a real sense the cement of the overall relationship.[21]

Before a wider foreign policy audience, such statements help to construct an image of Korea as the successful embodiment of market democratic ideals in a region where skepticism of such ideals still remains. The May 14, 2003, joint statement between Presidents Bush and Roh—entitled "Common Values, Principles, and Strategy"—made useful strides in this direction. Specifically, the statement reversed the order in which we have grown accustomed to thinking about the alliance—all strategy and few values—and focused the key message not on North Korea, but on the alliance's comprehensiveness: "Noting that 2003 marks the fiftieth anniversary of the US-ROK Mutual Defense Treaty, the two leaders pledged to work together to promote the values of democracy, human rights and market economy shared by the people of both nations and to build a comprehensive and dynamic alliance relationship for continued peace and prosperity on the Korean Peninsula and in Northeast Asia."[22] This common ideational grounding not only gives the relationship permanency, but also provides the glue that prevents these alignments from being washed away by the region's geostrategic currents after unification. In this regard, Washington and Seoul at the highest levels need to forge a common agenda of issues and actions, which will become the centerpiece of the alliance's broadening significance beyond the peninsula. This document should state the global issues on which the two leaders and their countries will unite, as well as the material efforts, individual or joint, they have already made to resolve these issues. The United States should also consciously promote Korea's political evolution as an example to newly democratizing countries in international institutions and other forums, such as the "Club of Madrid." Washington, Seoul, and Tokyo also should forge a new institutional forum for democracy in Asia that includes government officials, experts, and scholars who focus on issues of democratic development, transitional justice, and equity and regulation within open societies.

China

One of the alliance's biggest challenges is conjoining its continued resiliency with growing Chinese influence in the region. China will look on a consolidation of the US-ROK alliance after unification as a form of containment. South Koreans also hold a historical affinity for China that discounts the more recent half-century of Cold War hostilities as "aberrant" (the term used in their 1992 normalization), and celebrates the common Confucian heritage and traditional tributary relationship. China has been catching up to the United States as South Korea's primary trading partner. In 1995 Korea's total trade with the United States was $54.5 billion, versus that with China at a paltry $16.5 billion. By 2002, total trade with the United States was $55.8 billion; trade with China stood at $41.1 billion. And in 2003, China emerged as South Korea's largest export market, surpassing the United States, which has been the main market for Korean products since 1965.[23] While South Korean exports to the United States grew at 2.7 percent, that with China grew by 48 percent in 2003. Semiconductor exports to China grew at 120 percent compared to 2002. Computer products and mobile telecommunications equipment grew at 85 percent.

Table 2. ROK Trade with the United States and China

Year	ROK imports from US	ROK exports to US	Total value of bilateral trade
1995	$30,403,515,184	24,131,473,504	54,534,988,688
1996	33,305,378,793	21,670,464,688	54,975,843,481
1997	30,122,178,215	21,625,431,768	51,747,609,983
1998	20,403,276,346	22,805,106,108	43,208,382,454
1999	24,922,344,101	29,474,652,517	54,396,996,618
2000	29,241,628,233	37,610,630,128	66,852,258,361
2001	22,376,225,624	31,210,795,079	53,587,020,703
2002	23,008,634,858	32,780,188,163	55,788,823,021
Five-year totals (1998–2002)	119,952,109,162	153,881,371,995	273,833,481,157

Year	ROK imports from China	ROK exports to China	Total value of bilateral trade
1995	$7,401,196,380	9,143,587,605	16,544,783,985
1996	8,538,568,223	11,377,068,035	19,915,636,258
1997	10,116,860,682	13,572,463,052	23,689,323,734
1998	6,483,957,641	11,943,990,428	18,427,948,069
1999	8,866,666,765	13,684,599,051	22,551,265,816
2000	12,798,727,524	18,454,539,579	31,253,267,103
2001	13,302,675,219	18,190,189,650	31,492,864,869
2002	17,399,778,956	23,753,585,754	41,153,364,710
Five-year totals (1998–2002)	58,851,806,105	86,026,904,462	144,878,710,567

Source: Korea International Trade Association (KITA),
http://www.kita.org
All values are in US$.

Polls show that South Koreans overwhelmingly view China as their most important economic partner over the next decade (see Table 3). This combination of economics and geographic propinquity could pull the Korean peninsula strategically away from the United States and toward its Asian mainland neighbor. South Korea (unlike Japan) has never allowed the Dalai Lama a visa. Moreover, South Korea was the only US ally in the region uninterested in joining US missile defense architectures.

Despite the ROK-China affinity, I believe that China will not fundamentally obstruct the growth of the US-ROK alliance after unification. First, the extent to which unification creates zero-sum choices for Seoul between the two great powers will be determined by the nature of US-China relations at that time. If US-China relations continue on the more constructive, pragmatic path that emerged after 9/11, and if Washington and Beijing are seen to be cooperating closely in resolving the North Korean nuclear problem, then the US-ROK alliance's consolidation may prove less threatening to Beijing.

Second, regime type matters. China's economic influence over the peninsula is one thing, but a full-blown political and strategic relationship that replicates and replaces what South Korea has with the United States is unlikely if China's political system remains as it is today. There are natural limits to how closely liberal democracies like South Korea can link themselves with nondemocracies. Moreover, despite the historical tributary relationship between the two countries, China has never provided the type of security guarantee that the United States has granted to Korea. Surrounded as they are by great powers, South Koreans will continue to find it in their interest, post-unification, to ally with the biggest and most distant power. South Korean polls confirm this eventuality. Even at the height of anti-American demonstrations in 2002 and 2003, South Koreans saw their economic future with China, but overwhelmingly viewed the United States as their primary strategic partner over the next decade.

Table 3. South Korean Views of Closest Economic Partner in 5–10 Years

	June 1996	April 1998	May 2000	July 2002
China	38%	43%	55%	53%
United States	18%	13%	17%	14%

Source: Obtained from INR, State Department May 2003. For similar poll results, see *Ambivalent Allies? A Study of South Korean Attitudes toward the US*, Eric Larson and Norm Levin (Santa Monica, CA: RAND, December 2003).

Table 4. South Korean Views of Closest Security Partner in 5–10 Years

	June 1996	May 2000	July 2002
China	12%	13%	11%
United States	52%	60%	60%

Source: Obtained from INR, State Department May 2003. For similar poll results, see *Ambivalent Allies? A Study of South Korean Attitudes toward the US*, Eric Larson and Norm Levin (Santa Monica, CA: RAND, December 2003).

Building the ideational aspect of the alliance is critical in this respect. If one takes a traditional definition of alliances that suggests they only arise when faced with a threat, then post-unification, the US-ROK alliance will be forced into a zero-sum trade-off between targeting China or falling apart. However, if one defines an alliance in more fluid terms—as an institution that also stands for values and ideals—then a non-zero-sum equilibrium may be attainable between China and the US-ROK alliance.

Persuading China to "Free-Ride"

It is important to remember that China's geostrategic preferences on the Korean peninsula and in the region must be seen in relative terms. In absolute terms, China would probably like to be the dominant power in the region, and would oppose any unification scenario that keeps the United States on the peninsula. Realistically, however, Beijing's choices are not absolute but relative. If the alternative outcome for China is Korean unification with a heavy US ground-troop presence in the northern part of the peninsula, then China may be less opposed to a recessed US presence south of the 38th parallel, with primarily air and naval hubs.

The latter point underlines how important it is to recognize the absence of any deterministic predictions about China's role in the region. There is a "China-threat" school of thought that views a collision course between the United States and the region's most dynamic economic and growing military power.[24] Given demographic and other indicators, there is no denying the credibility of these arguments. The historical experiences of Britain, Germany, Imperial Japan, the Soviet Union, and the United States show that major powers undergoing rapid economic development also simultaneously experience the most expansionist phases of their foreign policies.

An alternative view argues for a less ambitious and more pragmatic position for Beijing vis-à-vis the United States. This perspective, offered by some American and Chinese scholars, argues that China's interests are best served by not undertaking a revisionist posture toward the balance of power in the region and challenging the American position.[25] Instead, the theory goes, China should continue as it has done since the early 1990s: to focus on its own development and growth provided by the markets and stability in Asia. This "free-riding" thesis implicitly means that Beijing neither desires nor aspires to underwrite prosperity and stability as the lead power in the system, instead preferring to cede that role to the US-based alliance system in Asia. "All this," according to the Beijing media, "is part of a newly adopted 'development strategy of peaceful ascendancy,' a strategy which is aimed at integrating China positively into the existing world system despite differences in political systems, levels of economic development, and cultural traditions, and 'seeking multilateral and constructive cooperation,' instead of confrontations, with the world powers in solving differences and conflicts during China's 'ascendancy.'"[26]

Corollary propositions emerging from this school, as Jing Huang states, are that first, China has not contested America's unipolar predominance in the international system. It accepts American unipolarity, but not American unilateralism. Second, people may not like China's free-riding, invoking arguments about long-term power transition and imperial overstretch, but the flip-side of free-riding is that China now accepts that the United States has historical and legitimate interests in Asia. As recently as December 2003, Chinese foreign ministry officials stated for the *first* time that "the US military presence in the Asia-Pacific is caused by historical process."[27] As one scholar interpreted this statement, "This is a significant change indeed, for until 1999, 'withdrawal of foreign troops in Asia' had been a principle in China's foreign policy."[28] Third, Huang observes that if China wants to free-ride on the status quo, then its primary concern vis-à-vis regional strategy is not the continuing US presence, but some concatenation of forces that might lead to Japanese military rearmament on a grand scale.

Whether the "truth" about Chinese intentions lies with either of these schools of thought is beside the point. In China, there are elements of both the "hegemon on the horizon" and the "free-ride" thesis. What matters is that US actions can shape which grand strategy will prevail in Beijing. An overwhelming deportment of US power, coupled with a resilient Northeast Asia alliance system, will "convince" China that any desires for dominance in the region take a back seat to peace and stability. There is no denying that the potential gains to China in becoming the dominant power in the region, displacing the United States, could be great. But with continued US power and US alliances, these gains for China are uncertain, and would come at great costs. On the other hand, Beijing could assure itself certain (though smaller) gains by recognizing the US position in the region as vital and legitimate, and continuing to benefit from this American system. By maintaining the Northeast Asian alliance system and US stature in the region, the free-riding thesis becomes the "rational" choice for China despite any grander aspirations it might harbor. Such an outcome is also best for the continued resiliency of the US-Korea alliance.

Why Now?

Why must the United States contemplate these changes now? Many critics and supporters of the alliance have argued that the timing does not work in the alliance's interests, creating fears of abandonment in Seoul. Others have suggested that the timing raises the specter of radical policies by the United States toward North Korea (the "preemptive attack" thesis), hence creating entrapment fears in Seoul.

First, the notion that the United States is drawing back forces on the peninsula for the purpose of preemptive attack is not credible. The United States has a significant expatriate population (plus allies and US bases in Japan) that would be held hostage by North Korea artillery. The so-called unilateral nature of the US posture review is itself a poor way to impute US intentions. Historically, the United States has made its own decisions about the disposition of its troops on the peninsula; more recently it has done so in consultation with allies.[29] The fact that North Korea has disavowed earlier threats made in April 2003 that it might transfer WMD capabilities to others also reduces the sole likely contingency under which the United States might contemplate attack.

Second, to argue that now is not the time to pull back forces begs the question: when is it the time? Frankly, there is *never* a good time to contemplate such changes and allied anxieties about abandonment are never really avoidable. In addition, as Tom Christensen has suggested, the US decision to rebalance forces in the aftermath of military operations in Iraq and Afghanistan actually offers the closest thing to ideal conditions under which to contemplate such changes. This is so because the United States can undertake such changes with little speculation about whether it remains willing to fight for a cause or an ally. That US-China relations and US-Japan relations are as strong as they have been in recent years also provides a window of opportunity to contemplate major changes in force posture with minimal allied anxieties.[30]

All Is Not Lost ... Yet

Skeptics might argue that the new political reality in South Korea inveighs strongly against the alliance's future. The demonstrations of 2002 and 2003 led many to believe that public opinion in Korea had shifted markedly against the United States, which boded ill for alliance relations.[31] Anger over a US military court's acquittal of two US soldiers for the accidental vehicular death of two Korean schoolgirls fueled many of the protests.

But Korean public opinion may be set against the United States indefinitely. Since the announcement of the rebalancing plan, South Koreans have taken a more realistic view of the alliance's utility. Polls in June 2003 (one year after the schoolgirls' deaths) show that those expressing a negative view of the United States declined most significantly among the 20–30-year-old age group. This group had previously been most strongly opposed to the United States.

Table 5. South Korean Attitudes toward the United States (June 2003)

	Negative	Positive	Neutral	Comments
June 2003	27.6	25.4	46.9	December 2002 negative perceptions of United States for 20-year-olds = 76%

Source: *JoongAng Ilbo* (English edition), July 26, 2003, p. 8.
Sample size: 1032.

Table 6. South Korean Attitudes toward Bush Administration Policy toward North Korea (June 2003)

	Strongly disapprove	Generally disapprove	Strongly approve	Generally approve
June 2003	9.4%	39%	11.2%	37.3%

20-year-olds positive = 36.7% / 50+ = 65%
20-year-olds negative = 63.3% / 50+ = 29.5%

Source: *JoongAng Ilbo* (English edition), July 26, 2003, p. 8.

More significantly, there exists a "silent majority" of Koreans with a right-of-center political orientation who still view the US-ROK alliance as critical to South Korea's long-term interests. In early 2003, these groups countered anti-American demonstrations—which numbered in the hundreds of thousands—with pro-American demonstrations that numbered in the millions.

In both South Korea and in the United States, there remains a substantial percentage of people who are "undecided" or "have no opinion" on questions related to the alliance. For example, the June 2003 polls (*Joongang Ilbo*) showed some 47 percent of South Koreans saying they had "neutral" feelings about the United States. In the United States, there is general ignorance about Korea, beyond *M*A*S*H** or the World Cup. There is thus a "soft middle" of impressionable opinion in both countries that can swing positively or negatively, depending on the course of events.

The long-term scope of this discussion does not diminish its urgency. Formulating a mutually agreeable vision and strategic rationale for the alliance ensures that future revisions to the force presence occur in the right political context and are not misinterpreted. If action is not taken now, the US-ROK alliance runs the risk of entering its middle age as a brittle Cold War relic, in danger of being overtaken and outpaced by events.

APPENDICES

Results of the First Meeting of the "Future of the ROK-US Alliance Policy Initiative"

http://www.usfk.or.kr/en/future_initiative_01.php
Joint Statement on the "Future of the ROK-US Alliance Policy Initiative," April 9, 2003.

1. The first meeting of the "Future of the ROK-US Alliance Policy Initiative" was held in Seoul on April 8–9, 2003. Lieutenant General Cha Young Koo, Deputy Minister for Policy of the ROK Ministry of National Defense, Mr. Shim Yoon Joe, Director General, North American Affairs Bureau of the Ministry of Foreign Affairs and Trade, Mr. Richard P. Lawless, the US Deputy Assistant Secretary of Defense (DASD) for Asia-Pacific Affairs, and Mr. Christopher LaFleur, Special Envoy of the US Department of State, led their respective delegations, which included members of the ROK MND [Ministry of National Defense] and the US Department of Defense, as well as the ROK Ministry of Foreign Affairs and Trade and the US Department of State.

2. The "Future of the ROK-US Alliance Policy Initiative" was agreed upon by the ROK Minister of National Defense and the US Secretary of Defense during the 34th Security Consultative Meeting (SCM) on December 5, 2002, to adapt the alliance to reflect changing regional and global security circumstances.

3. The US side conveyed the US Government's special appreciation for the ROK's decision to dispatch engineer and medical units to support the Coalition's effort in Iraq.

4. Acknowledging that this year marks the 50th anniversary since the official establishment of the ROK-US alliance, the two sides assessed the bilateral relations between the ROK and the US, and concurred that the ROK-US alliance made significant contributions to national security and development of Korea. In order to further enhance deterrence through the solidarity of the ROK-US alliance and to ensure a strong alliance for the future, the two sides agreed on the following basic principles for their joint consultation.
    i. Both agreed on the need to adapt the alliance to the new global security environment and to take into account the ROK's status as a prosperous democracy.
    ii. Both agreed on the need for both countries to invest in an enduring alliance.

5. The two sides shared a common view that the ROK-US alliance must be developed in ways to best contribute to security on the peninsula and beyond. Accordingly, both parties agreed in principle to expand ROK forces' role in defense of the Peninsula and to enhance US forces' contribution to regional stability. In the context of the ROK's own military transformation, it will assume responsibility for selected missions. The US presented a plan to invest in the future of the alliance by further developing twenty-first-century war-fighting capabilities.

6. The two sides agreed to consult on modernization of the ROK and US military capabilities in an effort to further enhance the ROK-US combined defense posture and deterrence capabilities.

7. The two sides agreed to consolidate the USFK base structure in order to preserve an enduring stationing environment for USFK, to achieve higher efficiency in managing USFK bases, and to foster a balanced development of ROK national lands. Both sides agreed to continue discussion on the timing of the overall realignment process. The US side expressed an understanding of the concerns of the Korean people regarding the alignment of USFK, including 2ID. The two sides agreed that there would be no compromise in the combined deterrence of their forces throughout the process of realignment.

8. Recognizing the need to foster a balanced development of the Seoul Metropolitan Area, to resolve inconveniences to Seoul citizens, and to provide a stable stationing environment for USFK, the two sides agreed to relocate Yongsan Garrison as soon as possible.

9. As a part of this process, the ROK JCS [Joint Chiefs of Staff] and the US JCS will consult regarding key topics required in developing concepts related to changes in the security environment, such as the development of ROK and US combined military capabilities. Additionally, they will form a consultative group to conduct a study of the ROK-US combined command relationship in the mid and long term.

10. Assessing that the first meeting has contributed to further strengthening the ROK-US alliance, the two sides agreed to hold the second meeting in the US in May.

Results of the Second Meeting of the "Future of the ROK-US Alliance Policy Initiative"

http://www.usfk.or.kr/en/future_initiative_02.php
Joint Statement on the "Future of the ROK-US Alliance Policy Initiative," June 5, 2003.

1. The second meeting of the "Future of the ROK-US Alliance Policy Initiative' was held in Seoul on June 4–5. Lieutenant General Cha Young Koo, Deputy Minister for Policy of the ROK Ministry of National Defense (MND), Mr. Shim Yoon Joe, Director-General, North American Affairs Bureau of the Ministry of Foreign Affairs and Trade (MOFAT), Mr. Richard P. Lawless, the US Deputy Assistant Secretary of Defense (DASD) for Asia-Pacific Affairs, and Mr. Christopher LaFleur, Special Envoy of the US Department of State (DOS), led their respective delegations, which included members of the ROK MND and the US DoD, as well as the ROK MOFAT and the US DOS.

2. The first meeting of the "Future of the US-ROK Alliance Policy Initiative" was held in Seoul on April 8–9.

3. The two sides reaffirmed that the US-ROK Summit between President Roh Moo-hyun and President George W. Bush in Washington, DC on May 14 provided the basis for further promoting and developing the US-ROK Alliance for the twenty-first-century, making the bilateral relationship closer and stronger as the two nations celebrate the fiftieth anniversary of the alliance.

4. The two sides agreed on the need to develop detailed plans to carry out the vision of the two presidents on modernizing the alliance. They reaffirmed the relocation of Yongsan at an early date and the consolidation of US forces in Korea around key hubs, taking careful account of the political, economic, and security situation on the peninsula and in Northeast Asia. In this regard, they agreed to begin work on several important implementation plans with the goal of completing them by the Security Consultative Meeting (SCM) in late September:

- An Implementation Plan for Capability Enhancement
- An Implementation Plan for Yongsan Relocation
- An Implementation Plan for the Transfer of Military Missions
- An Implementation Plan for the Realignment of US forces in the ROK

5. The two sides had very productive and in-depth consultations on major issues for the transformation of the current ROK-US alliance. They agreed on a number of items designed to enhance, shape, and align the alliance.

6. Both sides agreed that our fundamental goal is to enhance deterrence and security on the Korean peninsula and improve the combined defense. The US side reiterated Deputy Secretary of Defense Wolfowitz's recent statements on the US commitment to improving the ROK-US alliance. Both sides also agreed on the importance of structuring US forces in a manner that further promotes regional stability.

7. The US side presented a detailed explanation of its plan to invest in over 150 enhancements to the combined defense, valued at over $11 billion, over the next four years. Both sides agreed that this is a substantial US investment in the future of the alliance and the security of the Republic of Korea. The ROK side indicated that it would substantially enhance ROK military capabilities to strengthen the Alliance. The two sides agreed to detailed consultation between the ROK and US JCS on transformation of combined forces.

8. The two sides agreed to proceed with transfer of certain missions between US and ROK forces, in conjunction with the ROK-US combined capabilities enhancement. Both sides agreed that this is in keeping with the agreement at the summit meeting that the ROK's growing national strength provides an opportunity to expand the role of the ROK military in defending the Korean peninsula. The two sides reaffirmed their agreement to study possible mid- and long-term changes to command relationships.

9. In order to support the early movement of US forces currently located in Yongsan out of Seoul and the overall realignment of US forces in Korea, to include those north of the Han River, both sides agreed that the ROK government would start procuring appropriate land in 2004. Once the implementation plan is finalized selected facilities can be returned in the first year. The consolidation will take a number of years and proceed in two phases. Under the first phase, US forces north of the Han River will consolidate in the Camp Casey and Camp Red Cloud area. In phase two, US forces north of the Han River would move to the key hubs south of the Han River. The two sides agreed to sustain a US military rotational training presence north of the Han even after the completion of phase two.

10. The two sides agreed to hold a ROK-US Defense Ministerial Talk in Washington, DC soon to consult on follow-up measures to the ROK-US Summit and the recent visit by Deputy Secretary of Defense Paul Wolfowitz on enhancing, shaping, and aligning the Alliance.

11. Assessing that the second meeting has contributed to further strengthening the ROK-US alliance, the two sides agreed to hold the third meeting in the US in July.

Results of the Third Meeting of the "Future of the ROK-US Alliance Policy Initiative"

http://www.usfk.or.kr/en/future_initiative_04.php

1. The third meeting of the "Future of the ROK-US Alliance Policy Initiative" (FOTA) was held in Hawaii 22–23 July, 2003. Lieutenant General Cha, Young-Koo, Deputy Minister for Policy, ROK Ministry of National Defense (MND); Mr. Wi, Sung-Lac, Director-General, North American Affairs Bureau, Ministry of Foreign Affairs and Trade (MOFAT); Mr. Richard P. Lawless, US Deputy Assistant Secretary of Defense (DASD) for Asia-Pacific Affairs; and Mr. Christopher LaFleur, Special Envoy of the US Department of State (DOS), led their respective delegations which included members of the ROK MND and the US DoD, as well as the ROK MOFAT and the US DOS.

2. The two sides reaffirmed the basic aims of the "Future of the ROK-US Alliance Policy Initiative" are to further strengthen the ROK-US alliance and its combined defense capabilities, provide a stable long-term stationing environment for the USFK, and ensure a robust alliance for the future. In particular, the US side reiterated its commitment to the maintenance of security on the Korean peninsula.

3. Both sides shared a common view that the ROK-US Defense Ministerial Talks held in Washington, DC on 27 June solidified agreements from the ROK-US Presidential Summit regarding the future direction of the ROK-US alliance and furthered their combined consultations. Both sides agreed to actively pursue consultations, so that the ROK Minister of National Defense and the US Secretary of Defense could approve relevant FOTA implementation plans at this year's Security Consultative Meeting in October 2003.

4. Both sides used the meeting to reaffirm their commitment to ROK and US force enhancements of the alliance. In the meeting the two sides agreed that the combined military capabilities enhancements and additional force improvements for both ROK and US forces will continue. Additionally, the two sides verified that force enhancements are proceeding.

5. Both sides discussed plans to transfer some military missions from the US to ROK forces. The two sides reached agreement on the timing of the transfer of several of these missions and agreed to continue consultations for the timing of the remaining missions, with a view toward reaching agreement before the October SCM. Both sides agreed to consult on missions transfer with a view to establishing a more predominant ROK role in defending the peninsula and enhancing US forces' contribution to security on the peninsula and beyond.

6. Based on the agreement of the ROK and US presidents to relocate Yongsan Garrison at an early date, the two sides agreed to work jointly for relocation by the target year of 2006. In doing that, the two sides agreed to start jointly drafting a relocation Master Plan this year. Land acquisition for relocation and facilities design will start in early 2004, to be immediately followed by the start of construction. The two sides also agreed to conclude all necessary implementation planning for the relocation of the US forces out of the Seoul metropolitan area prior to the Security Consultative Meeting in October 2003.

7. Both sides reaffirmed the agreement reached at the ROK-US Defense Ministerial Talks in June 2003 to align US forces, including the US Second Infantry Division, into key hubs south of the Han River in a two-phased process. In phase 1, units north of the Han River will consolidate into bases in the Dongducheon and Uijongbu areas while facilities are prepared south of the Han River. The second phase will be implemented through close consultation between the ROK and the US. The two sides reaffirmed their commitment to sustain a US military rotational training presence north of the Han River even after the completion of Phase 2. Both sides agreed on the need to promote the awareness of the Korean public on this relocation's value to ROK security and to the future of the US-ROK alliance. Both sides reaffirmed the importance of continued US presence on the Korean peninsula.

8. The two sides reaffirmed agreements from the previous "Future of the ROK-US Alliance Policy Initiative" meetings to study the ROK-US combined command relationship in the mid- and long-term. The two sides agreed to report the results at the Security Consultative Meeting in 2005.

9. The two sides agreed to hold the fourth meeting in Seoul in early September.

USFL Force Enhancement Initiatives

http://www.usfk.or.kr/en/future_enhance.php

SEOUL, Republic of Korea (USFK) May 31, 2003—Gen. Leon J. LaPorte, Commander United Nations Command, Combined Forces Command, US Forces Korea, met with Cho, Young-kil, Minister of National Defense and Gen. Kim, Jong Hwan, Chairman of the Joint Chiefs of Staff to discuss future force enhancements for US Forces in Korea.

During the meeting, Gen. LaPorte discussed the operational requirement for both ROK and US capability improvements to enhance Combined Forces Command's capability to deter aggression and to guarantee the security of the Republic of Korea. Gen. LaPorte then highlighted plans for US capability enhancements to be implemented over the next three years.

"These enhancements represent a more than $11 billion US investment in peninsula security and regional stability," said Gen. LaPorte. "Our upgrades in capabilities demonstrate our firm US commitment to the long-standing ROK-US alliance."

Gen. LaPorte outlined several near-term enhancements during his meetings with Minister Cho and Gen. Kim, including upgrades to the intelligence collection systems, increased numbers of improved precision munitions, rotational deployment of the Army's newest Stryker unit to improve responsiveness, and additions to Army pre-positioned stocks to increase readiness to defend the Republic of Korea.

Minister Cho, Gen. Kim, and Gen. LaPorte agreed that enhancing both the Republic of Korea and US deterrence military capabilities is critical to ensure the ROK-US alliance is postured to meet the requirements of the future. They also agreed to continue consultations as near-term enhancements are implemented on the Korean peninsula and plans for long-term force enhancements are developed.

NOTES

[1] Kim Kyung Won, "What Makes and Sustains Alliances in Asia," paper presented at the IISS 38th annual conference, Dresden, Germany, September 1-4, 1998, pp. 3–5.

[2] For historical overviews, see Don Oberdorfer, *The Two Koreas* (New York: Basic Books, 2001), and a forthcoming book, Young Whan Kihl, *Transforming Korean Politics: Democracy, Reform and Culture* (M.E. Sharpe, forthcoming).

[3] These indicators are borrowed from Dr. William Perry, "Comprehensive Remarks," in *Alliance Tomorrow: Security Arrangements after the Cold War*, Yoichi Funabashi, ed. (Tokyo: Tokyo Foundation, 2001), pp. 295–98. Alliances serve the purpose not just of providing for one's security, but doing so in an efficient and relatively less costly manner than would otherwise be the case. In this vein, an alliance's success is measured by the extent to which it serves as a facilitator of power accretion and projection; operates as a unified command; enables common tactics and doctrine through joint training; promotes a division of security roles; facilitates cooperation in production and development of military equipment, and elicits political support among domestic constituencies.

[4] For elaboration, see Victor Cha, "The Ambivalent Alliance," *Current History* (September 2003).

[5] For one of the few detailed histories of US forces in Korea, see James P. Finely, *The US Military Experience in Korea, 1871–1982: In the Vanguard of ROK-US Relations* (Command Historian's Office, Secretary Joint Staff, Hqs., USFK/EUSA, APO San Francisco 96301, 1983).

[6] Victor Cha, *Alignment Despite Antagonism: The United States–Korea–Japan Security Triangle* (Stanford, CA: Stanford University Press, 2000), chapter 3.

[7] Michael Armacost, "Asian Alliances and American Politics," APARC Working Paper, February 1999, pp. 5,12. See also Tom Berger, "Set for Stability? An American Perspective on the Prospects for Conflict and Cooperation in East Asia," Presentation at the Graduate Institute of Peace Studies, Kyung Hee University, Seoul, September 24–26, 1998), pp. 24–25.

[8] Dibb, "The Strategic Environment in the Asia-Pacific Region," in *America's Asian Alliances*, p. 14.

[9] Ralph Cossa, "The Role of US Forces in a Unified Korea," *International Journal of Korean Studies* 5.2 (fall/winter 2001), p. 131. In a related vein, another often-cited mission is for the US presence in Asia to "shape" the region. One study defined this in a fashion that obscures more than clarifies:

> The United States must also seek to maintain stability in the region through "shaping" activities aimed a providing positive incentives for cooperative behavior and disincentives against the use of force to achieve geopolitical goals. These shaping activities must seek to convince nations of the region that their security will be attained more easily if the United States maintains an active military role in the region than would be the case if it did not. (Zalmay Khalilzad, et al., *The United States and Asia: Toward a New US Strategy and Force Posture* [Arlington, VA: RAND, 2001, pp. 43-44.])

[10] Gen John H. Tilelli (Ret.) and Maj. Susan Bryant, *Keeping the Calm: Northeast Asian Regional Security* (Arlington, VA: Association of the United States Army, 2002), pp. 39–40.

[11] James Kelly and Michael McDevitt, "In Search of Stability: Designing for a Better Peace in East Asia," in Ralph Cossa, ed., *US-Korea-Japan Relations: Building toward a Virtual Alliance* (Washington, DC: CSIS, 1999). See also Michael McDevitt in Eberstadt and Ellings, *Korea's Future and the Great Powers* (Seattle, WA: University of Washington Press, 2001), p. 286.

[12] This is not my own view of how the region will or should evolve. It is merely a representation of the most commonly accepted concerns about how international relations might progress after unification. For others who share these concerns on Japan, see Cossa, "The Future of US Forces," p. 123; Charles Wolf, *Asian Economic Trends and Their Security Implications* (Santa Monica, CA: RAND, 2000); Nicholas Eberstadt, *Prosperous Paupers and Other Population Problems* (Brunswick, N.J.: Transaction Publishers, 2000); Robert Ross, "The Geography of Peace: East Asia in the 21st Century," *International Security* 23, 4 (Spring 1999); and Michael Armacost and Kenneth Pyle in Eberstadt and Ellings (2001), p. 126. On China and Korea, see Jiyul Kim, "Continuity and Transformation in Northeast Asia," *Korean Journal of Defense Analyses* 13.1 (Autumn, 2001); David Kang, "Hierarchy and Stability in Asian International Relations" in G. John Ikenberry and Michael Mastanduno, eds., *International Relations Theory and the Asia-Pacific* (New York: Columbia University Press, 2003); Robert Manning and Jim Przystup, "The Great Powers and the Future of Korea," *http://www.columbia.edu/dlc/ciao/wps/mar02/*; *Global Trends 2015: A Dialogue About the Future with Nongovernment Experts* (Washington, DC: CIA, 2000); Tilelli and Bryant, *Northeast Asian Regional Security*, p. 34; and Khalilzad, *The United States and Asia*, pp. 10–16, 48–9.

[13] Ashton B. Carter and William J. Perry, *Preventive Defense: A New Security Strategy for America* (Washington, DC: Brookings Institution, 1999), p. 14.

[14] Victor Cha, "The Future of American Alliances in Asia: The Importance of Enemies or Ideas?" Paper presented at the APSA annual meeting, Philadelphia, August 2003.

[15] See Stephen Walt, "Why Alliances Endure or Collapse," *Survival* 39:1 (Spring 1997), p. 168. Walt, however, is skeptical about the causal role of identity in alliance commitments.

[16] See Karl Deutsch et al., *Political Community and the North Atlantic Area* (Princeton, NJ: Princeton University Press, 1957), p. 5.

[17] Historical precedents for identity-determining behavior in international relations were classical empires and colonialism, where common identification of remote territories with the core often led to imperial wars over objectively insignificant things. See G. John Ikenberry and Charles Kupchan, "Socialization and Hegemonic Power," *International Organization* 44: 2 (Summer 1990); and Kupchan, *Vulnerability of Empire* (Ithaca, NY: Cornell University Press, 1994), p. 258.

[18] Victor Cha, "Focus on the Future, Not the North," *The Washington Quarterly* (Winter 2002–2003); and Mike Mochizuki and Michael O'Hanlon, "A Liberal Vision for the US-Japanese

Alliance," *Survival* 40: 2 (Summer 1998), pp. 127–34.

[19] For theoretical elaboration, see Cha, "The Importance of Enemies or Ideas?"

[20] Statement by Dr. Kurt Campbell, Hearing on US Policy Toward the Korean Peninsula, Subcommittee on East Asian and Pacific Affairs, Senate Committee on Foreign Relations, September 10, 1998.

[21] "The Korean-American Relationship: Continuity and Change," Address before the Korean-American Society and the American Chamber of Commerce, January 23, 1998, Seoul (*http://usembassy.state.gov/seoul/wwwh0100.html* Also see public statements by Peter Tarnoff and Edward Royce in C. Fred Bergsten and Sakong Il, eds., *The Korea–United States Economic Relationship* (Washington, DC: IIE, 1997); and "Perspectives on US-Korea Relations," *US-Korea Tomorrow* 1: 1 (August 1998).

[22] See *http://www.whitehouse.gov/news/releases/2003/04/20030409-5.html.*

[23] Korea International Trade Association, *Bridging the Pacific*, No. XXXIV (January 2004).

[24] Representative works include Denny Roy, "Hegemon on the Horizon? China's Threat to East Asian Security," *International* Security 19: 4 (Summer 1994); Richard Bernstein and Ross Munro, "The Coming Conflict with America," *Foreign* Affairs 76: 2 (March/April 1997); Aaron Friedberg, "Ripe for Rivalry: Prospects for Peace in a Multipolar Asia," *International Security* 18: 3 (Winter 1993/94).

[25] Alastair Iain Johnston, "Is China a Status Quo Power?" *International Security* 27: 4 (Spring 2003).

[26] Jing Huang, "China and America's Northeast Asian Alliance: Approach, Policy, and Dilemma," January 2004, paper presented at APARC Northeast Asia Alliances conference, January 14–15, 2004, p. 4.

[27] Speech by Wang Yi, Vice Minister of Foreign Affairs, at CSCAP meetings, December 12, 2003, *http://news.sina.com.cn/c/2003-12-15/14091346610s.shtml.*

[28] Jing Huang paper, p. 10

[29] Cha, *Alignment Despite Antagonism*, chapter 3; and Nam Joo-Hong, *America's Commitment to South Korea* (Cambridge: Cambridge University Press, 1986).

[30] Victor Cha, "Not Bad for a Non-Policy," *Financial Times*, October 22, 2003.

[31] For a good new study, see Eric V. Larson and Norman D. Levin with the assistance of Seonhae Baik and Bogdan Savych, "Ambivalent Allies? A Study of South Korean Attitudes Toward the US" (Santa Monica, CA: RAND Corporation), DRR-3225-SRF, December 2003.

THE UNITED STATES AND SOUTH KOREA: AN ALLIANCE ADRIFT

Donald P. Gregg

As an American asked to assess the current status of the US–South Korean alliance, I find myself looking for an appropriate image to begin with. Three come quickly to mind. The first is Humpty Dumpty, having fallen from a wall and lying in pieces at its foot. That image does not work well because I cannot picture "all the king's horses and all the king's men" standing around anxiously. The alliance may be in pieces, but no one seems to recognize that fact, or, more ominously perhaps, no one seems anxious to try to put it back together.

The second image is of an old, traditional Korean house which having suffered lots of wear and tear over the years has been carefully disassembled and lies on the ground in pieces prior to being put back together by artisans with some new and stronger elements being added to the old parts. This image also does not work. The alliance has not been systematically disassembled; it has at least in part collapsed. Furthermore, I do not see policy artisans standing around with any capability of building a new and improved alliance structure.

The third image seems to work best. It is an image of the alliance as an old wooden warship too long at sea, leaky and barnacle-encrusted but still afloat. That raises the question of who is at the helm, and I'm afraid that I do not see anyone like "master and commander" Jack Aubrey in the vicinity.

During my time as ambassador, 1989–1993, President Roh Tae-woo used to express the hope that the US–Korean alliance could play the role in Asia that the US-UK alliance has long played in Europe and the Middle East. During the first Gulf War, that seemed to be a viable possibility. Today, it would be impossible for any South Korean to even voice that concept.

The American perception of Korea has been strongly influenced by press reports of what appear to be increasingly hostile views of the United States held by Koreans. I would hasten to add that press reports are an inexact measure of anti-US feelings. For example, in the three and one half years that I served as ambassador in Seoul, I was never able to make a publicized appearance on a university campus. As soon as it became known that I had been invited to appear as a campus speaker, radical students would threaten to riot, and the invitation would be withdrawn. These non-events were never reported in the press, and so the impression was conveyed that things on the anti-American student front were more tranquil than they actually were.

The fact is that there has always been a lot of anti-US feeling in South Korea, and it has been getting worse by leaps and bounds over the past several years. In 1998, for example, a poll of 220 university students in Seoul showed that 65 percent felt that the alliance was deteriorating, 70 percent felt that there should not be an American military presence in Korea after North-South unification, only 2 percent felt that the United States was favorable to Korea in economic terms, and less than 15 percent felt that the United States was being helpful to Korea in dealing with the so-called IMF crisis.

More recent reporting, by the Pew Global Attitudes Country Profile of South Korea (May 2003), produced some shocking statistics:

• Only 24 percent of those polled supported the US war on terrorism, and 58 percent said they were disappointed that Iraqi armed forces had not put up more of a fight against America and its coalition allies.
• 46 percent viewed America favorably, 50 percent viewed us unfavorably.
• Three in ten said they had considered boycotting US products to protest American foreign policy. (This was by far the largest figure on this issue found in the non-Arab world.)

At a Georgetown University conference on anti-Americanism in Korea held earlier in 2003, a strong consensus emerged among the participants that official attitudes on the part of both governments mask deep fissures in the relationship that need to be directly addressed. Koreans spoke of the current relationship as being more a façade than a pillar, and stressed that the façade hides a variety of tensions, antagonisms, and emotions.

An opinion leaders seminar on US-Korea relations held last summer by the Korea Economic Institute found that trust between the two countries had never been lower. The view was strongly expressed by distinguished Korean participants that "9/11 has changed everything in the US," and that this has badly damaged Seoul's relations with Washington. By this the Koreans meant that Americans seemed to be obsessed by the war on terrorism, and that we were mistakenly looking at the situation on the Korean peninsula through that prism.

Five factors have made major contributions to the deterioration in the alliance.

First has been South Korea's radically changing view of North Korea. This was largely triggered by the North-South summit meeting of June 2000. Since then, North Korea has metamorphosed in South Korea's perspective from an implacable enemy to something like a long-lost brother, who has acquired some bad habits and is in need of help and rehabilitation, not punishment. This major shift in the Korean view places US Forces in Korea (USFK) in an awkward position. Our force's long-range utility to Korea is now doubted by many

Koreans, particularly those under forty, and toleration of accidents involving USFK personnel has been reduced to almost the zero level.

The second factor is the Bush administration itself, particularly the way it is playing its role as the only global superpower. The Clinton administration had had some very difficult days in dealing with Seoul, around the time of the major nuclear crisis of 1994. Toward the end of his term, however, Clinton had appointed a distinguished former secretary of defense, William Perry, to assess our relations with North Korea. Perry did his work so well that by the fall of 2000 a declaration ending hostile relations between North Korea and the United States had been signed in Washington, and President Clinton came very close to making a visit to North Korea in the last weeks of his presidency.

It was expected in both Seoul and Pyongyang that the Bush administration would take up where Clinton left off (Secretary of State Powell said as much) but such was not the case. Bush entered office with contempt for anything that President Clinton had achieved, and a seething, ad hominem hostility to Kim Jong-il that he did nothing to hide. The Sunshine policy of Kim Dae-jung went into eclipse and a bristling new phase of US–North Korean relations opened up.

The third factor is the political maelstrom in South Korea. President Roh Moo-hyun is threatening to hold referenda that have had no previous place in Korean politics, and openly questions America's hard-line policy toward North Korea. With a National Assembly election looming in April 2004, South Korea seems headed for a period of intensive, inward-looking political infighting, with President Roh's future effectiveness as a national leader very much at stake.

At a conference on Cheju Island, held on 31 October 2003, President Roh showed just how strongly he feels on the North-South issue. In a small Q-and-A session former defense secretary William Perry asked what could be done to stop the slide in trust and understanding between the United States and South Korea, which had taken relations to the lowest point Perry had ever seen.

President Roh replied without hesitation that North Korea is the only issue on which Washington and Seoul disagree, but that in regard to that issue a wide perception gap exists. Roh stated that half a century ago, Korea had endured a horrible fratricidal war in which millions had died. He said that any repeat of that tragic experience must be avoided at all cost. Roh added that most South Koreans believe that Pyongyang will renounce and abandon its nuclear weapons programs once its security has been guaranteed. He urged both the United States and Japan, which were represented at the Cheju conference, to engage North Korea directly in substantive dialogue. Roh ended his response to Perry by asking, "Why does the US insist on such a hard-line policy, when it puts at risk so many lives?" Roh then asserted flatly that it is the US policy toward North Korea that causes the current high level of anti-American feelings in his country.

The fourth factor is Secretary of Defense Rumsfeld's decision to reposition the 2nd Infantry Division (2ID) from its position close to the DMZ to a more southerly location. This decision is part of the defense secretary's global program to make US forces more mobile, harder hitting, and highly technically competent. Rumsfeld believes that repositioning the 2ID will give it a more flexible role in defending South Korea against a North Korean attack, and would make our forces more easily adapted to a regional defense role. To South Korea's citizens, already deeply concerned about what an American attack on North Korea might mean for them, the shift of the 2ID away from the DMZ is seen as putting the main bulk of US forces out of range of North Korea's missiles and artillery so that we would be less constrained in launching a pre-emptive strike against North Korea's nuclear weapons facilities.

The fifth factor is that South Korea is rapidly integrating into the larger Asian economy and is seeking to capitalize on that integration by becoming a business hub for Northeast Asia. Although this process began when South Korea normalized relations with Japan in 1965, complete integration was only possible after relations were normalized with China in 1992. China has rapidly become the largest customer for South Korean exports and will soon displace the United States as South Korea's major trading partner. Moreover, South Korea was the third largest investor in China during 2003, ranking behind only Hong Kong and Japan. Indeed, the growth in trade with China has played a substantial role in South Korea's recovery from the 1997 economic crisis. A major disruption in this new relationship—such as might be caused by a conflict with North Korea or even growing instability in the North brought about by sanctions—would have serious negative economic and political ramifications for South Korea. Any US policy that is even perceived as increasing tensions with North Korea is therefore subject to criticism in South Korea as being inimical to important South Korean economic interests.

Given its new but substantial economic interests in China, South Korea's moves to reinforce stability on the peninsula by strengthening its commercial ties with North Korea and encouraging North Korea to modernize its economy are interlocked with South Korea's efforts to integrate into the larger Asian economy.

The *New York Times* on December 17, 2003 quoted the then South Korean foreign minister Yoon Young Kwan as follows: "The key of our North Korean policy is helping North Korea adopt market mechanisms. That will help them rebuild their own economy, which will in turn bring about some positive domestic impact and some positive impact in terms of North Korea's international behavior."

Asked by the *Times* whether he thought DPRK chairman Kim Jong-il could play the reformer's role in North Korea that Deng Xiaoping had played in China, Minister Yoon replied without hesitation, "I think so."

The same *Times* article quoted Deputy Unification Minister Park Chan Bong on parallels between Kim Jong-il and Deng. Mr. Park said, "In the case of China, reforms were made possible because Deng maintained strong leadership and political stability. In the case of North Korea Kim is in full control of North Korea. If he decides to reform, then I think he can do it."

With South Korea's economic presence and influence burgeoning in North Korea, and with roads and railroads being reconnected, any US consideration of coercive options against the North becomes more problematical. The spectrum of realistic American options vis-à-vis North Korea has narrowed to the point where any sort of pre-emptive military action seems completely out of the question. South Korean president Roh put this very bluntly on 18 December when he spoke to a group of foreign reporters. Roh said that his country "…would not remain idle if the United States tries to resolve the DPRK nuclear crisis with fists."

Contrast these Korean views with some thoughts of Deputy Secretary of Defense Paul Wolfowitz, cited in the *Washington Post* of December 23. Wolfowitz, in many ways the intellectual godfather of the Iraq war, was commenting on the removal of Saddam Hussein. He placed Saddam in the same league as Hitler, Stalin, and Kim Jong-il. Wolfowitz opined that men of that deeply evil character were never content to inflict their horrors on their own people alone. Sooner or later their evil work spills out over their borders, making them international security threats that must be dealt with.

President Bush has distanced himself from rhetoric of this sort, and now speaks of diplomacy as being the preferred option in dealing with North Korea. This presidential preference has not yet, however, been clearly translated into a viable policy toward North Korea. The administration, or at least part of it, remains fixated on "not rewarding bad behavior on the part of North Korea," and "not submitting to North Korean blackmail."

I personally had the opportunity to see how these rigid policy tenets played out at a "track two" six-party meeting held in Qingdao, China, in early September. The meeting had been arranged by Susan Shirk of the University of California as one of a long series of unofficial multiparty meetings designed to shed additional light on knotty policy issues affecting Northeast Asia. China was the host of the meeting, and it was led by Ambassador Fu Ying. Some of the Russian and Japanese attendees had been at the official six-party talks held a few days previously in Beijing. The same issues were discussed at Qingdao as had been discussed in Beijing.

Fu Ying, one of China's leading female diplomats, summed up the situation succinctly, based on her participation in the Beijing talks. She said that all six of the countries represented, including North Korea, wanted a nuclear-free Korean peninsula to emerge from the six-party talks. All six countries also agreed that the final result of the talks should be a verifiably nuclear-free Korean peninsula, with issues arising from North Korea's legitimate security and economic concerns having been dealt with adequately. The problem, Ambassador Fu Ying asserted, was that no one had any idea how to get from the starting position to the end objective. Who was to make the first move? Could moves be made simultaneously? Should a sequenced series of moves be worked out in advance? She made it clear that US insistence that it "would not reward bad behavior or submit to North Korean blackmail" made it very difficult to get any negotiating process started. The best that the US representative could say in reply was, "Well, North Korea does not have to do everything before we do anything."

The core group at the Qingdao meeting comprised China, South Korea, and Russia, who seemed to be in agreement on all major issues. Three countries were isolated to one degree or another: North Korea because of its WMD programs; Japan because of nagging historic issues, such as the comfort women and other World War II atrocities; and the United States because no one could ascertain what our specific policy toward North Korea was—except that it was hostile.

Negotiations are now under way designed to produce a more positive agenda for the next six-party meeting. That meeting, originally scheduled for late fall 2003, has been put off indefinitely. On 28 December, however, the North Koreans signaled that they were ready to attend another six-party session to be held early in 2004.

The difficult position in which we find ourselves has been evolving for years. In 1994, having seized control of both houses of Congress in the off-year elections, the Republicans, under Speaker Newt Gingrich's strident leadership, refused to fulfill several obligations the United States had entered into less than two months earlier as part of the Agreed Framework with North Korea. Diplomatic relations with North Korea were not entered into, North Korea was not removed from the US list of terrorist nations, and we did not start to develop economic relations with North Korea.

In 1998, after North Korea surprised us by firing a multistage rocket, a report by Donald Rumsfeld on missile threats to the United States made North Korea the poster child for national missile defense. A foundation of hostility between the Republican Party and North Korea had been laid.

Then came the Pyongyang summit of June 2000 between Kim Dae-jung of the South and Kim Jong-il of the North. In July of that year, I was asked by a Korean-language paper in Seoul to assess the summit meeting from an American perspective.

In my article, which appeared in Korean on 1 August 2000, I cited the Pyongyang summit and the French defeat at Dien Bien Phu in 1954 as two events that had ushered in new eras by creating paradigm shifts that required the United States to reevaluate its role in the regions concerned. As I put it in the article, "The relevant question is whether the US will do better in dealing with the changed situation in Northeast Asia that the Pyongyang summit is producing than it did in reacting to developments in Southeast Asia in the wake of France's defeat and withdrawal from Vietnam."

In mid-2000 warning signs were already quite clear that we were heading for new tensions in the US–South Korean alliance. As I put it: "Initial public Korean reactions to the Pyongyang summit have in some cases included open opposition to a continuing US military presence in the country and anti-American demonstrations have once again erupted. The initial American reaction to the summit was seen by some Koreans as being too negative and skeptical. This had suggested to them that our main concern about the Pyongyang summit was that it might weaken the rationale for a continuing military presence in the region, and the deployment of a national missile defense system."

My article ended with these words: "In President Kim Dae-jung we have a staunch friend and ally whose creative diplomacy with Korea's neighbors and with North Korea has released new forces in the region. The next American president, whoever he is, can use President Kim's final two years in office as a time to create a new posture for the United States in Northeast Asia. How well he does this will largely determine the future pattern of America's relations with Korea and its neighbors in the era that is now beginning."

What has eventuated in the three and one-half years since those words were written has been far more negative than positive in terms of US-Korean relations.

• President Kim's first meeting with President Bush, held in March 2001, did not go at all well. President Bush made it clear that he did not trust Kim Jong-il, and that an American policy review had to take place before any endorsement of President Kim's Sunshine policy could be made.

• The US policy review was completed in late spring 2001, endorsing a continuation of engagement with North Korea. The review stipulated, however, that some of the most difficult policy issues, such as North Korean troop deployments along the DMZ, had to be dealt with early in any resumption of engagement. This was a marked change from what had been worked out by President Kim with the Clinton administration. This change in priorities did not go over well in either North or South Korea.

• The terrorist attacks on the United States of September 11, 2001, came before any contacts between the United States and North Korea had taken place. The United States became preoccupied with the war on terror.

• In his State of the Union speech in January 2002, President Bush placed North Korea in an "axis of evil," along with Iran and Iraq. This infuriated the North Koreans, and shocked the South Koreans.

• In June 2002, during the height of the World Cup tournament, one of South Korea's most triumphant moments was marred by the accidental death of two young girls, killed by a US armored vehicle as they walked along a narrow country road on their way to a birthday party. As far as South Korea's younger generation is concerned, the US government has never properly addressed this tragedy.

• In October 2002, the Bush administration held its first meeting in Pyongyang with North Korean government officials. The sole purpose of the meeting was to inform North Korea that through intelligence sources, the United States had come to believe that North Korea, with the aid of equipment acquired from Pakistan, was developing a highly enriched uranium program in direct violation of the 1994 Agreed Framework.

• Over the next several months, in a series of retaliatory moves, the United States and North Korea moved to a posture of confrontation. The United States cut off oil shipments to North Korea required by the Agreed Framework. North Korea evicted IAEA inspectors, withdrew from the NPT, and began reprocessing plutonium fuel rods.

• North Korea asked for a nonaggression pact with the United States. The United States refused to talk directly to North Korea on this or any other issue, as that would have been "rewarding bad behavior" on their part.

• Taking advantage of its improved relations with China, the United States has asked Beijing to convene and manage a series of six-party talks, designed to solve the North Korean nuclear question. The world now awaits the scheduling of the next session in Beijing.

Where does that leave the Korean-American alliance, and US relations with other Northeast Asian countries?

The South Korean government is clearly interested in maintaining the alliance with the United States. The latest evidence of this is Seoul's decision to send troops to Iraq. This was not an easy decision to make, and is an admirable extension of support to an ally (the United States) dealing with a difficult political/military situation. The United States for its part also wants to continue the alliance, although with a different deployment pattern for USFK. These hopes are held hostage by the widely diverging views of North Korea held by the Roh and Bush administrations. Only a cooperative and ultimately successful joint approach to Pyongyang by Seoul and Washington will allow the alliance to continue in anything like its current form.

Seoul will never acquiesce to the preemptive use of force by the United States against North Korea. The United States, so far at least, refuses to enter into direct negotiations with North Korea. North Korea for its part feels fundamentally under threat from the United States, and will not dismantle its WMD programs in advance of a US security guarantee and extension of economic assistance. With the passage of time, North Korea moves closer and closer to becoming a full-blown nuclear power. This pattern of events brings into clear focus a time when the Bush administration may feel vulnerable to the politically devastating charge that it sat idly by while North Korea joined the "nuclear club." What, if anything, the Bush administration intends to do to avoid such a charge is not at all clear. Sanctions associated with the so-called proliferation security initiative will not come close to solving this dilemma for Washington, despite enthusiastic vocal support from neoconservatives in the Bush administration.

The Bush administration scored a significant success in its efforts to convene the six-party talk process. These talks take advantage of the historic fact that for the first time ever, China, Russia, Japan, and South Korea are at peace with each other. Intraregional trade is flourishing, and there will never be a better time to draw North Korea out of its isolation and make it part of an economic boom in Northeast Asia. The fundamental problem is that Washington sees North Korea essentially as a proliferation threat that must be disarmed, while China, Russia, and South Korea see the North as a neighbor and potential economic partner in regional development.

None of North Korea's neighbors want it to become a nuclear power. They all believe that direct negotiations involving Pyongyang and Washington can solve the current impasse. If the Bush administration continues its refusal to negotiate, and North Korea declares itself a nuclear power, its neighbors, with the possible exception of Japan, will adjust to that reality through accommodations. The US position in South Korea will be drastically undercut, and the alliance will almost certainly cease to function in any significant way. Beijing and Seoul will move closer in terms of trade and policy coordination.

American influence on the mainland of Asia will be markedly diminished, and we will be forced to place greater reliance on our bases in Japan in order to maintain a significant military presence in the region.

The long-range costs of not talking directly to North Korea now would appear to be so high and so evident as to force Washington to rethink its moralistic policy of stiffing Pyongyang. But as we proved in our catastrophic misreading of the new situation in Southeast Asia that began at Dien Bien Phu in 1954, we are capable of strategic miscalculations of enormous consequence. Will this same pattern repeat itself in Northeast Asia, exactly fifty years later? The answer to that question is now being shaped by debates and discussions within the Bush administration.

CHALLENGES FOR THE ROK-US ALLIANCE IN THE TWENTY-FIRST CENTURY

Won-soo Kim

The alliance between the Republic of Korea (South Korea) and the United States has endured, with impressive achievements and through resilient adjustments, for the last fifty years. The deterrence provided by the alliance enables South Korea to accelerate its economic development and political maturity. The alliance has been clearly a cost-efficient mechanism contributing to peace and prosperity for South Korea and the Northeast Asian region. It has also managed to make occasional adaptations, geared to the changing environment at global, regional, and peninsular levels, and has taken into account the changing dynamics within the alliance, most notably the growth of South Korea.

In 2003, however, the alliance encountered an unexpected turn of events, even as it celebrated its fiftieth anniversary. The tragic death of two young schoolgirls in June[1] sparked a nationwide anti-American protest, leading to a series of massive candlelight vigils on the streets in the run-up to the presidential elections in December. The protest was generally assessed as the highest both in the number of protesters and the sustained intensity of demonstrations during the fifty years history of the alliance.

The protest sparked heated debates, both in South Korea and the United States, on a number of issues, ranging from the sources of such a surprising outburst of anti-American emotions, to the factors that sustained it for so long, and the possible cures. These debates were also entangled with the nuclear drama that unfolded in October, as North Korea disclosed its secretive uranium enrichment program for nuclear weapons. The alliance governments have been careful in handling this problem so that it will not develop into a full-fledged crisis with damaging spillovers into other areas.

Despite the damage-control efforts, the North Korean nuclear problem escalated in November, when North Korea announced its intention to restart the nuclear facilities in Yongbyon. Soon afterward, both issues—anti-American sentiments and the North Korean nuclear problem—seriously affected the political campaign for South Korea's presidential elections. Surprisingly, the election result indicated that the problems in the alliance relationship played a more significant role than did North Korea, a threat common to both South Korea and the United States.

This finding defies conventional wisdom on two counts. First, prior to the 2003 election, it was believed that an event or crisis highlighting the North Korean security threat boosted the standing of candidates with conservative credentials. The most cited example of this phenomenon was the bombing of a Korean Airlines plane by North Korean agents, on the eve of the 1987 election,[2] which was deemed to favor the former president Roh Tae-woo, a retired general and the then-presidential candidate. Second, the security threat from North Korea has the effect of cooling down political differences between South Korea and the United States. The South Korea–US alliance has never been free from political differences. Among the three pillars of bilateral relations, politics, security, and economics, domestic political issues dominated until the late 1980s, when South Korea began to move toward genuine democratization. All of these issues relate to irregularities with power transition, the unpredictability of democratization programs, various political scandals such as Korea-gate, or alleged human rights violations (including the treatment of dissidents in South Korea). The North Korean threat, as perceived by the alliance, had actually kept many of these political differences from surfacing to the public and facilitated the management of those differences through a quiet and mutually acceptable diplomacy.

The events of 2003 called into question the viability of the South Korea–US alliance. Many opinions and policy recommendations have been offered about the alliance's future, but even these postmortem analyses expose a wide divergence of views not only in South Korea but also across the Pacific.

Notwithstanding this divergence, it is not contested that the alliance is now in serious distress. None of the challenges looks easy to tackle. In South Korea, anti-American sentiment has been expressed in three different forms, ideological, policy-oriented, and emotional. But these are the symptoms, not the causes. The candlelight vigils in 2002 were a unique hybrid case in which all three types of anti-American sentiment combined in reaction to a single incident.

As to what lies behind these symptoms, a number of populist myths have been floated. A closer look at these myths reveals that they do not offer explanations for the real causes, but merely oversimplified pictures with ill-based prescriptions. This paper examines the four myths about problems with North Korean policy: two that blame the South Korean and US governments; one that blames the generational change in South Korea; and one that blames the basic difficulty of the North Korean nuclear problem. This paper shows that these myths are not only inaccurate, but also counterproductive. Blaming their own policy is the last thing the allies should do, and blaming generational change or the nuclear problem is putting the cart before the horse. If the allies cannot handle common challenges, whether internal (generational change) or external (the nuclear problem), something deeper must amiss in the relationship. The challenges themselves are not the issue.

This paper identifies four structural factors which have been simmering for some time to cause the recent rise of anti-American sentiment in Korean society. These are:

1) diverging security perceptions;
2) discord in the alliance rationale;
3) presence fatigue; and
4) inadequate cultural awareness.

None of these factors is easy to overcome. What makes their handling more difficult is their dual interface with the domestic political developments in South Korea and the United States and the dynamics of the North Korean nuclear problem. Still, the fundamental interests of both countries point to the need for strengthening the alliance. Whether this need will be translated into reality depends on how effectively the two governments tackle the challenges together. This paper concludes with a detailed suggestion of what should be done toward this end.

I. Three Types of Anti-American Sentiment

1. Ideological Anti-Americanism

Ideological anti-Americanism has the strongest roots among student and left-wing activists in South Korea, who have viewed the United States as the main obstacle to realizing their ideologically driven socialist vision of one Korea. These groups remain relatively small in number, but tend to be the most active and often violent. Their involvement in anti-American demonstrations dates back to the 1980s, the most shocking of which was a burning incident at an American cultural center. This type of anti-Americanism garnered little popular support, and waned as the Cold War ended in the early 1990s, along with the consequent retreat of socialist ideologies. Even so, these groups have adapted and survived, continuing to produce left-wing slogans and anti-American propaganda.

2. Policy-Oriented Anti-American Sentiment

Policy-oriented anti-American sentiments are a relatively recent phenomenon. They became evident among liberal intellectual and civil society groups in South Korea after the Bush administration took office in 2000.

Such policy-oriented groups are not anti-American per se; they might be more accurately labeled anti-Bush policy.[3] Comprising a variety of diverse nongovernmental organizations (e.g., human rights advocacy, environmental protection, economic transparency, and greater political participation), these groups are generally regarded as more moderate in their views and more centrist than the ideologically driven group described above. Accordingly, their socio-political campaigns garnered relatively larger popular support from the South Korean people. One example was the successful campaign by a civil rights group, the Participatory Coalition, in the 2000 parliamentary elections.[4]

Policy-oriented groups object to the Bush administration's policies toward North Korea, as well as stances on other foreign policy issues that they perceive as too unilateral and hawkish to justify the world's sole superpower's moral leadership. These groups come mostly from the South Korean civil society, who strongly supported the political and social agenda of former president Kim Dae-jung, and particularly his Sunshine policy toward North Korea. Many in these groups were angered by the way they perceived the Bush administration to have treated, or mistreated, then-president Kim on his visit to Washington in March 2001. In their view, the US relations with North Korea began to deteriorate soon after, and the South–North Korea relationship also got into trouble. These groups tend to blame this worsening situation on the Bush administration, and further argue that once the United States changes its North Korea policy, anti-Americanism will dissipate in South Korea.

3. Emotional Anti-American Sentiment

Emotional anti-American sentiment does not usually materialize unless other factors come into play to mobilize it. The death of the two schoolgirls was a good example of an unexpected incident unleashing public anger and anti-American energy.

Emotional anti-American sentiments are more dangerous than their ideological and policy-oriented counterparts for two reasons. First, they may be easily manipulated by opportunistic leaders or groups with hidden political agendas. Second, they are the most powerful, and can be massive in their expression, when mobilized. In short, those engaged in this type of anti-Americanism are the swing bloc. Without a catalyst, they remain silent with relatively neutral views. When an issue arises, their reaction largely depends on how they perceive the issue's merits. The need for the government, political and social leaders, and the media therefore to provide an objective picture of the alliance—and an educated assessment of what should be done in the best interests of the South Korean people and state—cannot be stressed enough.

In 2002, we witnessed an exceptional hybrid case, in which all three types of anti-American sentiment combined to explode over a single incident, that of the death of the two schoolgirls. In one (marginal) quarter, student activist groups raised radical anti-American slogans. In another, ordinary citizens—middle-aged parents together with their young children—mourned the deaths with candles in their hands. Both conspicuous and problematic was the fact that the supposedly small group of ideologically oriented activists appeared to take control of events, even though the majority of protesters did not share their same anti-American fervor. In fact, many joined the demonstrations out of a mixture of sympathy for the deceased girls and anger over the perceived injustice of releasing the American soldiers involved in the incident. This public anger mostly arose (and was often misconceived) from a lack of understanding about differences in the American and South Korean legal systems. Nevertheless, it was embraced not only as a miscarriage of justice, but also as evidence of the unequal South Korea–US relationship, in which South Koreans were treated as junior partners.

It is not clear what these emotional participants wanted to do about the alliance. Later polls showed that the majority of South Korean people still supported the continued presence of US troops on Korean soil.[5]

Over fifty years, a variety of grievances and perceived inequalities in the alliance relationship had accumulated in the minds of South Koreans; the schoolgirl incident merely sparked the fire. It is noteworthy that one mishandled incident could mobilize so many people under one banner. From a policy perspective, this has two implications. First, among the South Korean people, the level of latent emotions critical of, or at least not favorable to, the United States could be higher than conventional wisdom previously expected. Second, if a similar incident happens again, much more serious collateral damage could be done to the alliance.

II. Four Myths

In South Korea, foreign policy discussions tend to juxtapose the alliance relationship with the North Korean problem, along dichotomous lines—pro-alliance or pro-nation; pro-war or pro-peace; or pro-denuclearization or pro-stability. This polarizing tendency of foreign policy debates makes it more difficult to handle anti-American sentiment in South Korea.

These either-or debates usually offer overly simplistic explanations, which do not fit with real-world situations in which many gray area options exist between two extremes. A pro-alliance or pro-nation dichotomy pits South Korea–US relations against the South–North Korea relations. But in the real world, these two issues might well be worked out together and simultaneously. For instance, measures generally perceived to increase the likelihood of war could also end up compelling the other side to behave, thereby promoting peace. Measures for denuclearization are also likely to avoid a nuclear arms race, thereby contributing to the maintenance of strategic stability.

A by-product of such polarizing debate is a variety of populist myths that are intended, in a simplistic way, to explain what lies behind the emerging distress in the ROK-US alliance. The four myths are examined below.

1. The current trouble was caused by the Sunshine policy of former South Korean president Kim Dae-jung.[6]
Argued by conservatives in Seoul and echoed by neo-conservatives in Washington, this view argues that the Sunshine policy is based on an incorrect premise—that North Korea will change and should be encouraged to do so through more outside help. It further argues that the Sunshine policy does not produce the result it intends, but rather brings trouble to the alliance by weakening the South Korean perception of the North Korean threat.

This view goes to the heart of the South Korean people's changing perception of North Korea, as a complex mixture of an enemy and a brother. This mix may change over time and over generations. Currently, however, North Korea is perceived as a country whose economy has been declining for more than a decade, with serious shortages in food, energy, and hard currency. While it is true that Kim Dae-jung took bold steps to initiate inter-Korean reconciliation, his critics unwittingly give his policies too much credit, claiming that they had brought about a sea change in the minds of the South Korean people. A policy cannot have such an impact unless it reflects the prevailing views of its adherents.

A more accurate assessment might be that the Sunshine policy reflected a fundamental and preexisting change in South Korean perceptions of North Korea. This change could have resulted from media imagery that depicted an increasingly vulnerable North that badly needed South Korean help. Containment appeared to be an undesirable approach, given that it might have backed North Korea into a corner from which it could have lashed out in desperation.[7]

2. The current trouble is a result of the Bush administration's hawkish policy toward North Korea.[8]

The converse of blaming the Sunshine policy is the argument that blames the Bush administration's policy. Liberal intellectuals in South Korea, who tend to express policy-oriented anti-American sentiment, have held this view, echoed by the Democrats in Washington who were involved in Korean affairs during the Clinton administration. This view looks right in pointing to the allergic reaction that conservative Republicans have long shown for the Geneva Agreed Framework (AF) since its conclusion, and in the Bush administration's strong distaste for some Clinton policies, popularly known as "ABC: Anything But Clinton." But this view also runs the risk of oversimplification. Nobody knows for sure how a Democratic administration would have reacted to the 9/11 terrorist attacks, nor how it would have treated the North Korean violation of the AF with its secretive pursuit of a uranium enrichment program.

One cannot rule out the possibility that a Democratic administration would have reacted more strongly to North Korea's cheating, in order to co-opt Republican criticism against the AF. It is also likely that security imperatives following 9/11 would have forced a Democratic administration to take tough stances against North Korea, in order to prevent nuclear weapons material landing in terrorists' hands. The US concern about nuclear weapons and other weapons of mass destruction (WMD) has certainly increased after 9/11. In this respect, North Korea is clearly the *worst* case, since it is the most advanced among a group of countries of concern, in nuclear weapons, other WMD capability, and in missile technology for WMD delivery.

In fact, those involved in handling North Korean affairs during the Clinton administration now tend to argue for a not-so-soft approach that will leave all options open, including a military solution, while pursuing a negotiated settlement.[9] In case the latter fails, they further argue, all options should be employed to deal with the North Korean nuclear problem.

Republicans and Democrats seem to share the same strategic objective for denuclearization of the Korean peninsula, although they may differ over a detailed methodology to achieve it. One such difference supposedly lies in the conditions for a negotiation to take place. The Bush administration clearly abhors the idea of providing North Korea with any carrots to get them to the negotiating table. They see the negotiation itself as a reward to the outlawed North Korean regime, and do not want to entertain any impression of giving in to North Korean blackmail by offering pre-negotiation incentives. On the other hand, Democrats and a number of Korean experts do not subscribe to this view. They instead argue for the need to increase dialogue with the North Korean regime, at least as a way to test North Korea's real intentions and move toward the next step.[10]

3. The strain in the alliance was caused by generational change going on in South Korean society—the emergence of a younger generation which did not experience the Korean War in the early 1950s.
According to one survey, those under the age of twenty-nine constitute around 46 percent of Korean society, and this group shows the highest rate of dislike of the United States.[11] This finding offers a confusing and troublesome scenario for two reasons. First, this age group grew up in the most affluent environment and under the heaviest influence of American pop culture, as represented by Hollywood movies, video games, hamburgers, Coca-Cola, and the like. This leads one to wonder where the popular dislike of the United States among this age group comes from. It is not easy to digest this seemingly contradictory cultural orientation: on the one hand, they enjoy American culture, while on the other, they do not like *American-ness*. Second, if the anti-American trend of this generation is not reversed, emotional anti-American sentiment will continue to rise and to dominate South Korean society for many years to come, as this group gets older.

Presidential elections in 2002 also highlighted generational politics in South Korea. A clear generational cleavage manifested itself in preferences for candidates with liberal or conservative credentials. With those in their mid-forties as a dividing line, those under that age preferred a liberal candidate, while those above it leaned toward a conservative one. One simplistic argument ascribes this ideologically driven generational cleavage to the fact that the younger generation did not experience the Korean War. It goes on to argue, therefore, that this cleavage will persist for the next several decades. Another equally simplistic argument is that younger voters supported the liberal candidate, because, as a younger politician from a political minority group, he is more likely to bring about change. The fact is that the motivation for the younger generation's electoral behavior in 2002 is hard to decipher. It remains to be seen whether the voting tendency along age lines will be sustained and whether this group's political orientation will hold over time.

Without empirical data, the answer to these question remains elusive, and only a wait-and-see approach for the next several elections will yield more insight. As often happens, the political orientation of the young generation may evolve and change as they age and mature. In the future, the younger generation might even split the vote if they must choose between candidates of the same age, but with liberal and conservative orientations, respectively.

4. The North Korean nuclear problem made coordination of policies difficult for the alliance. The North Korean nuclear problem should therefore be blamed for stress in the alliance; its resolution will ease the stress.

The North Korean nuclear problem resurfaced at a time when difficulties in the South Korea–US alliance were also on the rise. This coincidence, combined with the complexity of the nuclear problem, led to a popular belief that the nuclear problem was the main culprit for stress in the alliance.

If the alliance is unable to deal with something it is intended to handle, the viability of the alliance itself is called into question. If this is so, then something serious must *already* have damaged the alliance, before the external challenges, such as the nuclear problem, came to the fore. In this case, a more plausible explanation would be that, after the nuclear problem resurfaced, its complexity highlighted *existing* distress in the alliance by further complicating the already strained policy coordination. It also follows that, unless the real sources of the existing strain are tackled, alliance coordination will remain difficult, both on more mundane security and foreign policies and on particular policy related to the North Korean nuclear problem.

III. Four Sources of Distress

The above examination of the four myths indicates that factors such as policy differences, generational change, or an exogenous variable such as the North Korean nuclear problem do not explain the whole story. Closer scrutiny is required to identify deep-seated structural causes at both the domestic and the alliance level.

1. Diverging Threat Perception

During the Cold War, Seoul and Washington's threat perceptions were identical, since it was in the alliance's interest to deter the threats represented by the former Soviet Union and North Korea. With the end of the Cold War, this picture began to change. The end of the Cold War expedited South Korea's pursuit of the Northern Policy, which resulted in normalization of relations with both the former Soviet Union (1991) and China (1993), two erstwhile North Korean allies. It also conicided with the simultaneous entry of both South and North

Korea into the United Nations (1991) and the conclusion of the inter-Korean agreements on basic relations and nonaggression (1992).[12]

The inter-Korean detente reached a stalemate in early 1993, when the North Korean nuclear crisis intensified. In contrast, South Korea's relations with Russia and China continue to develop both in quantity and quality. North Korea's relations with the United States and Japan have yet to normalize, and those with Russia and China lag far behind where they were in the Cold War era. These developments, together with South Korea's continuous economic growth and the continuous decline in North Korea's economy, helped to change the South Korean people's threat perception of North Korea. Now, the majority of the South Korean people see an increasingly weak and vulnerable North Korea as an entity to be engaged rather than contained.

On the other hand, Washington's perception of the North Korean threat has not changed much since the Cold War, mainly due to North Korea's continuous pursuit of WMD, including nuclear weapons. As noted earlier, US concern about North Korea's WMD capability may even have increased following 9/11, given the possible nightmare scenario of WMD falling into terrorists' hands.

These divergent perspectives opened a gulf, or more accurately, signaled a change in priorities between South Korea and the United States in their threat perceptions of North Korea. Seoul was more concerned with the conventional threat posed by North Korea, while Washington focused on the North Korean WMD threat. This gulf was tacitly reflected in the agenda-setting of US–North Korean relations that forced Seoul to accept, reluctantly at first, direct negotiation between Pyongyang and Washington on the nuclear problem in 1993–94, the Kumchangri (suspected nuclear site) problem in 1999, and missile issues in 1999 and 2000.[13]

The South Korean people tend to perceive the threat posed by North Korea in conventional military terms. Their biggest fear has been the military scenario of North Korea's raining artillery shells onto Seoul, a "sea of fire" image. Seoul took seriously the first nuclear crisis in 1993, as well as North Korea's testing of the Taepodong missile in 1998. Seoul's sense of seriousness, however, did not match the degree of shock that Japan and the United States felt over North Korea's display of its ability to wreak havoc on them. Put another way, Seoul's perception of the seriousness of the WMD threat may be relatively less in qualitative terms, since it has long been exposed to the artillery threat, which it views as the greatest cause for concern. Washington and Tokyo's level of apprehension is likely much higher, since they are exposed to North Korea's long range and direct threats for the first time.

As described above, the security perception of the South Korean people is complex and evolving. This is mainly due to a dynamic interplay of triple fears: (1) abandonment; (2) the security dilemma; and (3) exclusion. Ever since the Korean War erupted in 1950,[14] the fear of being abandoned by the United States has remained alive in the minds of many South Koreans. A recent example is the public reaction to the reported redeployment of US forces in

Korea (USFK) south of Seoul, which has been interpreted as weakening the USFK's "tripwire"[15] role.

The sticking point in the alliance's dealings with the 1993 nuclear crisis was South Korea's exclusion from the negotiation process with North Korea over important issues affecting peace and stability on the Korean peninsula. This time, the South Korean people's biggest worry seems to stem from the security dilemma the nuclear problem poses. Measures intended to enhance security (for nonproliferation) may inadvertently increase the likelihood of a conflict (a scenario they seek to avoid through the deterrence provided by the alliance), whether by miscalculation or misunderstanding of the other side's intention due to poor communication. South Korea would then once again be a battlefield in a conflict that would bring immediate devastation. Behind this concern there is the US's new security strategy,[16] which emphasizes the doctrine of preemption. The possibility of a unilateral preemptive strike by the United States against North Korea seems to loom larger in South Korean people's minds whenever tension rises, although in reality this scenario is unimaginable without South Korean consent.[17]

So, this time, unlike a decade ago, Seoul's sensitivity about the format of negotiation is secondary to its focus on the desirability of a negotiated settlement. In other words, South Korea's main concern lies in reducing the security dilemma by addressing the nuclear problem through peaceful means. All of this, in turn, runs counter to Washington's mood. US doubt about the negotiated settlement increases with the perceived failure of the AF, which reduces its eagerness for negotiation and raises its sensitivity about the format of negotiation.

2. Discord over the Alliance Rationale

The end of the Cold War and the demise of the overriding common threat blurred the rationale of the alliance relationship at the global level. As a result, almost all of the alliance systems underwent serious readjustments, many of which are still going on. The anti-terrorism campaign following 9/11 added a new trend: a coalition of the willing that depended on the context of situations requiring collective intervention. Today, it is fair to argue that the alliance relationship in general is in flux, and its ultimate form remains unclear.

In the meantime, coalition-building among the willing nations seems to be taking over the fixed alliance in handling international crises. Given the changing dynamics in modern warfare technology, context-specific coalition-building could be a more efficient and less costly method. The strategic importance of forward bases is changing as projection capabilities improve. Terrorism also makes the threat diversified and harder to deter, and requires a more agile and flexible response. This new requirement does not fit well with conventional conceptions of an alliance that is formed with a single focus to deter a predetermined threat in a specific theater.

The trends of peacekeeping, peacemaking, and peace-enforcing in the 1990s in general, and the anti-terrorism campaign that ensued after 9/11 in particular, show that the United States is increasingly depending on ad-hoc coalition-building, taking into account the geopolitical context of each military intervention and trying to solicit participation from its traditional allies whenever possible. The invitation is not limited to them, however, and the United States shows readiness to go without them when necessary. For the United States, the focus of the alliance is now more global, which also means that the US forces stationed in one theater under a specific alliance could be deployed in other areas should it become necessary.

The South Korean people, by contrast, tend to see the alliance through a more peninsular lens. Although South Korea's threat perception of North Korea is changing, that threat still dominates its strategic calculations. This apparent contradiction manifests itself in the South Korean people's mixed reaction to the possible relocation of the US forces to the south of Seoul.

While some in South Korea are arguing that South Korean forces should increase their role, and US forces decrease theirs, others strongly oppose any move in that direction. The majority of South Koreans support the continued US presence[18] and are uncomfortable with the idea of initiating a premature restructuring of the USFK at a time critical for peace and security on the peninsula.

The narrow geographical definition of the South Korea–US alliance treaty[19] also makes it harder to justify South Korea's participation in a US-led military campaign in a third area. For example, Australia invoked its alliance treaty in joining a campaign in Afghanistan, while South Korea acted in the "spirit" of the treaty, even though the action was largely endorsed at the UN. The recent controversy over South Korea's participation in the Iraqi campaign highlights the difficulty of justifying a campaign in another region to the domestic audience. This difficulty seems to arise most frequently when a campaign is launched without UN authorization.

3. Presence Fatigue

The USFK has been stationed on South Korean soil, in large numbers, for more than five decades. The length of its stay, combined with a focus on ground troops, has inevitably resulted in many incidents or accidents involving the US soldiers on the one hand and South Korean soldiers and civilians on the other. It has also given rise to a steady stream of complaints from local residents about traffic violations, environmental contamination, disturbances from military firing exercises, and so on.

The local South Korean community increasingly views the presence of the US bases as an obstacle to regional development. Many restrictions are placed on local residents, which they view as a burden—examples include the increasing direct costs of environmental cleaning and the opportunity costs of stagnant real estate. Now, it is incumbent on both governments to devise a joint scheme to alleviate the US presence fatigue, and to recast the USFK as a plus to local economies and environments. Both governments should also take joint measures to create the impression that the Status of Forces Agreement (SOFA) is dealing with complaints from local residents as expeditiously and equitably as possible.

4. Inadequate Reciprocal Awareness of Cultural Diversity

The protest following the schoolgirls' deaths in 2002 escalated out of proportion, in part due to mishandled public relations about the incident. Early mistakes in media and public relations were damaging, and the measures taken to allievate public fury tended to come late, weakening their impact. In large part, the public anger was fed by the perceived inequality in treating the victims and the accused soldiers. At bottom, the two militaries and governments misread or underestimated public emotions, and failed to lead them. The majority of South Koreans simply could not accept a verdict that acquitted the acccused, with no punishment, while the victims were dead. Many South Korean parents and students were overcome with sympathetic feeling for the victims and their families. This instant assimiliation of pain may well be unique to a country with one people and one culture.

Differences in the two countries' legal systems also contributed to the downward spiral. The criminal code of South Korea holds anyone involved in traffic accidents with a loss of a life criminally accountable with immediate detention. Under US law, traffic accidents are usually not subject to criminal charges unless backed by other criminal activities, such as reckless driving, speeding, or the use of drugs or alcohol. The jury system of the United States also contributed to public suspicion about the verdict's objectivity, because the jury was composed of fellow US soldiers.

Overall, for a host of reasons, the Korean public never developed an objective perspective on the situation. The fracas that followed clearly shows that poor reciprocal knowledge of an ally's culture can not only dent social relations between two countries, but also cause devastating damage to the crucial political relationships.

IV. Conclusion: Tasks Ahead

As discussed above, the sources of disagreement relate to almost all areas of bilateral relations—security, political, social, and cultural. Accordingly, an urgent, comprehensive plan for joint action must take shape. Stopgap measures will only aggravate the trouble. But addressing the key points of disagreement will be a tall order. The two governments should recommend a blueprint to address specific, long-term measures, ranging from security and political to social and cultural. This vision should extend even beyond the possible reunification of Korea.

Below is a list of principles and recommended measures that should be stressed in devising a master plan for revitalizing the South Korea–US alliance in the twenty-first century. The rule of thumb is to highlight strong points, while downplaying weak ones. Currently, the balance sheet of strong fundamentals to weak spots in the alliance is in the black. It is therefore incumbent upon policymakers and opinion leaders in both countries to provide the general public with a comprehensive, redefined rationale for a revitalized alliance, one that stresses partnership, peace, and prosperity, and that is easy for the public to understand.

1. Addressing the Sources of Distress

A. Bridge the gap in threat perception: Readjust priorities and realign perceptions

The two allies cannot have identical priorities in their respective threat perceptions nor in their strategies to deal with them. What really matters is whether they can devise a joint security strategy that accommodates both sides' concerns and interests in a mutually agreeable manner. Differing priorities in handling threat perceptions at the global, regional, and peninsular levels should be fully discussed and reflected in a joint strategy.

In devising a strategy to deal jointly with conventional and WMD threats from North Korea, special attention should be paid to the need to accommodate both sides' concerns equally. In other words, the South Korean fear of a conventional conflict breaking out on the peninsula, and the US fear of WMD proliferation in general as well as WMD transfer to terrorists in particular, should be treated with equal sensitivity.

Peace and nonproliferation should be the alliance's guiding pillars. It should be noted here that peace is not just a means to a higher objective, but an end in itself to the South Korean people. Accordingly, the allies should devise a strategy that will convince the South Korean people that, before taking any forcible measures (e.g., sanctions), all other avenues have been tried and exhausted to preserve peace. Likewise, greater sensitivity and understanding should be given to the US need to deal with the global terrorist threat.

In this regard, two points should be highlighted. First, any readjustment or restructuring of the USFK ought to be done in genuine consultation with the South Korean government, since it will have a major impact on the primary South Korean security concern, a conventional North Korean military threat. At this critical juncture, any US move that the South Korean people perceive to be unilateral will be damaging to the alliance. It would fuel South Korean grievances, working on the triple fears of the South Korean people. Some may interpret it as a sign of US abandonment. Others may interpret it as an indication of US unilateralism preparing for a preemptive attack—by moving the USFK out of harm's way—thereby substantiating the combined fears of security dilemma (by increasing the risk of a conflict) and exclusion (by not being fully consulted).

Second, the alliance may ultimately face the difficult question of whether to pursue denuclearization of the peninsula through regime change in North Korea, in the event that peaceful avenues do not lead North Korea to more compliant behavior. Given the North Korean regime's unique characteristics, seeking its change as a policy objective will not be feasible without risking a conflict. At least for now, South Korea, China, and Japan appear reluctant to entertain that risk, for fear of a conflict and its potential spillover effects in the region.

B. Redefine the alliance rationale: A comprehensive value-based partnership for the twenty-first century

In the post–Cold War world, a viable alliance must move toward a more comprehensive partnership with multiple focuses. Dealing with diverse threats requires broadening the alliance focus and redefining its rationale. But the real challenge is how to redefine the rationale in a manner that accommodates both partners' seemingly conflicting priorities, global and peninsular. The new rationale should specify joint goals for the alliance to achieve on the Korean peninsula, in the Northeast Asian region, and beyond, through jointly employed means.

Such redefinition can be done in a positive way, in order to achieve something, rather than in a negative manner, intended to work against or prevent something. It will be far more effective to base the redefinition of the alliance rationale on common values, and on securing broad support, not only from the peoples of both countries but also from the international community, including major powers in the region. The redefinition of the USFK's role will require careful consultation between the two governments. Whether the USFK assets will be allowed to be used in a theater beyond the peninsula will be a sensitive issue, and should be treated delicately.[20]

C. Reduce presence fatigue: Improve SOFA implementation and carefully reconfigure the force structure

Emotional anti-Americanism has deep roots in the US forces' extended presence in the region. Complaints from local residents are inevitable, as are grievances occurring over unexpected accidents or incidents involving US soldiers. What matters more, however, are the efforts to reduce the likelihood of such complaints, and to establish mechanisms to control damage as soon as it occurs. Overall, the current SOFA with South Korea, as revised in 2000, is no less equitable than the other SOFAs of the United States. If the current SOFA provisions are implemented as well as intended, then most public grievances will dissipate. It is particularly important to show to the Korean people that the SOFA's operation is being substantively improved, in order to dispel popular misconceptions that the terms of America's SOFA with South Korea include more concessions in criminal jurisdiction and other provisions than those with Japan or Germany.

A wide range of joint measures can be examined with respect to reducing presence fatigue. These include (1) rebasing in a less populated area; (2) improving the local environment for a smoother presence; (3) strengthening the soldiers' code of conduct; (4) improving the SOFA implementation, including a 24/7 emergency standby; (5) upgrading coordination for military exercises with the local authorities; and (6) devising a joint scheme for local employment. Through these efforts, the US presence could become a benefit to the local economy and environment, not a burden.

D. Improve mutual understanding through cultural awareness programs and targeted public diplomacy

A variety of programs should be institutionalized to address this persistent and sometimes explosive problem. These include (1) increasing the cultural awareness of US citizens and soldiers before and after their arrival in South Korea; (2) expanding interactive community relations of the US military with the local community; (3) strengthening public diplomacy toward weak spots such as local media, students, and labor activists; and (4) launching a specially timed, nationwide campaign about better understanding each other's culture and social systems. This campaign could productively be timed to coincide with the anniversary of the two countries' diplomatic relations, or to highlight the sacrifices of the US soldiers on such occasions as the Korean War anniversary.

2. Getting Back to Basics

A. Restore strong, joint leadership

When facing a complicated problem, it is always a good idea to return to basics to solve it. Strong leadership is most needed at times of troubling transition. In the case of the South Korea–US alliance, both governments must take a leading role to address and successfully implement the urgent tasks that lie before them.

For instance, a military restructuring plan would be difficult to sell to a domestic constituency without the support of the media and the civil society. Due to the growing political maturity of the South Korean society, managing government–private sector relations becomes more important for any policy to succeed. Due to the country's changing demographics, the importance of educating younger generations has also risen. In fact, some blame the young generation's anti-American tendency on the generally liberal inclination of teachers in South Korea. Whether or not this is true, it is impossible to overemphasize the importance of education, since the alliance's future lies on the shoulders of the younger generation.

Government leadership is all the more crucial, given that 2004 will be a volatile year in terms of domestic politics. Both South Korea and the United States will be consumed by electoral politics almost all year long. The coming general elections of South Korea in April will be politically critical in many respects, and as will the US presidential elections in November. Given these significant distractions, both governments should do their best to maintain domestic bipartisanship on South Korea–US relations, before, during, and after the electoral process.

B. Highlight the alliance's existing strong fundamentals for a comprehensive partnership: Hedging against uncertainty
A comprehensive examination of the South Korea–US relationship clearly shows that a strong partnership serves both countries' interests—political, security, economic, and socio-cultural. For South Korea, the US presence on its soil not only provides a deterrent against North Korean adventurism, but also a base for its peace and prosperity. Were the United States to withdraw, it would place a huge financial burden, both direct and indirect, on South Korea. Directly, it would drain the South Korean budget, which would have to compensate for the withdrawn strategic assets of the United States. Indirectly, the US withdrawal will also be a serious blow to investors' confidence in South Korea's stability.

The United States' presence in South Korea provides a valuable forward base and continues to allow America to play the role of balancer in Northeast Asia, one of the tripolar economic centers of the world. A US withdrawal would cause a big security vacuum in the region, with increased uncertainty for Japan in particular. South Korea is a good example of success in the US alliance systems in that South Korea has grown into a market economy with an increasingly mature democracy. The South Korea–US alliance can become a model of a comprehensive partnership based on common value perceptions as well as national-interest calculations.

Put simply, the South Korea–US alliance is an efficient, cost-effective tool for maximizing both countries' interests and increasing their respective roles in a security equation in the region and beyond. A revitalized alliance will serve both as a regional balancer and a hedge against future uncertainty.

C. Improve policy coordination: Working out policy differences in private and maintaining one voice
As discussed above, policy differences should not be blamed for the alliance's current troubles. Allies cannot have identical priorities in foreign and security policies. The important thing is coordinating differing priorities in a mutually beneficial way.

The process of recent policy coordination between the governments of South Korea and the United States has not been smooth. These disagreements over policy gave rise to the 1999 creation of the trilateral policy coordination process among the United States and the two US allies, South Korea and Japan.

This process improved policy coordination significantly,[21] but much remains to be done.

One recent problem between the allies has been a pattern of uncoordinated leaks or premature announcements to the press which create public policy differences that might be better kept private. Although such announcements are usually followed by a denial from the government in question, they create serious problems for alliance management regardless of their truth, since the public tends to take them at face value. To be sure, enormous damage can be caused by a single press leak, but to make matters worse, each country's commentary invites the other to respond, thereby perpetuating a vicious cycle. Each government should do everything possible to make policy announcements only after both the intra- and intergovernmental coordination process has concluded. To achieve this goal, it would be worth appointing a senior policy coordinator within the US government[22] who would oversee Korean affairs and directly report to the president. The danger of premature announcements is that the public might compare the final result with earlier announcements, and use them as a yardstick to gauge success or failure in obtaining concessions from the other side. Generating unfavorable public opinion in this manner makes negative emotional perceptions of the alliance much more likely.

Maintaining one voice before an inquisitive and skeptical public is a difficult public relations exercise. It is vital, however—not only for sustaining domestic support, but also for ensuring the effectiveness of any policy chosen by the alliance vis-à-vis its main target, North Korea. The North is well known for its strategy to drive a wedge between Seoul and Washington whenever possible, and to wait and see how it works to its advantage. Only when North Korea realizes there is no room for a wedge will it begin to move toward compromise. Preserving an outwardly unified voice is strategically important as a hedge against the North Korean wedge.

D. Broaden the support base: Network-building

One noticeable problem of late is the weakness of a network that connects leading figures from major sectors of both countries. Despite a long period of ever-increasing exchanges at many levels, the network-building lags behind the needs of the times.

A more closely knit network should be in place, and should include opinion leaders both within and outside the government, as well as from conservative and liberal factions of the two societies. This should be done sooner rather than later, since it takes time to build a network and to reap its benefits. Therefore, network-building should begin immediately, and be targeted toward middle-aged opinion-makers from the government, politics, academia, media, and civil society in both South Korea and the United States.

V. Concluding Remarks

The ROK-US alliance now stands at a crossroads. Which road the alliance takes from here will depend on *how* the two governments jointly address structural factors and handle common challenges. Symptoms of anti-American sentiment in South Korea are likely to get worse unless the root causes are addressed. Many of these causes relate to the internal transition that South Korea is now undergoing. The country's economic growth and political democratization has transformed South Koreans' perceptions of themselves, and of their relationships with the United States, their most important ally, and North Korea, a complicated mix of brother and security threat. A clear new consensus has yet to emerge in South Korean society. To the extent that the alliance is experiencing distress, it is because South Korea is in serious transition.

In times of transition, the prerequisite for addressing the causes of alliance stress is to maintain—or more accurately *restore*—the unity of the two governments on policy priorities. Care should thus be given to the South Korean people's growing demand for more equitable recognition and treatment as an alliance partner. Modalities should be refined to ensure that South Korea is genuinely consulted on common challenges and issues affecting the alliance, and that differences can be sorted out as quietly as possible. Through such consultation, the two governments should present a redefined rationale of the alliance for the twenty-first century that looks beyond the Korean peninsula, is in tune with the South Korean people's changing perceptions, and takes into account the evolving US security imperatives following 9/11. This requires a comprehensive strategy both to accomplish the short-term tasks and to present a long-term vision that looks beyond the reunification of Korea.

The tasks suggested above are easier said than done. Joint, strong government leadership is all the more vital given the uncertainty arising from both allies' fluid domestic politics in 2004 and the unpredictability associated with the North Korean problem. Fundamental interests demand that the alliance to rise to the occasion. Serious efforts should begin now, to educate the younger generation and to build a stronger network for the alliance's future as a vehicle for peace and prosperity in Northeast Asia for the next fifty years.

NOTES

[1] On June 13, 2002, two Korean middle-school girls were killed by an armored mine-clearing vehicle during a US military exercise. Two US soldiers, the driver and the commander of the vehicle, were put on trial by the US military court in accordance with the SOFA (Status of Forces Agreement), which allows the US side to exercise criminal jurisdiction over on-duty crimes. They were later found not guilty on charges of negligent homicide on November 20 and 23. These rulings sparked mass rallies to protest their acquittals and to demand the revision of the SOFA to return criminal jurisdiction in similar cases to the Korean side.

[2] For details of the incident, see Don Oberdorfer, *Two Koreas: A Contemporary History*, pp. 183–86 (Basic Books, 2002). Oberdorfer discusses the incident in the context

of North Korean attempts to sabotage the 1988 Seoul Olympics, and does not comment on its possible impact on the presidential election.

³ These groups are composed of diverse entities from South Korea's civil society, but are loosely connected in consultative capacities. This enables them to form coalitions, and thus enhances their impact on certain issues.

⁴ This movement for "non-nomination and non-election" attracted significant public support by designating certain candidates for national assembly seats as ineligible, whether for party nomination or election.

⁵ See the survey done by the *Joongang Ilbo* in June 2003. The survey shows that Korean perceptions of the United States have bounced back from the lowest point of winter 2002. For example, those who supported the revision of the SOFA have dropped from 64 percent in December 2002 to 29 percent in June 2003. In another poll conducted by the *Joongang Ilbo* in cooperation with the Center for Strategic and International Strategy (CSIS) in September 2003, over 90 percent of respondents considered the relations with the United States as "important" and about 63 percent supported the continued presence of the US forces.

⁶ In a poll conducted by the *Joongang Ilbo* in September 2003 (see note 5, above), about 24 percent of respondents pointed to the "inter-Korean rapprochement" as a factor contributing to the weakening of the alliance.

⁷ For a detailed discussion of cost-benefit analysis of various options, see Victor Cha, "Hawk Engagement and Preventive Defense on the Korean Peninsula," *International Security*, Vol. 27, No. 1 (Summer 2002), pp. 40–78. Cha argues that "the 'default' prescription for North Korea remains engagement. The alternatives—containment-plus-isolation or containment-plus-coercion—only increase North Korea's rational incentives for engaging in hostilities even though victory is unlikely." (p. 70)

⁸ In a *Joongang Ilbo* poll (see notes 5 and 6, above), about 27 percent pointed out the "US hard line policy toward North Korea" as a factor contributing to the weakening of the alliance.

⁹ See William Perry, "It's Either Nukes or Negotiation," *Washington Post*, July 23, 2003, p. A23, and "US, N. Korea Drifting Toward War, Perry Warns," *Washington Post*, July 15, 2003, p. A14.

¹⁰ See the Report of an Independent Task Force, sponsored by the Council on Foreign Relations: Morton Abramowitz and James T. Laney, "Testing North Korea: The Next Stage in US and ROK Policy" (2001). The report recommends a comprehensive approach whose essence is to trade economic benefits and security assurances for threat reduction and the prospect of change in North Korea. It also argues that a dialogue must start at the level of vice foreign minister or higher and that North Korea's intentions must be tested.

¹¹ Sook-Jong Lee, "The Roots and Patterns of Anti-Americanism in Korean Society: A Survey-Based Analysis," Unpublished paper presented to the Fourteenth US-Korea Academic Symposium, "The US and South Korea—Reinvigorating the Partnership," APARC, Stanford University, October 2003.

¹² For details, see Oberdorfer, *Two Koreas*, pp. 260–65.

¹³ For details of the development of these problems and the allies' dealings with them, see Oberdorfer, *Two Koreas*, pp 409–41.

¹⁴ In 1949, US Secretary of State Dean Acheson stated that the Korean peninsula was outside the US line of defense. This declaration was generally considered to be one of the factors probably taken into account by Stalin prior to his endorsement of the North Korean plan to wage a war on South Korea. Before his endorsement, Stalin seemed to have turned down Kim Il-sung's war plan at least twice. See Don Oberdorfer, *Two Koreas*, p. 9.

[15] "Tripwire" is the term used to describe the situation in which the physical presence of the US forces in Korea near the Demilitarized Zone would automatically trigger the US involvement in any military confrontation initiated by the North. Now, with evolution in modern warfare strategy, this term is generally considered inappropriate in defining the role of the USFK. Nonetheless, it shows well the symbolism that the South Korean people attach to the USFK presence as a guarantee to avoid US "abandonment."

[16] "The National Security Strategy of the US," the White House, September 17, 2002. Section V, entitled "Prevent enemies from threatening us, our allies and our friends with WMD," states that "the United States has long maintained the option of preemptive actions to counter a sufficient threat to our national security. The greater the threat, the greater is the risk of inaction—and the more compelling the case for taking anticipatory action to defend ourselves, even if uncertainty remains as to the time and place of the enemy's attack. To forestall or prevent such hostile acts by our adversaries, the United States will, if necessary, act preemptively."

[17] One of the most popularly raised, though without substantive basis, scenarios for South Koreans is that the United States may preemptively respond to North Korean brinkmanship without prior consent of or full consultation with South Korea, and North Korea may react by pouring artillery shells on South Korea. Then South Korea will be a battlefield in a conflict that it does not initiate. This scenario is a combination of fears of exclusion and security dilemma.

[18] Recent polls continue to show that majority support still exists for the US presence. See, for example, a poll conducted by the *Joongang Ilbo* (note 5, above) in September 2003.

[19] See Article 3 of the Mutual Defense Treaty between the Republic of Korea and the United States, 1954. "Each Party recognizes that an armed attack in the Pacific area on either of the Parties in territories now under their respective administrative control, or hereafter recognized by one of the Parties as lawfully brought under the administrative control of the other, would be dangerous to its own peace and safety and declares that it would act to meet the common danger in accordance with its constitutional processes."

[20] For example, if part of the USFK or its assets were deployed in a potential hot spot such as the Taiwan Strait, it would have huge domestic and regional implications, particularly vis-à-vis China.

[21] The result of the 1999 trilateral coordination in 1999 was the so-called Perry Process. For details, see the unclassified report by William J. Perry, US North Korea Policy Coordinator and Special Advisor to the President and the Secretary of State, *Review of United States Policy Toward North Korea: Findings and Recommendations*, Washington, DC, October 12, 1999.

[22] For a similar recommendation in dealing with the North Korean nuclear problem, see the Report of an Independent Task Force, sponsored by the Council on Foreign Relations: Abramowitz and Laney, "Meeting the North Korean Nuclear Challenge" (2003), pp. 37–38.

US-ROK DEFENSE COOPERATION[1]

William M. Drennan

By any objective standard of evaluation, the US-ROK alliance has been a big success. It has succeeded in preventing a renewal of the Korean War and provided the security upon which South Koreans have built one of the world's leading economies from the devastation of the 1950–53 war. Despite this success, the alliance partners have been described as "the closest of strangers," and the alliance as a marriage of inconvenience, irreverent observations that contain grains of truth: the alliance has always been "high maintenance," with more than its fair share of tensions and controversies.

This paper will examine adjustments to the alliance that have occurred in the past and attempt to illuminate other changes the Bush administration is likely to promote in the near term. Some analytical and concluding thoughts are offered in the last two sections.

I. What adjustments have occurred in recent years in the operational arrangements underlying US-ROK defense cooperation?

Background

Defense cooperation between the United States and the Republic of Korea (ROK) dates from July 14, 1950, when President Syngman Rhee placed ROK forces under the "operational command" of General Douglas MacArthur in his capacity as commander-in-chief (CINC) of the nascent United Nations Command (UNC) following the North Korean invasion. For twenty-five years following the signing of the Armistice in 1953, the US-led UN Command had the missions of maintaining and managing the Armistice for the allies, deterring further aggression by North Korea (and its allies, China and the Soviet Union), and defending the ROK if deterrence had failed (in which case CINCUNC would once again have become the "warfighter" leading United States, ROK, and allied forces in the defense of South Korea).

With the signing of a mutual defense treaty on October 1, 1953, the United States and the ROK entered into a security alliance that forms the basis for the continuing defense cooperative relationship; that relationship is now entering its fifty-first year. In agreeing to a unique military command arrangement in which the defense of South Korea is a responsibility shared by the ROK and the United States, South Korean authorities ceded a degree of national sovereignty in exchange for the security that a defense partnership with the United States afforded (in the words of a former CINC, "the most remarkable concession of sovereignty in the entire world").

This command arrangement—with the United States leading a multinational military command that both complemented and underwrote the US commitment to help defend South Korea—remained unchanged between 1953 and 1978. Stability in military command arrangements, however, tended to mask what was clearly a contentious US-ROK relationship. Ties between Washington and Seoul were tested on a number of occasions:

• The 1961 military coup led by Major General Park Chung-hee overthrew an elected government, in the process violating UNC rules by using South Korean units under CINCUNC's operational control (OPCON) to effect the coup.

• The Nixon (Guam) Doctrine and the subsequent withdrawal of the US 7th Infantry Division from the ROK shocked South Korea, as did Nixon's subsequent opening of relations with the People's Republic of China, leading to a short-lived thawing of relations between South and North Korea.

• The transition in the early 1970s away from providing South Korea with military assistance via grants and to a loan-based arrangement under the US foreign military sales program.

• The clandestine program by President Park to produce nuclear weapons, an effort that was discovered and stopped by the United States.

• The initiative by President Carter to withdraw all US forces from South Korea (later reduced to the withdrawal of all remaining ground forces). While ultimately unsuccessful, Carter's troop withdrawal initiative fed into South Koreans' fear of abandonment, a fear that had been heightened by the US withdrawal from the Republic of Vietnam and its subsequent conquest by North Vietnamese forces.

Partly as a result of Carter's attempt to withdraw US forces, the first major change in military command arrangements was initiated in 1978 with the creation of the US-ROK Combined Forces Command (CFC), which assumed the deterrence and defense responsibilities of the United Nations Command (with UNC retaining responsibility for maintaining the Armistice). CINCCFC became the new "warfighter," reporting to two masters—the National Command and Military Authorities of both the United States and the ROK[2]—and exercising operational control over those military units assigned to CFC by US and ROK authorities.

As was the case in the initial twenty-five years of the defense relationship, the first sixteen years of CFC's existence (1978–1994) proved challenging for US-ROK defense cooperation, beginning with the assassination of President Park in October 1979. Park's death led to a rolling coup by Major General Chun Doo Hwan, whose seizure of the ROK military in December 1979 began a process that culminated in his takeover of the ROK government in 1980. Similar to Park's violation of UNC OPCON to carry out his coup in 1961, Chun violated CFC OPCON in December 1979 in his takeover of the ROK military. His disinformation campaign following the suppression of the uprising in the southwestern city of Kwangju in May 1980—in which he falsely claimed to have had US backing for his actions—was a betrayal whose aftershocks are felt to this day, both in terms of relations between the US and ROK militaries and in the rise of anti-Americanism among South Koreans in the years since.

Other challenges to defense cooperation in the 1978–1994 timeframe included:

• The effort—begun at the ROK government's request in 1988—to relocate United States Forces Korea (USFK) facilities and especially those at the 660-acre Yongsan Garrison out of Seoul (more on relocation below);

• The East Asia Strategy Initiative (EASI) of 1990, designed unilaterally by the first Bush administration to move the United States from a leading to a supporting role in the bilateral relationship;

• The first nuclear confrontation with North Korea (1993–94), a crisis in which policy coordination between the two allies proved to be extremely difficult, a crisis that almost led to war with the North.

Concerning the relocation of US facilities out of Seoul, the effort never really got off the ground (save for the return of the Yongsan golf course), despite the signing of a comprehensive bilateral memorandum of understanding in 1990 codifying the agreement, listing the responsibilities of each side, and establishing a timetable to complete the move by 1996. The project initially stalled over concerns about the costs involved (under the terms of the MOU, the move was to be made at no cost to the US government) and second thoughts among ROK policymakers about the wisdom of removing the US military from Seoul. Concerns about North Korean nuclear weapons also led to EASI being suspended after completion of Phase I, in which a small number of noncombatant troops were withdrawn from Korea.

The US decision in 1993 to engage North Korea directly on its nuclear weapons program strained relations between Washington and Seoul, but with the signing of the US-DPRK Agreed Framework on October 1994, allied cooperation improved as the United States and South Korea worked closely with their international partners on the Korean Peninsula Energy Development

Organization light water reactor project. In 1996 the allies jointly proposed the convening of four-party peace talks (South Korea, North Korea, the United States, and China), and the Clinton administration supported President Kim Dae-jung's Sunshine policy. Kim's hope for reconciliation between the two Koreas seemed to have been realized when he visited Pyongyang in June 2000 for the first-ever summit meeting between the leaders of South and North. Seoul's engagement policy was mirrored by Washington's, leading to the October 2000 visit of Marshal Cho Myong-nok to Washington, followed by Secretary of State Albright's trip to Pyongyang and talk of President Clinton visiting North Korea in the waning days of his administration.

Policy Context

In retrospect 2000 was a watershed year in US-ROK relations. The euphoria felt in much of South Korea over the June 2000 inter-Korean summit had a darker side, with latent anti-Americanism in the ROK coming to the surface as South Koreans began to question the need for the 37,000 US troops in South Korea in the new era of (assumed) South-North reconciliation. The new orthodoxy in South Korea following the summit—that North Korea is a partner for peace and is as committed to reconciliation and peaceful coexistence as is the South—was questionable from the beginning, certainly from the US standpoint, and quickly became an issue between the allies following the November 2000 US presidential election.

George W. Bush entered office skeptical of Kim Dae-jung's Sunshine policy, a skepticism made public during Kim's star-crossed visit to the White House in March 2001. Kim was determined to visit Washington as early as possible in an effort to enlist Bush's support for Sunshine, but the rush to Washington served neither side well. The Koreans had soured the mood of the summit through two missteps just days before leaving for Washington: implicitly criticizing national missile defense—a Bush priority—by agreeing officially with Russia that the 1972 ABM treaty, from which the United States would soon withdraw, was "the cornerstone for strategic stability"; and announcing its intention to sign a "peace declaration" with the North, a proposal having potentially momentous implications for the US position in Korea, and about which Korean officials could provide no details, because there were none. These missteps only reinforced the impression of amateurish ROK diplomacy under President Kim, and his subsequent embarrassment on these two counts was compounded when he appeared to be rebuked by Bush—indirectly but publicly—on his approach to North Korea. Three years later, US-ROK relations have yet to recover.

Allied Divergence

If June 15, 2000, was a watershed date for South Korea, September 11, 2001, was a turning point for the United States; both have had serious implications for US-ROK defense cooperation. Despite efforts to paper over their differences, the two allies are no longer pulling in harness nearly to the extent that they used to.

The foundation for the alliance, the shared perception of a common threat from North Korea, has been seriously weakened since the Pyongyang summit.

South Korea has been operating since the summit on the assumption of a new benign intent on the part of North Korea. Kim Dae-jung returned from Pyongyang declaring that "the greatest achievement of the inter-Korean summit talks is the disappearance of the threat of war on the Korean peninsula," and South Korea has adhered to a policy of unreciprocated assistance to the North ever since.

The US position, on the other hand, is that the summit and its aftermath have had no measurable impact on the security situation on the peninsula. For the United States North Korea remains a clear, present, and—with its two nuclear weapons programs—growing danger to the ROK and to US interests.

The divergence in positions of the alliance partners became public when the Kim Dae-jung administration disputed the analysis of the North Korean threat provided by CINCCFC in congressional testimony in the spring of 2001. For the first time in the history of the alliance, the professional judgment—and even the motives—of the military commander charged by both governments to deter the North and defend the South were called into question by ROK authorities. The rift has yet to be healed.

The US position would appear to have been vindicated in light of the revelation that the Kim government paid the North at least $500 million under the table to host the Pyongyang summit (and has continued to pay for engagement since). But Kim stuck with his Sunshine policy for the duration of his presidency, a policy that has been continued by his successor, Roh Moo-hyun (whose only adjustment was to rename it the Peace and Prosperity policy).

Recent Operational Adjustments

Three significant adjustments have occurred in recent years (i.e., during the presidencies of Kim Young-sam (1993–98) and Kim Dae-jung (1998–2003).

Peacetime OPCON. In December 1994, in recognition of political sensitivities and rising nationalism in South Korea, peacetime OPCON of ROK forces was transferred from CINCCFC to ROK authorities, with a new arrangement called Combined Delegated Authority (CODA) devised to ensure that the CINC would be able to continue to meet his deterrence and defense responsibilities. Peacetime operational control of the ROK military thus has resided with ROK authorities for the last nine years.

Arms Upgrades. US Forces Korea have undergone a significant upgrade of equipment in the last decade, with older equipment being replaced by newer, more capable gear (the Army Tactical Missile System—ATACMS, counter-battery radar, Apache helicopters, newer tanks, the Stryker combat vehicle). These upgrades have significantly enhanced the combat power of USFK.

The ROK has also embarked on a major upgrade of its equipment, agreeing to purchase F-15K fighters to replace older F-4s, and has plans for modern replacements for the other services as well, including tanks, helicopters, artillery, tactical missiles, destroyers, and early-warning aircraft.

As a result of these upgrades, long-standing gaps in the combined defense structure are being addressed, interoperability is being enhanced, and the overall combat capabilities of US and ROK combined forces are being significantly improved.

The Land Partnership Plan (LPP). At the 2001 Security Consultative Meeting the allies agreed to a sweeping adjustment to the US military "footprint" in South Korea. The US agreed to a major consolidation of its existing base structure in the ROK, enabling it to return approximately half of the forty-one major installations currently in use to the ROK, representing over 54 percent of the total amount of land USFK occupies. The LPP addresses not just the Yongsan Garrison and the US 2nd Infantry Division (2ID) in the area north of Seoul. Installations in other major cities will be consolidated or closed as well, including those in Pusan, Taegu, Chunchon, and Inchon, all of which have been the subject of protests by local residents objecting to the presence of US military installations in or near their cities. Existing facilities in Osan-Pyongtaek and a few other areas south of Seoul will be expanded to handle the influx.

II. What additional changes is the Bush administration likely to promote?

Despite a growing divergence in threat perception and therefore policy among the allies in the last ten years (and especially since the Pyongyang summit), the military structure of the alliance remained stable.

It appears that that is about to change. The next several years are likely to see major adjustments in the US military presence and in the roles and responsibilities assigned to each partner. When completed, these changes will reshape the alliance in fundamental ways.

Under the "Future of the Alliance Policy Initiative" (FOTA) begun in the spring of 2003, the allies have embarked on a major restructuring of the combined military structure. The FOTA process, though, has become controversial, as the US presses for significant changes in the near term and the South attempts to slow the entire process down.

The changes being pushed by the United States include:

Elimination of the "tripwire." The essence of deterrence for fifty years has been the presence of US ground troops between the DMZ and Seoul. Their vulnerability (coming under fire and taking casualties with the opening salvo of a renewed war) is designed to ensure that the US will join the fight if North Korea attacks. The necessity—indeed, the morality—of this "mission" has been rejected by the Bush administration, contributing to the decision to move the division south.

Consolidation. In the first phase of the move, elements of 2ID currently dispersed at numerous posts between Seoul and the Demilitarized Zone will be consolidated at Camp Red Cloud and Camp Casey, beginning as soon as possible, with 2006 as the target date for completion.

Relocation. In the second phase of the consolidation, the division will move to new bases south of Seoul (most likely to Camp Humphreys in the vicinity of Pyongtaek).

In addition, Yongsan will be vacated, with the headquarters of USFK moving to Osan Air Base and the Eighth US Army to Camp Humphreys. Originally, the headquarters of Combined Forces Command and the United Nations Command were to remain on a small portion of Yongsan, along with about a thousand US military personnel, but, since the United States and ROK were unable to agree on the amount of land to be retained, the US announced that CFC and UNC will also relocate to the Osan-Pyongtaek area as well, and in early 2004 the ROK government agreed. US installations in cities other than Seoul (see above) will also be closed.

Transformation. Presidents Bush and Roh have signaled their shared intent to take "advantage of technology to transform both nations' forces and enhance their capabilities to meet emerging threats" with lighter, more agile and adaptable forces. This is consistent with the Bush administration's desire to transform the US military around the world (see "The war on terrorism" below), to include moving away from "static defenses" tied to large bases.

Force reductions. While officials have yet to confirm it, there are strong indications that the US plans to withdraw some of its forces currently stationed in the ROK during the consolidation and relocation process. In testimony before the Senate Armed Services Committee in February 2003, the secretary of defense indicated as much, with some experts speculating that as many as a third of the 37,000 US troops currently deployed to the ROK will be withdrawn, a view echoed by CINCCFC in remarks at a conference in Seoul in early 2003.

Force enhancements. The United States has committed to a program of further enhancing the defense capabilities of the ROK, pledging $11 billion to the effort over the next three years and encouraging the ROK to continue to take advantage of advances in military technology as well. In Defense Secretary Rumsfeld's view, "It's not the numbers, but the capability to impose lethal power where needed with the greatest flexibility" that is needed.

Mission transfers. The United States has announced its intention to transfer responsibility for up to ten specific missions from US to ROK forces. These include guarding the Joint Security Area; decontaminating chemical, biological, and radioactive materials in southern areas of the ROK; laying land mines in emergency situations; preventing naval infiltration of North Korean special operations forces; countering the North's tactical missiles and long-range, hardened artillery; and search and rescue missions. Consolidated, relocated, and resized US forces would take on more of an expeditionary role, capable of executing missions both on and off the peninsula.

Command arrangements. CINCCFC is reported to have suggested that wartime operational control of ROK forces could be returned to Korean authorities, and at its first meeting in the spring of 2003 the FOTA agreed to form a joint consultative body to conduct a study of combined command arrangements. Transferring wartime OPCON to the ROK would almost assuredly mean disbanding Combined Forces Command and moving toward a command arrangement similar to that in Japan, where US Forces Japan (USFJ) and the Japanese Self-Defense Force have separate chains of command. In addition, there have been public reports that the US four-star position in South Korea will be downgraded to three stars to match the rank of the commander of USFJ.

Taken together, these adjustments—and especially the transition of USFK from a peninsula-only mission to a regional, power-projection role—represent a historic, fundamental alteration to the US approach to the defense partnership with the ROK.

III. Analysis

Noting "the opportunity provided by the Republic of Korea's growing national strength to continue expanding the role of the ROK armed forces in defending the Korean peninsula," Presidents Bush and Roh agreed in May 2003 to "work closely together to modernize the US-ROK alliance" and to "work out plans to consolidate US forces around key hubs and to relocate the Yongsan Garrison at an early date." The two chief executives also agreed that the "relocation of US bases north of the Han River should be pursued."

In that regard 2006 is shaping up as an important year in the relocation effort. US authorities are pushing for the 2ID and Yongsan relocations to be completed that year, and for the ROK to take over responsibility for the JSA and other missions currently assigned to USFK as well. During his visit to the ROK in November 2003, the secretary of defense said he agrees with President Roh's vision of a South Korea that takes more responsibility for its own defense. "It is time for [South Koreans] to set a goal for becoming somewhat more self-reliant," Rumsfeld said, and the United States seems intent on pressing ahead with relocation despite ROK reluctance.

Despite the understanding reached between presidents Bush and Roh in May (and reaffirmed at the APEC meeting in October 2003), the pace and scope of these changes ensures that they will be controversial; indeed, they are troubling both to some officials of the ROK government and to many South Korean citizens as well, which has made it difficult to get beyond general "agreements in principle" to proceed in a coordinated manner to implement these changes. Currently ROK officials are balking, insisting on the need for more time.

• The prime minister has publicly opposed the move of the 2ID, insisting that the tripwire function must be maintained.

• Led by the majority opposition Grand National Party, more than half of the 273 members of the National Assembly have signed a resolution opposing the relocation of USFK.

• The governor of Kyonggi province, which encompasses the area around Seoul up to the DMZ, also opposes the move, concerned about the economic impact on the province and the security implications of removing the screening force of US ground troops.

• The senior Blue House aide for defense matters voiced his opposition as well before being replaced early in 2004.

In the face of significant opposition, the United States is persisting with the changes out of a recognition that the context in which the alliance operates is quite different now than it was during its first half-century. At least three main reasons for this can be discerned.

The war on terrorism. The imperative to combat terrorism with a global reach has stretched US military capabilities, particularly those of the Army. Currently the Army has only ten active-duty divisions (down from eighteen at the end of the Cold War); nine have been, are, or soon will be deployed to Iraq or Afghanistan. Only the 2ID in Korea has been unaffected by the war on terror. As part of a larger effort to transform the US military for the threats of the new century, Pentagon planners are reported to be looking at the war plan for Korea with an eye to capitalize on growing ROK national strength and technological advances in weaponry to free up US ground forces in South Korea for missions off the peninsula.

The growth in ROK capabilities. South Korea has more than double the population of the North, and an economy thirty times greater. It can and should do more for its own defense.

Domestic changes in the ROK.

Threat Perception. Nations form security alliances to counter common threats. When the threat diminishes or disappears, or when an alliance member's perception of the threat declines, the foundation for the alliance is weakened and possibly destroyed. As mentioned above, South Korea after the Pyongyang summit appears determined to operate on the assumption that the North has fundamentally changed and that a new cooperative relationship has been forged. For the United States, however, North Korea remains a threat, part of the axis of evil, and a potential supplier of weapons of mass destruction to anyone willing to pay for them.

The US-ROK alliance cannot long endure in its current form if the United States is seen as more concerned with the security of South Korea than are South Koreans themselves. Recent polls show that a majority of South Koreans think the United States benefits more from the alliance than does the ROK, and that only 9 percent of South Koreans consider North Korean nuclear weapons to be a major concern. Another poll shows Americans, Europeans, and Australians more worried about North Korea's going nuclear than are South Koreans.

Demographics. The older conservative majority with memories of the Korean War and its aftermath has been supplanted by politically active younger generations whose views of the two countries of greatest importance to the security of the ROK—the United States and North Korea—are decidedly different from those of their parents and grandparents. Voters in their twenties and thirties now make up 50 percent of the electorate; when those in their forties are included, they exceed 70 percent. They are educated, affluent, nationalistic, skeptical of (if not outright hostile to) the United States, and see the North more as an object of pity than as a threat. While currently a (bare) majority of South Koreans supports the continued presence of USFK, the numbers are steadily declining as the population becomes more "progressive."

Pressures on USFK. After half a century, South Korea is becoming less hospitable to US forces. Lingering embarrassment over not being self-reliant in defense matters often manifests itself as resentment against the presence of USFK. US military installations that used to be in the countryside have been enveloped by urban sprawl. A "not in my backyard" sentiment has surfaced—while Yongsan is the best known, it is not the only installation that is the target of protests by local citizens objecting to the presence of foreign military bases in their cities. The area between Seoul and the DMZ is increasingly urbanized and congested, making it harder for US ground forces to train. The chances of accidents happening, such as the deaths in June 2002 of two schoolgirls run over by a US armored vehicle on maneuvers, will only increase.

The South Korean media, some of it government controlled, **have** added to the pressure, accentuating the negative aspects of hosting US forces. The Status of Forces Agreement has become a lightning rod, with denunciation of the "unfair SOFA" a staple in the media. (Polls show that more than 85 percent of South Koreans want the SOFA to be revised; they also show that two-thirds of Koreans admit to knowing nothing about the provisions of the agreement.)

The above, coupled with a long-standing reluctance on the part of ROK governments to intercede with their citizens on controversial issues associated with the presence of USFK, have left American forces in the untenable position of trying to contend with local concerns that clearly are the responsibility of the host government.

Mainstreaming of Anti-Americanism. The "candlelight" demonstrations in 2002–2003 were different from previous outbreaks of anti-Americanism in South Korea. For the first time, members of the critically important middle class joined elements in South Korea long opposed to the US (and USFK). Individual Americans—and especially US military personnel—were subject to abuse and assault. Moreover, neither the government nor any of the candidates in the 2002 presidential election—including the candidate from the right—defended the alliance or criticized the excesses of the anti-American demonstrations, perhaps foreshadowing the future of ROK politics.

For the first time in the five-decades-old relationship, anti-Americanism in South Korea elicited a reaction in the United States. Protests in Korea received an unusually large amount of press coverage in the United States, triggering a reaction in post-9/11 America. There does not appear to be much patience for an ally long protected by the United States who is seen as turning away from its alliance partner and toward its principal adversary. Former supporters of South Korea in the United States began publicly questioning the utility of continuing to protect people who seem not to value or desire that protection. There are indications that anti-Americanism accelerated the Korea portion of the global transformation of the US military that the administration already was planning.

Accusations of an "unfair SOFA" are now being countered by US officials, who cite the "unfair" (and immoral) tripwire. In answer to demands from anti-American protesters for "American forces out of Korea," a Pentagon official asserted just before the initial meeting of the FOTA that USFK could be gone "in a day" if that was the desire of Koreans.

IV. Conclusion

US plans for a major adjustment to the defense relationship and the anti-Korea backlash in evidence in the spring of 2003 seem to have gotten the attention of the Roh Moo-hyun government as well as many ROK citizens. Anti-American demonstrations have largely died out, at least temporarily. President Roh, who as an opposition member of the National Assembly had once advocated the withdrawal of USFK, now emphasizes the continuing importance of USFK and the need to modernize the alliance. His visit to the White House in May 2003 was a success, and he and President Bush seem to have established a good working relationship. In the face of strong public opposition, he has ordered an additional 3,000 ROK troops to Iraq to augment the 500 medical and support personnel already there.

His political position at home is precarious, however. A year after his election, Roh's approval rating has plummeted to the 30 percent range, with half of his former supporters saying in December 2003 that they regretted having voted for him. Relations with the opposition-dominated National Assembly are strained, and allegations of corruption swirl around him, his family, and his presidential staff. Roh has weakened his own political standing by publicly questioning his own ability to govern, going so far as to propose a referendum on his leadership (something for which there is no provision in the constitution).

The United States is contending with the North Korean nuclear challenge while trying to prevent further deterioration of its alliance with the ROK as it simultaneously attempts to make historic changes to the nature of the alliance. The deep divisions within South Korean society compound the difficulty of these tasks—President Roh presides over a South Korea badly split on ideological, generational, and regional lines, conflicted over how to deal with the North, and ambivalent about the alliance with the United States. (Incredibly, a poll taken in early 2004 showed that 39 percent of South Koreans viewed the United States as the biggest threat to South Korea's security; only 33 percent identified North Korea. Koreans in their twenties chose the United States over North Korea by a 3 to 1 margin, those in their thirties by a 2 to 1 margin.) And while other polls show a majority still considers the presence of USFK to be necessary, the numbers are down significantly in recent years, and even larger majorities have an unfavorable opinion of the United States, with two-thirds of those in their twenties and thirties saying that they either dislike or hate the United States.

To borrow a phrase from Wall Street, the Korean peninsula is "in play," and it is far from clear what the future holds for the US-ROK alliance or for the security of South Korea. One thing, though, is increasingly clear: by the end of President Roh's term in 2008, the US presence in South Korea and the US-ROK alliance will look substantially different than it looks today.

NOTES

[1] The views expressed in this paper are solely those of the author writing in a private capacity.

[2] The National Command and Military Authorities are the secretary of defense and the president on the US side and the minister of national defense and the president on the ROK side.

CHANGES IN THE COMBINED OPERATIONS ARRANGEMENT IN KOREA[1]

Kim Jae-chang

The United States and the Republic of Korea (ROK) established an effective alliance during the Korean War and formalized that alliance following the war by signing the US-ROK Mutual Defense Treaty. The essence of this treaty calls for the two nations to maintain a strong military alliance.[1] Based on this agreement, the United States dispatched combat units to the Korean peninsula and formed combined forces with the combat units of the ROK. During the Cold War, the alliance successfully maintained security on the Korean peninsula, which contributed to the regional stability of Northeast Asia. Although they have not yet resolved the Korean question, both nations have expressed their intent to maintain the alliance even after the reunification of the peninsula.[2]

During the Cold War, the alliance used a strategy of deterrence against North Korea even as both nations prepared to defeat the enemy in case deterrence failed. This strategy worked well for both partners of the alliance because the US and the ROK wanted the *status quo* on the peninsula.

After the Cold War, however, neither alliance partner felt bound to the restrictions required for maintaining the *status quo* on the peninsula as they had previously. In January 2002, President Bush declared the North Korean regime a member of the "axis of evil"; this statement sent a strong message to both nations on the Korean peninsula. The ROK did not remain passive in its relations with North Korea, but adopted an engagement policy in an attempt to reduce military tension and to achieve a peaceful solution on the peninsula.

Both partners of the alliance are now using their own dynamic methods in dealing with North Korea in contrast to the more static modes used during the Cold War. During the Cold War, North Korea was an important part of the Soviet bloc and thus played a bigger role in the United States' policy of containment of communism. Now, from the US perspective, it is no more than a rogue state that is located adjacent to one of its key regional alliances. The US also views North Korea as an adversary in its global war on terrorism. Thus the US deals with North Korea from a global or regional perspective while the ROK must consider the implications of dealing with a neighbor who also resides on the same peninsula. Because of the difficulties associated with a reunited Korea, the ROK government is determined to achieve a peaceful unification with the North.

The operational arrangements reflect the strategy of the country they serve. The US strategy is based mostly on a global perspective whereas the ROK's strategy is focused more on the Korean question. For the US-ROK Combined Forces Command (CFC), planning for operational employment on the basis of two different strategic visions is proving difficult. In the coming decades the CFC must attempt to harmonize the changes in each nation's operational force arrangements to serve the combined objective on the Korean peninsula.

Historical Background

When the Korean War ended in 1953, there were 302,000 US troops in Korea deployed along the Military Demarcation Line (MDL). In 1954 the US began to withdraw a major portion of the forces that participated in the Korean War, leaving only two divisions along the western corridor of the Korean peninsula. In 1969, President Nixon declared that US allies would bear the primary responsibility for their own security.[3] By March 1971, one of the two US divisions of the US Forces Korea, amounting to 20,000 troops, withdrew to the United States and an ROK army division took over the sector.

The two governments took the prudent measure of creating the US-ROK Combined Corps Headquarters in order to fill the gap created by the reduction of US ground troops.[4] The Third Tactical Fighter Wing of the US Air Force was also created at Kunsan. This new headquarters took charge of the defense of Seoul. The two governments also began combined exercises: Focus Retina, Freedom Bolt, and Team Spirit. These exercises demonstrated not only US commitment to Korea but also US capability of rapid deployment of combat troops from the US continent to Korea in case of hostilities.

In 1977, President Carter devised a force withdrawal plan from Korea, but the US canceled this plan before it was completed. The plan consisted of three phased withdrawals of US forces from Korea. The first phase of the plan was implemented starting in June 1977, and by December 1978, 3,400 ground forces troops had returned to the United States, leaving 37,000 US troops in Korea. In 1978, the two governments created the US-ROK Combined Forces Command, which took charge of the entire defense of the Korean peninsula. In late 1979, President Carter reassessed the strategic situation in Northeast Asia and finally scrapped his withdrawal plan.

Current discussions of the US troop redeployment in Korea reflect the North Korean nuclear threat, the change in the South Korean threat perception, and advancements in military technology.

Changes in Korea's Strategic Environment

Increased North Korean Military Threat

Kim Jong-il's regime persistently pursues a military-first policy for North Korea. Despite its miserable economic conditions, North Korea allocates 20–25 percent of the nation's GNP to sustaining and improving its armed forces. According to statistics, in 2003 Kim Jong-il visited 87 places in North Korea to deliver direct teachings to North Korean workers and officials. Among them, 61 military units were included, thus accounting for 70 percent of all his activities outside of his office.[5] With their alleged nuclear weapons, North Korean missiles threaten not only the ROK but also all neighboring countries. Military experts claim that the North Korean military threat has grown bigger, closer, and deadlier since 2000.

North Korea's Psychological Offensive

Since the division of the Korean peninsula, there have been indigenous communist activist groups and pro-Pyongyang sympathizers in the South. During the Korean War, North Korea's attempt to subdue the South through a combination of armed attack and an activist-led uprising in the South failed miserably. Now, it is clear that North Korea is trying to use this sympathy in the ROK to drive a wedge between the US and the ROK. If North Korea adopts Sun-Tzu's theory of warfare, then disrupting the alliance between the US and ROK will have a higher priority than destroying the armed forces of South Korea.[6] It is clear that the North Koreans never miss an opportunity to use anti-American rallies in the South to show up the problems in trying to maintain the US-ROK alliance.

Advancement in Military Technologies

The US-ROK alliance is determined to defend Seoul from a possible North Korean attack. Since Seoul is located less than forty miles from the DMZ, it is vulnerable to North Korean surprise attack. Tactically, it made sense for the Combined Forces to deploy as many troops as possible to the forward area for the defense of Seoul. Advancements in modern military technology, however, have enabled us to change the concepts, organization, processes, and equipment used to achieve gains in operational effectiveness, operating efficiencies, and cost reductions. The US confirmed the need for military transformation and new concepts during the recent Iraqi war. The time has come to rethink operational arrangements in Korea in light of the advantages of modern military technologies.

Discussions on Changes in Operational Arrangements

Defense officials in the United States and South Korea began discussing redeployment of the US forces in Korea in early 2003. For the last fifty years the US has deployed its combat units north of the Han River close to the MDL, providing a strong defense capability in the event of a renewal of hostilities. These forces are thus at significant risk from North Korean artillery. Taking advantage of advances in military art and science, the Pentagon has proposed redeployment of the US ground forces further south in Korea.

Redeployment of US Combat Units South of the Han River

In the 35th Security Consultative Meeting between Secretary Rumsfeld and Minister Cho, both nations reaffirmed the principle of realignment and consolidation of the US forces in Korea into two hubs south of the Han River. Both men said that although realignment of the ground units would begin as soon as possible, the timing of the relocation would be determined by the highest national authorities. The US 2nd Infantry Division and its supporting units, which are deployed north of the Han River and oversee one of North Korea's major avenues of approach to Seoul, would be the largest US combat force that would move south.

Although Pentagon officials have said that repositioning US forces away from the DMZ will actually increase deterrence and correct an outdated deployment plan from Cold War days, the move alters the security equation on the peninsula. First, since the new locations are out of the range of North Korean artillery, the US ground assets would be better protected in the beginning of an outbreak of hostilities. From an operational perspective, keeping the US ground forces in the rear area comparatively safe in the first stage of conflict increases efficiency in the use of forces in the Korean theater. This is positive.

Second, relocating US ground units south of the Han River also warns North Korea of the increased possibility of a preemptive strike, at least from the North Korean perspective, on its nuclear facilities. On July 6, 2003, North Korea's Radio Pyongyang claimed that the redeployment of the 2nd Infantry Division was an attempt by the US to position its forces to launch preemptive strikes on North Korea. Secretary Rumsfeld helped to confirm North Korean fears when he said that "with North Korea threatening war, a US threat to strike against Yongbyon will not be credible while American forces remain deployed in positions vulnerable to North Korean rocket and artillery attack."[7]

Third, the redeployment of US forces is compatible with the concept that the US takes a leading role in regional stability and the ROK a supporting role, whereas the ROK takes a leading role in the security of the Korean peninsula and the US a supporting role. The new arrangements certainly increase the strategic flexibility of the US in Northeast Asia, while they place a greater burden on the ROK for its defense. In order to create this new arrangement, the US will have to transfer selected missions to the ROK military. Military experts are now trying to determine how the ROK army can effectively take over the missions that the US ground units maintained in the forward area, especially the counter-artillery measures.

Fourth, the expectation that relocation of US combat units further south will reduce anti-American sentiment among South Koreans may not be well founded. Those who lead anti-American rallies are not the people living around the US forward camps but are usually from somewhere else. Actually, those who live in the forward area are more sensitive to the North Korean military threat and have maintained good relations with the US troops. US troops and local residents have had a long time to adjust themselves overcoming their cultural differences. Although South Korea has a few US units in the rear, an increased number of ground troops there will create new civil-military issues and will require time for mutual adjustment.

Fifth, successful deterrence rests in theory on the counterbalance provided by the combined forces. The effective combination of the US capability of maneuver warfare supported by long-range precision weapons and that of the forward-deployed Korean army would create enhanced deterrence. In practice, however, deterrence relies more on North Korea's perception of the new operational arrangements and US intent concerning defense of the Korean peninsula than on the counterbalance of the combined forces. Considering North Korean paranoia over the illusion of unification by means of military force and its military-first policy, redeployment may send the wrong signal to the North.

Relocation of US Forces from the Seoul Metropolitan Area

The two governments reviewed agreements for the relocation of US forces from the Seoul metropolitan area during the Security Consultative Meeting in Seoul last November. In Seoul are the command structures of the US forces and their supporting units: United Nations Command (UNC), US-ROK Combined Forces Command (CFC), US Forces Command in Korea (USFK), and the Eighth United States Army (EUSA). Seoul was a small city with a population of 2 million at the end of the Korean War when USFK established bases in Yongsan, a suburb on the outskirts of Seoul. In the last fifty years the city of Seoul has grown to 17 million people and the Yongsan Garrison is now in the middle of the Seoul metropolitan area. Large numbers of US forces based in Seoul, stationed on prime real estate, have become a focal point for anti-American demonstrations. The two governments agreed to work jointly on relocation of the Yongsan Garrison at the earliest possible date.[8]

Compared with the relocation of the combat units, the move of the command group has political and psychological implications. First, the location of USFK's command group has symbolic meaning for the alliance: its presence helps to demonstrate US resolve on deterrence. In deterrence is rooted the stability of the Korean peninsula for the last several decades, which provided a favorable environment for economic prosperity and political development. Deterrence was built on the combination of the demonstrated resolve of the US government to defend the Korean peninsula and its ability to reinforce forward deployed forces with continental-based US forces. In that sense, the location of the USFK command group in Seoul has not only its real military value but also uncountable symbolic meaning. Although the US and South Korea agreed that relocation of the Yongsan Garrison would serve the overall interests of both governments, measures are necessary to help ease the psychological concerns of those who fear that relocation will weaken the bond between the two partners.

From the ROK perspective, it is better to have the operational command element of the alliance, US-ROK Combined Forces Command, close to the Korean national command authority. From the military operational perspective, the CFC is the link between the two military organizations in peace and in war. Since the Joint Chiefs of Staff of the Korean armed forces is located in Seoul, locating CFC away from Seoul would not serve the effective coordination between the two alliance partners. In the event of a crisis it might be hard to coordinate between political objectives and military means if the operational command were located far from the national command authority.

Increasing the Quality and Decreasing the Quantity of the US Forces in Korea

The US plans to invest $11 billion to enhance the combat power of the US forces in Korea over the next three years: this program includes upgrading missile systems and reinforcing military intelligence assets. Military experts believe that the improvements the US military has made in firepower, accuracy, and rapid force deployment capabilities mean that fewer US forces are required on the Korean peninsula. They believe the US force in Korea will be more agile and more lethal in the near future although it will be smaller.

To achieve effective teamwork, both partners will need to take proactive measures. First, ROK forces need to prepare to take over missions from the US forces in the forward area of operations. Second, the ROK needs to transform its military to more effectively adapt to the new environment. Third, the relocation of the US ground units should be timed in connection with the progress of the military transformation of the ROK forces so as not to create a defensive gap in the process of relocation.

Further Adjustments Required

Although both partners of the alliance are pressuring North Korea to take measures to show positive change, the most important goal of the US-ROK alliance is to prevent a repeat of the Korean War. Deterrence capability is essential to sending the proper signal to the North that the alliance has both the intent and the capability to defend the Korean peninsula. In the 1970s, when the US withdrew 20,000 troops from Korea, it was necessary to make North Korea understand that the US had the capability of rapid force projection in case of hostilities. Combined exercises were one of the effective tools for communicating US commitment and capability. In Focus Retina, the US demonstrated its force projection capability by moving 2,500 troops to Korea from the US continent in only 31 hours by mobilizing seventy-seven C-130 aircraft. Furthermore, the US and ROK decision to locate the 2nd Infantry Division north of the Han River and close to the DMZ conveyed a clear signal to the North. These measures certainly contributed to the deterrence of war even though the alliance reduced the number of troops in Korea. In deterrence, perceptions matter as much as capability.

The redeployment of US troops south of the Han River is distinguished from the operational changes of the 1970s in terms of effective deterrence. Military experts say that the goal of realignment is to most effectively deter a North Korean attack and defend South Korea should an attack come. From North Korea's perspective, however, consolidation and relocation of the US troops into two hubs south of the Han River might be interpreted as a weakening of the intent of the US. Based on the experience of the 1970s, proper measures are required to convey the right signal to the North of both US intent and capability concerning the defense of the Korean peninsula.

Conclusion

Redeployment of US ground troops in South Korea to the south of the Han River will open a new era in the security alliance between the US and the ROK. Although the alliance has not solved the Korean question, it is undertaking a new operational arrangement for a new division of labor in Korea. For regional stability, the US takes a primary role whereas the ROK takes a supporting role; and for the security of the peninsula, the ROK takes the primary role whereas the US takes a supporting role. Although advances in modern military technology have made these changes possible, measures for preventing North Korea from misunderstanding them are necessary.

NOTES

[1] According to Article 4, "The Republic of Korea grants, and the United States of America accepts, the right to dispose United States land, air, and sea forces in and about the territory of the Republic of Korea as determined by mutual agreement."

[2] See the Joint Research Report by Jonathan D. Pollack and Young Koo Cha, *A New Alliance for the Next Century: The Future of US-Korean Security Cooperation* (Santa Monica, Calif.: RAND, 1995).

[3] The Nixon Doctrine. In 1969, President Nixon claimed that although the US would honor all the commitments it had made in the quarter of a century since the end of World War II, its allies, outside of Western Europe and Japan, would bear the primary responsibility for their own security. Douglas J. Murray and Paul R. Viotti, eds., *The Defense Policies of Nations* (Baltimore: The Johns Hopkins University Press, 1994), p. 25.

[4] The Corps was named the First Corps (ROK-US) Group in 1971 and renamed as Combined Field Army (ROK-US) in March 1980 and decommissioned after the ROK Third Army took over its mission in July 1992.

[5] Ministry of Unification, Weekly Report on North Korea, No. 673, Dec. 12–Dec. 18, 2003, p. 5.

[6] Roger Ames, trans., *Sun-Tzu, The Art of Warfare* (New York: Ballantine Books, 1993), p. 111.

[7] Robyn Lim, "Rumsfeld Warns China on Korea," *New York Times*, March 13, 2003.

[8] Joint Press Conference of the 35th US-ROK Security Consultative Meeting (November 17, 2003).

DOMESTIC POLITICS AND THE CHANGING CONTOURS OF THE ROK-US ALLIANCE: THE END OF THE STATUS QUO

Lee Chung-min

As the Republic of Korea and the United States celebrated their fiftieth anniversary in October 2003, both sides could rightfully claim to have built one of the most successful, unique alliances in the post–World War II era. To be sure, other alliances have also surpassed the symbolic half-century threshold—NATO and the US-Japan alliance are among the more prominent strategic relationships forged in the aftermath of World War II and the Korean conflict. The rebirth and reconstruction of Germany and Japan as democratic, economic giants in the postwar era would have been impossible without alliances that were conceptualized, led, and sustained by the United States. Likewise, the ROK-US alliance's overall success can be summarized as follows.

I. The End of the Status Quo

First, despite the accidental nature of the alliance, it has persevered and prospered for five decades. Although the ROK-US alliance continues to function as South Korea's key security pillar, virtually no one could have predicted in the late 1940s that South Korea would be enjoined firmly in an alliance with the United States well into the twenty-first century.[1] Second, notwithstanding the preponderance of military and security issues, the alliance has branched out incrementally since the late 1970s to cover increasingly important economic and trade issues as well. In the aftermath of the first North Korean nuclear crisis in 1993, the alliance has also coped with nonproliferation as a major security and political agenda, as illustrated by the ongoing second North Korean crisis. Third, the alliance has survived key political and generational transitions. These include South Korea's democratization since the late 1980s and Seoul's changing security consensus and threat perceptions vis-à-vis North Korea that began in earnest under the Kim Dae-jung administration (1998–2003). The latter only sharpened with the inauguration of Roh Moo-hyun in February 2003.

Despite a strong raison d'être for maintaining the alliance in the face of security and military threats emanating from North Korea and the uncertainties associated with the unification process, the alliance today is undeniably in the midst of major change and transformation. The arrival of the Roh government in February 2003—the most liberal regime to be voted into power in South

Korea since the country's founding in 1948—in many respects has hastened ongoing discussions to modify the alliance. However, even if the conservative opposition party had won the presidential election in December 2002, changes in the alliance would likely have been inescapable.[2] In other words, while there is little doubt that the Roh administration accelerated the pace of revamping the alliance (such as the recent decision to relocate the US 2nd Infantry Division to an area south of Seoul), adjustments in the alliance were, in many respects, long overdue.

In large part, the propensity for maintaining the status quo was shaped by the rigid nature of the inter-Korean and Northeast Asian strategic balance, coupled with successive South Korean and American governments that placed a premium on managing rather than modernizing the alliance. The rationale for maintaining an alliance with a focused mission—namely, successfully deterring the outbreak of another major war on the Korean peninsula—remains as valid today as it was five decades ago. Nonetheless, though deterring the outbreak of a second Korean conflict continues to drive the alliance, almost all of the central elements that contributed to a focused strategic outlook have changed over the past two decades. For example, North Korea's revelations since October 2002 that it was working on a highly enriched uranium nuclear weapons program, and intermittent assertions that it deserves the right to have nuclear deterrent capabilities have shifted the contours of the security debate on the Korean peninsula.[3] While Seoul has repeatedly stated that it would not tolerate a North Korea with nuclear weapons, it remains uncertain what South Korea would do if North Korea is verified to have nuclear weapons capabilities already.[4] Equally worrisome is the growing possibility of structural change in North Korea, including regime or state collapse. Worsening economic conditions, the rising number of refugees, high-level defectors, and Pyongyang's narrowing exit strategy suggest that the status quo within North Korea is probably not sustainable.[5] If so, the ROK-US alliance would be forced to reckon with a range of offline or nonlinear scenarios that would entail comprehensive crisis management, the reconfiguration of the US Forces Korea (USFK), and co-drafting post-unification alliance management requirements. In short, the "alliance menu" has broadened and both sides have to make new accommodations if the strategic partnership is to be sustained into the post-unification era.

The inauguration of the Roh administration also brought to the fore new political forces and agendas including a growing desire on the part of South Korea to foster a more balanced and equal alliance.[6] While President Roh Moo-hyun toned down his rhetoric vis-à-vis the alliance since entering *Chongwadae* (the official presidential residence), his limited foreign policy experience, coupled with populist streaks, caused significant unease throughout the summer and fall of 2003.[7] As a result, revamping or reengineering the alliance emerged as one of the new government's most important agendas. This impetus coincided with matching moves in the United States fundamentally to review the alliance, including the desirability of maintaining some 37,000 US troops in South Korea.

As an example, Secretary of Defense Donald Rumsfeld stated in February 2003 that a review of US troops levels in South Korea would be initiated once President Roh assumed office. More recently, Rumsfeld noted that the USFK could be moved away from the "Seoul area and from near the DMZ, and be more oriented towards an air hub and a sea hub." In late April 2003, when asked whether he expected to see some withdrawal of US forces from East Asia (including Korea), Rumsfeld answered that while he had no intentions of announcing such a move, "it's an appropriate time for us to review that [changing the status of US forces] and so we will be reviewing."[8] In addition, Secretary of State Colin Powell noted on February 25 after a round of meetings with Roh administration officials that the United States reaffirmed its security commitment to the ROK and "our intention to keep a presence in the region." Powell also went on to say, however, that *"we of course should constantly review that presence*, in close coordination and consultation with the South Korean government, and we should have transparency in these discussions and rules should be no surprises."[9] (emphasis added).

At the tail end of the Kim Dae-jung administration, the South Korean government maintained that no official discussions had yet taken place on relocating the US 2nd Infantry Division to an area south of Seoul. However, following the inauguration of the Roh government in April 2003, the ROK and the United States began the first round of the so-called Future of the Alliance Initiative dialogue. The first meeting took place in Seoul from April 8-9, and the second conference was held from May 6-7, just prior to the first Roh-Bush summit.[10] According to remarks made by a senior US defense official who participated in the first round of discussions, the future status of the US forces in South Korea was not a part of the official agenda. Rather, the primary impetus for the talks was to set the stage for "preparing the alliance to meet emerging challenges."[11] Nonetheless, by the time the third round of talks was held in June 2003, the two sides announced that a reconfiguration of the USFK would be implemented in a two-phased plan. In the first phase, US forces currently deployed in areas north of Seoul would be consolidated onto larger more modern camps, with final relocation into key hubs south of Seoul during the second phase.[12] Following the annual ROK-US Security Consultative Meeting (SCM) in Seoul in November 2003, Secretary Rumsfeld confirmed that the reconsolidation of the USFK would be implemented as part of a joint transformation effort. In particular, Rumsfeld noted that:

...Any changes to US military posture in Northeast Asia will be the product of the closest consultation with our key allies. Most important, they will result in increased US capabilities in the region. Whatever adjustments we make will reflect the new technologies that are available, the new capabilities, and they will strengthen our ability to deter and, if necessary, defeat any aggressions against allies such as South Korea. Above all nothing we do will diminish our commitment to Korea's security or our ability to fulfill our obligations under the Mutual Defense Treaty.[13]

II. The Limitations of Default Alliance Management

South Korea today confronts five interlocking challenges that are likely to drive the future shape, roles and missions, and political makeup of the alliance. Each of these tasks demands the closest of consultations and policy coordination with the United States, although it is equally important to note that both sides must contend with a significantly different political milieu. The critical issue for South Korea is to understand that henceforth, the choices it makes vis-à-vis the alliance will have direct consequences for its security as it heads into the unification tunnel.[14] A certain level of angst has always permeated the alliance, given Korea's historical mistrust of the great powers and growing desire to pursue greater security autonomy commensurate with its relatively increased national capabilities. The alliance has also weathered significant disagreements and tensions, such as the spillover from the so-called Koreagate affair in the late 1970s and the Carter administration's initial decision to withdraw US forces from South Korea. The enunciation of the Nixon Doctrine in 1969, the strategic opening with China and the withdrawal of the US 7th Infantry Division in 1972, and the fall of South Vietnam in 1975, among other developments, resulted in significant doubts about the depth of US commitment to the defense of South Korea.

If the Korean strategic template undergoes significant change, South Korea will have to grapple with a range of issues with which it has not contended before. Alliance management by design, rather than default, will become the hallmark of the Seoul-Washington relationship in the years to follow. Specifically, five major areas are going to drive alliance futures. First and most urgent is North Korea's nuclear quagmire and attendant consequences. Thus far, Pyongyang has been able to solicit significant assistance and aid from South Korea, the United States, Japan, the European Union, and selective international organizations, owing to its nuclear brinkmanship. If North Korea chooses not to roll back its nuclear weapons program and opts to make permanent its withdrawal from the nuclear Non-Proliferation Treaty (NPT), the United Nations Security Council (UNSC) would have to consider coercive measures, including economic sanctions.[15] Conversely, a comprehensive package could thwart North Korea's nuclear ambitions, provided that the Bush administration can convince the North that while it would not support the signing of a nonaggression pact, it would provide the North with equally strong political assurances. South Korea, the United States, and Japan could also entice North Korea by agreeing to provide their own version of a "Marshall Plan" toward the North if Pyongyang rescinds its decision to withdraw from the NPT and agrees to submit to IAEA safeguard agreement provisions.

Second, the status of the USFK (including its relocation south of Seoul), concomitant force improvement measures by ROK armed forces, and redefining roles and missions of the US-ROK Combined Forces Command (CFC) are bound to assume the lion's share of the alliance's forthcoming political and military discussions. To be sure, this is not the first time that changes have been sought in the US military presence in South Korea. Reassessing the optimal USFK footprint on the Korean peninsula dates back to 1949, when all US combat forces were withdrawn a year before the outbreak of the Korean War. In 1971, the Nixon Administration chose to withdraw the 7th Infantry Division in tandem with the so-called Nixon or Guam Doctrine.[16] During the 1976 US presidential campaign, Jimmy Carter asserted that given South Korea's growing economic edge, continuing US commitment to South Korea's defense, and ongoing force modernization program in the South Korean military, it was time to withdraw US ground troops from the ROK. In 1977, the Carter administration announced that it would begin just such as incremental withdrawal, pending close consultations with Seoul. In February 1979, Carter stated that "further troop withdrawals from the ROK would be held in abeyance pending assessment of a number of North Asian developments" after it was revealed that North Korea's military strength continued to grow in the late 1970s, contrary to earlier intelligence assessments.[17]

One major reason for concern is that new domestic political forces in South Korea are accelerating a change in Seoul's security consensus. These include sharp internal divisions on the reality of the North Korean military threat, the need for a sustained deployment of US forces in South Korea, and whether a US alliance is warranted in the post–Cold War era. Clearly, despite the rise in anti-American demonstrations in late 2002, following the accidental death of two South Korean students by US soldiers during a training exercise in June of that year, most South Koreans remain wary of a sudden US military withdrawal from South Korea. That said, if reengineering the alliance is driven primarily on the basis of South Korean sentiments such as growing nationalism, a desire for greater autonomy, and mismatched threat perceptions, the consequences for South Korea's long-term security could be high, and more importantly, irreversible.

Third, in order for Seoul and Washington to sustain the alliance well into the twenty-first century, both sides must jointly formulate a longer-term strategic rationale. As South Korea and the United States celebrated the alliance's fiftieth anniversary in October 2003, the two sides could have issued a comprehensive joint declaration akin to the April 17, 1996 "US-Japan Joint Declaration on Security: Alliance for the 21st Century," signed by President Clinton and Prime Minister Hashimoto. The joint declaration emphasized the need to accentuate bilateral, regional, and global cooperation, and concluded by noting that "the three legs of the US-Japan relationship—security political, and economic—are based on shared values and rest on the mutual confidence embodied in the Treaty of Mutual Cooperation and Security."[18] Moreover, during the fiftieth anniversary of the Atlantic Alliance in April 1999, the heads of state and government of the North Atlantic Council declared, in part, that "we will maintain both the political solidarity and the military forces necessary to protect our nations and to meet the security challenges of the next century." The joint declaration also noted that "our Alliance remains open to all European democracies, regardless of geography, willing and able to meet the responsibilities of membership."[19] The changing political and strategic contours of the ROK-US alliance mean that preparations should begin in earnest to enable the alliance to transition smoothly into the post–North Korean threat era. In this respect, it would also be worthwhile to pay serious attention to launching a "two plus two" foreign and defense ministers' conference between South Korea and the United States, akin to the annual US-Australian and US-Japanese foreign and defense ministers' meetings. Although the US-ROK SCM has been held annually since 1968 and the annual Military Consultative Meeting (MCM) since 1978, outstanding security issues dictate the need for a new format that would formalize a "two plus two" meeting.

Fourth, and perhaps most importantly in the context of evolving South Korean politics, is the need to begin a concerted public diplomacy campaign in South Korea to build a new consensus for the alliance. Public support for the alliance has shifted over the years but pronounced differences began to surface in the early 1990s, coincident with the end of the Cold War and South Korea's accelerated democratization. While the majority of South Koreans continue to believe in the need for a strong alliance that includes the presence of US forces, perceptions remain sharply divided across generational and ideological lines. The outpouring of unprecedented anti-Americanism in South Korea in fall 2002 was largely situation-specific, related to the public outcry against the two students' deaths and two US servicemen's subsequent exoneration. But it cannot be denied that deeper forces were also at work, notably South Korea's increasingly ambiguous perception of the North Korean threat. Indeed, although still a minority, some South Koreans believe that North Korea, as a sovereign state, should have the right to develop nuclear weapons, and moreover, that even if North Korea has nuclear weapons, it would not use them against fellow Koreans. Coupled with unease at the preponderance of American power in the post–Cold War era but particularly in the aftermath of the 9/11 attacks, many younger South Koreans no longer equate South Korean security as intimately tied to the ROK-US alliance.

Fifth, South Korea must set key policy priorities as it seeks to address a condominium of security interests and long-term threats. For the time being, the ROK has no choice but to focus its primary defense efforts on deterring threats from the North. Under the rubric of its "New Defense for the 21st Century," the Ministry of National Defense has emphasized its own version of defense transformation with a greater focus on capabilities-based defense planning.[20] The ROK envisions the creation of an "Advanced Elite Defense" structure based on an "omni-directional" defense posture. To this end, it seeks to implement force-restructuring schemes with a greater emphasis on more maneuverable, flexible forces. That said, South Korea must also set in place force planning measures that will enable it to meet short-term threats (principally from North Korea) and mid- to long-term threats (regional and unconventional)—all within very limiting budgetary constraints. By most indicators, the ROK armed forces have grown into a fairly robust force. Among seventeen nations in the Asia-Pacific region, South Korea's cumulative defense spending from 1998 to 2002 ranked fourth following Japan, China, and India.[21] In terms of troop strength, South Korea's 690,000 force level rank fifth in the Asia-Pacific region. Notwithstanding the importance of quantitative capabilities, however, South Korea has to think seriously about converting its force once unification occurs. For the past five decades, the ROK has devoted almost all of its force planning and defense contingencies to the North Korean threat, with a premium on its central military relationship with the United States. But domestic political change in South Korea, accelerated transformation in North Korea, or a combination of these two phenomena, could expedite South Korea's defense posture and strategies.

As the ROK seeks to exploit the advantages in emerging military technologies and selectively applies lessons learned since the early 1990s (such as the Gulf War, the NATO campaign in Kosovo, the ongoing Afghanistan campaign, and the recently concluded war in Iraq), it has little choice but to downsize its ground forces. More importantly, the ROK must also decide the type of forces it would require when the North Korean threat recedes significantly—in the event of rapid South-North reconciliation and rapprochement—or conversely, if North Korea collapses. In either case, for the first time since 1910, when Korea was colonized by Japan, a unified Korea would have to contend directly with the militaries of China, Russia, and Japan. Some have argued that a unified Korea should assume an equidistant security posture between the United States and China. Others advocate strict neutrality, so that Korea will no longer be entangled in great-power alliances. A minority of defense and security experts even emphasize the need for a unified Korea to possess nuclear weapons and long-range ballistic missiles to act as a counterweight against great-power ambitions and potential intervention on the Korean peninsula.

All of the options noted above, however, would most probably result in heightened security concerns for a unified Korea, despite the proclivity to weigh national sentiments in favor of more dispassionate calculations of Korea's core security interests in the post-unification era. If a unified Korea harbors nuclear weapons or other weapons of mass destruction (WMD), it would only compel the regional powers to pinpoint Korea as a central security threat, and in doing so, serve as a catalyst in spurring a dangerous new arms race in Northeast Asia. A nuclearized, unified Korea would also mean the de facto end of the ROK-US alliance. The prevalence of "nuclear naiveté" in South Korea—the belief in some quarters that a nuclear-armed North Korea should not concern South Korea since North Korea would never use nuclear weapons against fellow Koreans, or the equally fallacious argument that a nuclear Korea would provide a new strategic buffer against the great powers—does not serve its strategic interests in the event of unification. Thus, one of the principal challenges that South Korea must overcome in this transitional period is to distinguish clearly the costs associated with a national security strategy that places a premium on national sentiments, versus more objective assessments of its national interests. A unified Korea should forsake nuclear and other WMD options simply because it would not only downgrade significantly Korea's strategic posture, but would also force Korea to compete militarily, head-on, with the great powers at a time when many of its financial, technical, and manpower resources will be devoted to post-unification reconstruction. In other words, the ROK must set in place security and defense paradigms that would enable it to transition relatively smoothly into the post-unification era. For the time being, the ROK-US alliance offers the best security guarantee and the best option to aid in such a transition.

III. New Alliance Dynamics: Political Change and Strategic Consequences

The election of Roh Moo-hyun as South Korea's president in December 2002 ushered in a bold new era in South Korean politics, and by extension, in the ROK-US alliance. Changes in the alliance began to emerge during the presidency of Kim Dae-jung (1998–2003), when contrasting threat perceptions (particularly after the inauguration of the Bush administration in 2001) vis-à-vis North Korea and attendant policy prescriptions often soured the relationship. Roh's victory initially caused significant consternation within and outside South Korea given his relatively novice views on foreign affairs coupled with only limited contact with the United States. Indeed, when President Roh traveled to Washington for the ROK-US summit on May 14, 2003, it was his first-ever visit to the United States. In his earlier years as a human rights lawyer and a member of the National Assembly in the late 1980s, Roh advocated distinctly unfavorable views on the alliance and at one time, even called for the withdrawal of US forces.

Throughout the campaign in fall 2003, then-candidate Roh emphasized the need to construct a more balanced relationship. In September 2002, he stated that "the Korean-American alliance should be transformed into a horizontal alliance based on a mature partnership in an era of significant change."[22] He also noted that the alliance played a key role in deterring war during the Cold War, in addition to maintaining a security environment that was conducive to South Korea's economic development. But Roh also maintained that "it is time to define a new role for the alliance as a partner that is able to extricate the Cold War from the Korean peninsula."[23] In another speech delivered in October 2002, Roh said that if the revelations of a North Korean nuclear weapons program were true, it was necessary for the North to compromise on inspections and other aspects related to WMD. In return, he emphasized that "it is critical for the United States to desist from pursuing an adversarial posture towards North Korea" and that "once North Korea stops its nuclear weapons efforts and at the same time, the United States drops its adversarial stance towards the North, both sides can then move towards a comprehensive solution." Roh also stressed that "not only South Korea, but Japan can also play the role of a mediator" in order to resolve the nuclear problem between North Korea and the United States.[24]

Roh continued to advocate a new paradigm for the ROK-US as president-elect, although his rhetoric toned down significantly compared to his prepared and impromptu remarks during the campaign. In January 2003, Roh stated that "there is a lot of concern related to the candlelight vigils in the aftermath of the death of two middle-school students...including misconceptions of the candlelight vigils as being anti-American. The key demand of the candlelight demonstrations was to call for a revision of the SOFA [Status of Forces Agreement] with a parallel desire for a more mature ROK-US relationship, but keeping in mind for the continued need for the presence of US forces."[25] In his inauguration address, President Roh reemphasized the need for a strong ROK-US alliance.

> ... This year marks the fiftieth anniversary of the Korea-US alliance. It has made a significant contribution in guaranteeing our security and economic development. The Korean people are deeply grateful for this. We will foster and develop this cherished alliance. We will see to it that the alliance matures into a more reciprocal and equitable relationship. We will also expand relations with other countries, including traditional friends.[26]

Roh's rhetoric vis-à-vis the alliance began to shift in the aftermath of the May 2003 ROK-US summit in Washington, DC. In a joint statement issued after the summit, the two leaders announced that "they will not tolerate nuclear weapons in North Korea" and reiterated "their strong commitment to work for the complete, verifiable, and irreversible elimination of North Korea's nuclear weapons programs through peaceful means based on international cooperation."[27] President Roh mentioned at a press conference that "when I left Korea, I had both concerns and hopes in my mind. Now, after having talked to President Bush, I have gotten rid of all of my concerns, and now I return to Korea with hopes in my mind." During a second meeting that was held in Bangkok during the annual APEC meeting, Bush and Roh issued another joint statement which emphasized that they discussed the North Korean nuclear issue, Iraq reconstruction, and upgrading the ROK-US alliance. Roh's decision to dispatch an additional 3,000 troops to Iraq in addition to the 670 noncombatants already stationed in Iraq, as well as the first round of the Six Party Talks that were held in Beijing in August 2003, all contributed to a successful summit. However, the deployment of additional combat forces to Iraq continued to simmer in South Korea as a major political issue.

As President Roh marked his first anniversary in office in February 2004, significant aspects of alliance discord had been resolved. The most challenging issue facing the government now is how to offset its instinctively nationalistic sentiments vis-à-vis security dependence on the United States coupled with the need to foster a more cooperative relationship with Washington in the midst of the North Korean nuclear quagmire. But as noted below, the rise of new political forces in South Korea and increasingly polarized national security and foreign policy perceptions in South Korea (including the alliance with the United States) may well result in more, not less, turbulence in the years ahead.

IV. Shifting Public Attitudes on the ROK-US Alliance

One of the most interesting and vexing aspects of South Korea's shifting attitude toward the United States resides in parallel shifts in how the public perceives North Korea and the US's related role on issues vital to the future of the Korean peninsula. It is critical to understand that public opinion in South Korea has a tendency to change rapidly and is prone to reflect situation-specific phenomena such as the 2002 incident involving the two schoolgirls. At the same time, even in the midst of sporadic outbreaks of anti-American sentiment, the public at large continues to oppose any abrupt withdrawal of US forces. As a case in point, at the height of the anti-American demonstrations in the weeks preceding the December 17, 2002, presidential election, a *Munwha Daily* poll showed that 85.7 percent of the respondents felt that the upsurge in anti-Americanism was "inevitable in light of the need to revise the unequal nature of the Korean-American relationship" and only 8.7 percent felt that such feelings "were not desirable in the context of the ongoing South-North military confrontation since it could contribute to security instability."[28] According to an April 2003 survey conducted by the *Donga-Ilbo* (South Korea's third-largest daily), a majority of respondents felt that bilateral relations were not good (61.4 percent), but at the very same time 84.8 percent of the respondents answered that the USFK were important (44.2 percent replied "somewhat important" while 40.6 percent answered "very important").[29]

Other survey data bear out these bifurcated views. For instance, a joint US Gallup and Korea Gallup survey conducted in February 2002 and December 2001 respectively showed that 37 percent of Koreans "did not like" the United States, while only 37 percent said they "liked" the United States. Conversely, 58 percent of American respondents said that they "liked" Korea while 31 percent replied that they did not. Compared to an earlier Korea Gallup poll conducted in 1993, the percentage of Koreans who had favorable impressions of the United States fell from 66 percent in 1993 to 37 percent in 2001.[30] Still further, a poll conducted by the Sejong Institute in 1995 and a similar poll conducted by South Korea's MBC station illustrates South Korea's changing attitude toward both North Korea and the United States. In the 1995 poll, 53.7 percent of the respondents felt that North Korea could launch another war, while 36.8 percent felt that there was little or no chance of a North Korean attack. In the 2002 poll, 68 percent of the respondents felt that North Korea should be seen as a partner to pursue peaceful unification, while 30.6 percent replied that North Korea still pursued war aims. Insofar as the US forces are concerned, 41.5 percent of the respondents stated in the 1995 poll that US forces should continue to be deployed while 45.6 percent stated that they should be withdrawn incrementally. Only 5.9 percent called for their immediate withdrawal. In 2002, only 27.6 percent of the respondents said that US forces should continue to be based in South Korea, while 55.6 percent called for an incremental withdrawal, and 16.7 percent called for an immediate withdrawal.[31] In a January 2003 survey (after the election of Roh Moo-hyun), a KBS poll resulted in the following findings.

Poll 1: Alliance with the United States
Question: "The United States is the most important ally."

Agree Very Strongly	16.9%
Agree Strongly	44.4%
Agree Somewhat	25%
Not Really	10.6%
Not At All	3.2%

Source: "Survey on Korean-American Relations," January 16, 2003, KBS.

Poll 2: US Exploitation
Question: "The US exploits South Korea for its own interests."

Agree Very Strongly	48.2%
Agree Strongly	37.1%
Agree Somewhat	11.0%
Not Really	3.3%
Not At All	0.4%

Source: "Survey on Korean-American Relations," January 16, 2003, KBS.

Poll 3: The United States and Korean Security
Question: "The United States is necessary for Korean security."

Agree Very Strongly	22.8%
Agree Strongly	47.2%
Agree Somewhat	20.7%
Not Really	7.2%
Not At All	2.1%

Source: "Survey on Korean-American Relations," January 16, 2003, KBS.

Poll 4: Deployment of US Forces
Question: "US Forces should be deployed for Korean security."

Agree Very Strongly	22.7%
Agree Strongly	30.3%
Agree Somewhat	28.0%
Not Really	13.8%
Not At All	5.2%

Source: "Survey on Korean-American Relations," January 16, 2003, KBS.

Poll 5: US Forces and the Regional Balance of Power
Question: "US Forces are necessary to maintain stability in Northeast Asia since the presence of US forces contributes to the maintenance of a balance of power between Russia, China, and Japan."

Agree Very Strongly	17.5%
Agree Strongly	36.2%
Agree Somewhat	28.7%
Not Really	12.6%
Not At All	5.0%

Source: "Survey on Korean-American Relations," January 16, 2003, KBS.

If this poll can serve as a guide, one of the most interesting results is that anti-Americanism in South Korea is situation-specific. It is also shaped by "national sentiments" that the alliance is "unequal" or that the preponderance of American power is equated with American dominance over South Korea. At the same time, however, a majority of South Koreans—*over 80 percent*—believe in the need for the continued presence of US forces for South Korean *as well as* regional stability. In part, South Korea's anti-American sentiments can also be understood in the context of antiwar sentiments, both in the Korean and other contexts. For example, according to a March 18, 2003, Gallup Korea survey on attitudes toward the US war on Iraq, only 10 percent of South Koreans supported the impending US war against Iraq—down from a 37 percent support rate reported in a February 8, 2003, survey.[32] Public attitudes toward the South Korean government's decision to send an engineering battalion to Iraq were more evenly divided: 48.2 percent of respondents favored the deployment of noncombatant forces to Iraq, while 45.1 percent were opposed and 6.7 percent did not respond.[33]

Public attitudes in South Korea to the alliance reflect two equally strong strands. The first is pent-up frustration and resentment against the United States, owing to the perceived heavy-handedness of US policy, the prevailing public belief that South Korea's SOFA is unfair. The second, opposing view is a realistic, abiding appreciation for the importance of maintaining US forces in South Korea and a close strategic relationship with the United States. As noted above, these mixed attitudes toward the United States and the ROK-US alliance also stem from an increasingly bifurcated view of North Korea.

Most of the South Korean public continue to believe that North Korea cannot be trusted, yet they do not perceive North Korea as a central threat to the ROK. In a late March 2003 poll, the percentage of respondents who answered that they did not like the United States (29.5 percent) slightly outweighed those who said they did not like North Korea (29.1 percent). Equally alarming was the fact that the same percentage of respondents (23 percent) answered that they liked the United States *and* North Korea, while 46 percent were neutral in their feelings toward the United States and 45.9 percent were neutral in their feelings toward North Korea.[34]

A very wide generation gap is evident in virtually all polls, including this one, since 47.3 percent of respondents who said they did not like the United States were in their twenties, while 45 percent of those who answered that they liked the United States were in their fifties or above. At the same time, 24.8 percent of respondents who said they liked North Korea were in their twenties, while 17.7 percent of those in the fifties-and-over group answered that they liked North Korea. Of those respondents who said they did not like North Korea, 48.3 percent were in their fifties or above. In a subsequent poll taken in September 2003, however, 42 percent of respondents said they had a more favorable impression of North Korea, compared to 46.1 percent for the United States, or a slight decrease from the earlier poll.[35]

Since the beginning of the Roh presidency, public attitude toward the United States, the USFK, and the alliance has been affected by more objective perceptions of the United States, which relate largely to North Korea's continuing nuclear threats and reduced volatility in postwar Iraq. For the most part, however, deep feelings of ambiguity remain. The following polls, conducted in September 24, 2003 by Gallup Korea, illustrate some of these changes. For example, attitudes toward the USFK have improved slightly over the past year. Only 4.5 percent of respondents noted in September 2003 that the USFK should withdraw immediately, although 40.6 percent said that they should withdraw incrementally. Conversely, a very slight majority of 50.5 percent responded that the USFK should remain for a significant period of time, or continue to be deployed.

Poll 6: US Forces Korea
Question: "What are your feelings about the US Forces Korea?"

Withdraw immediately	4.5%
Incrementally withdraw	40.6%
Should be deployed for a significant period	31.2%
Continue to be deployed	19.3%
Don't know	4.3%

Source: Gallup Korea, September 24, 2003.

Poll 7: Feelings toward the US and North Korea
Question: "Between the United States and North Korea, toward which country do you have a more positive feeling?"

Much more toward the United States	14.7%
A bit more toward the United States	31.4%
Combined	**46.1%**
A bit more toward North Korea	28.4%
Much more toward North Korea	11.8%
Combined	**40.2%**

Source: Gallup Korea, September 24, 2003.

Poll 8: George W. Bush and Kim Jong-il
Question: "Between President George W. Bush and Chairman Kim Jong-il, which leader do you think is more threatening to peace in Korea?"

Kim Jong-il	42.1%
George W. Bush	38.0%
Don't know	19.9%

Source: Gallup Korea, September 24, 2003.

Poll 9: Approval of Roh Moo-hyun
Question: "Are you satisfied with the performance of President Roh Moo-hyun? Or not?"

Doing well	28.6%
Doing poorly	52.9%
Average	11.7%
Don't know	6.9%

Source: Gallup Korea, September 20, 2003.

While there was a slight improvement in public perception toward the United States and the role of the USFK between fall 2002 (at the height of anti-American demonstrations) and the end of 2003, it is startling to note that nearly 38 percent of South Koreans perceive President Bush as more threatening to peace on the peninsula, compared to 42.1 percent for Kim Jong-il. If the ongoing second North Korean nuclear crisis is resolved peacefully through the Six-Party Talks or parallel discussions between Washington and Pyongyang, South Korean public attitudes toward North Korea and Kim Jong-il could improve significantly. In such an instance, however, there is a strong possibility that positive attitudes toward the United States, and more importantly, toward the continuing need to maintain the USFK, could be diluted, perhaps even significantly.

In the future, it appears that the ideological and generational divide in South Korea will continue to pose serious challenges to building a national consensus on North Korean policy as well as ROK policy toward the United States. The key litmus test is likely to come if North Korea crosses the red line. For example, if Pyongyang refuses ultimately to accept International Atomic Energy Agency (IAEA) inspections and proceeds with its nuclear weapons program, test fires another long-range Taepodong-1 missile (as it did in August 1998), or conducts an underground nuclear test, it will be in serious breach of previous IAEA resolutions, the nuclear Non-Proliferation Treaty (NPT), the self-imposed moratorium on long-range missile tests, and the above-mentioned 1992 South-North Joint Denuclearization Declaration of the Korean Peninsula. In such an instance, South Korea will be forced to deal with two issues: whether it will continue to oppose a nuclearized North Korea, and the extent to which it will coordinate its policy with the United States, particularly in the event that North Korea crosses the red line. To be sure, the Bush administration is also in the midst of an intense debate on what to do with North Korea if Pyongyang ultimately refuses to give up its nuclear weapons program.

Before sanctions could be enacted against North Korea, the UN Security Council would have to vet the nuclear issue. Thus far, however, the council has not discussed sanctions in the context of the North Korean nuclear problem because China and Russia continue to oppose them. While negotiations are likely to intensify and Seoul hopes to increase its leverage in the multilateral talks, the key issue is how far the United States and South Korea will be able to formulate a joint roadmap. Notwithstanding South Korean ambivalence, the Bush administration also faces a gap between rhetoric and implementable policy choices. Assistant Secretary of State James Kelly testified before the US House International Relations Committee in February 2003 that US policy toward North Korea is based on four major pillars. First, the United States remains critically concerned about North Korea's plutonium, as well as its highly enriched uranium weapons program, since both programs violate the Agreed Framework, the NPT, the IAEA safeguards agreement, and the Joint South-North Declaration on the Denuclearization of the Korean Peninsula. Second, despite Pyongyang's rhetoric, the nuclear program is not "just a matter between the DPRK and the United States," since it impacts international security and the global nonproliferation regime. Third, in addition to its nuclear weapons program, North Korea has seriously to address its human rights problem, issues related to its appearance on the US State Department's list of states sponsoring terrorism, the proliferation of missiles and missile-related technology, and its conventional force configuration. Fourth, the United States is not going to reward North Korea for living up to its international obligations, although the United States remains "prepared to pursue a comprehensive dialogue about a fundamentally different relationship with that country, once it eliminates its nuclear weapons program in a verifiable and irreversible manner and comes into compliance with its international obligations."[36]

Kelly's benchmarks on the Bush administration's policy toward North Korea have remained relatively unchanged. In the aftermath of Libya's surprise announcement that it was ridding itself of WMD, some have alluded to the possibility of a similar policy decision by North Korea. For example, Deputy Secretary of State Richard Armitage stated in an interview in December 2003 that if North Korea followed Libya's example, it "would very rapidly find herself integrated into the vibrant community of East Asia." He added that "I don't think she is going to do that, but it would be wonderful."[37]

How South Korea reconfigures its relationship with the United States is likely to hinge significantly on a combination of four key issues: (1) whether the United States and South Korea will be able to convince North Korea to give up its WMD capabilities (including its nuclear weapons programs) in return for some type of a security guarantee and matching political and economic incentives; (2) the ROK government's shaping of the public debate over a range of security issues including its push for a more self-reliant defense posture while maintaining the ROK-US alliance; (3) continued politicization and exploitation of South Korea's relationship with the United States by civic groups, NGOs, and the media; and (4) the hold on power of a new generation of political leaders with growing disregard for the comprehensive strategic benefits flowing from a robust ROK-US alliance.

In conclusion, although it may be tempting for South Korea to contemplate a strategic future that includes a significantly reduced security dependence on the United States, such a move would entail major costs for the ROK or even a unified Korea under the auspices of the ROK. Beyond the financial, technical, and intelligence burdens that would be placed on South Korea if it chose to downgrade—however incrementally—its alliance with the United States, the most important cost would lie in foreclosing the critical support the United States would most likely play in fostering Korean unification. As the case of the former West Germany aptly illustrated in the period leading up to unification in 1990, it was Bonn's critical alliance with Washington that crystallized and finalized German unification, rather than West Germany's *Ostpolitik* or its growing ties with the former Soviet Union. Notwithstanding South Korea's burgeoning economic relationship with China or the latent promises of Seoul's Sunshine policy, South Korea must remember to balance the search for greater autonomy with a strong dose of realism as it enters the unification tunnel.

NOTES

[1] In June 1949, US forces that were stationed in South Korea during the period of US military occupation from 1945 to 1948 were withdrawn except for five hundred military advisors based on assessments made by the US Joint Chiefs of Staff. With the outbreak of the Korean War on June 25, 1950, however, President Truman decided to dispatch US forces to South Korea, resulting in a sharp policy reversal. The ROK-US Treaty of Mutual Defense was signed on October 1, 1953.

[2] Based on personal discussions with high-level US officials in July and December 2002. A Bush administration official commented in December 2002 prior to the South Korean presidential election that "whoever emerges as the next president [of South Korea], changes in the status of US forces are inevitable. If the South Korean government continues to assert that there really is no serious military threat from the North but the United States continues to advocate the opposite, we are willing to support the continuing 'Koreanization' of Korean defense but it also means that South Korea has to bear the consequences."

[3] During the course of trilateral discussions among the United States, China, and North Korea in Beijing from April 22 to 24, 2003, US Assistant Secretary of State James A. Kelly was apparently told by Deputy Director General Li Gun of the North Korean foreign ministry that "we already have a [nuclear] bomb" and "now what are you going to do about it?" See "North Korea Tells US It Has Bomb," *Financial Times*, April 25, 2003. Subsequent press reports, however, indicated that North Korea proposed a comprehensive deal with the United States, including a promise to accept international inspections and to discard its nuclear program if Washington restarts the shipment of oil and agrees to safeguard North Korea's security. A coordinated response from Seoul, Washington, and Tokyo, however, is unlikely to crystallize until the ROK-US summit slated for mid-May and parallel trilateral consultations have taken place.

[4] During his February 25, 2003 inauguration speech, President Roh stated that "North Korea's nuclear development can never be condoned. Pyongyang must abandon nuclear development. ... It is up to Pyongyang whether to go ahead and obtain nuclear weapons or to get guarantees for the security of its regime and international economic support." "President Roh Moo Hyun's Inauguration Address," Yonhap News Agency, February 25, 2003. Despite the president's strong warnings, which have since been reiterated after the

April trilateral meeting in Beijing, Seoul has continued to stress that dialogue is the best means to resolve the North Korean nuclear crisis.

[5] According to an Australian press report, a group of North Korean military and scientific elites, including top nuclear specialists, has defected to the United States since October 2002. Some twenty senior North Korean officials apparently defected under the codename of "Operation Weasel" through a network of NGOs and individuals spanning eleven countries. US officials have neither confirmed nor denied high-level North Korean defections. Martin Chulov and Cameron Stewart, "N. Korean Scientists Defect," *The Australian*, April 19, 2003.

[6] South Korean foreign minister Yoon Young Kwan stated on February 27, 2003, that "while we will continue to strengthen our alliance with the United States, our closest ally, we also seek to develop this relationship into a more balanced and mature one." See "Foreign Minister's Inauguration Speech," Ministry of Foreign Affairs and Trade, Office of Press Affairs, February 28, 2003.

[7] During the presidential campaign in fall 2002, then-candidate Roh stated on several occasions that he would not "kowtow" to the United States and that if necessary, South Korea should mediate between the United States and North Korea to resolve the North Korean nuclear issue. Coming on the heels of unprecedented anti-American demonstrations throughout the period preceding the December 12 election, candidate Roh accused his conservative opponent, Lee Hoi Chang, of being a "war-prone" candidate and asserted that if Lee was elected, South Korea would be enmeshed in an extremely serious crisis. He stated on December 15 that the election was about "war or peace" and that if Lee was chosen, the threat of war would be heightened on the Korean peninsula. "A New Seoul and a Peaceful Korean Peninsula," Office of the President, Republic of Korea, March 10, 2003, *http://www.president.go.kr/warp/app/pre_speech*.

[8] "Rumsfeld: US May Cut South Korea Forces," February 13, 2003, CNN: *http://cnn.worldnews.com*. See also "Secretary Rumsfeld Interview with the Associated Press," April 24, 2003, *http://www.defenselink.mil/transcripts*.

[9] "Powell Cites Asian Support for US Proposal on North Korea," Office of International Information Programs, US Department of State, February 25, 2003, *http://usinfo.state.gov*.

[10] "Korea, US to Resume Future of Alliance Talks," April 19, 2003, Ministry of National Defense, Office of Press Affairs.

[11] Comments made by a senior US official during a closed conference entitled "Managing Weapons of Mass Destruction and US-ROK-Japan Cooperation," co-sponsored by the Institute for Foreign Policy Analysis and Yonsei University on April 11, 2003.

[12] "Two-Phase Relocation Plan Reaffirmed," *News Release*, Seoul, UNC/CFC/USFK, July 24, 2003.

[13] "Rumsfeld Says US Troops Adjustments Will Benefit South Korea," *Washington File*, November 17, 2003, *http://usembassy.state.gov/seoul/wwwh41bd.html*

[14] The term "unification tunnel" refers to the process whereby the inter-Korean balance or the status quo begins to shift such that it could accelerate the pace of South-North unification. How South Korea emerges from the unification tunnel remains unknown. But, contrary to the prevailing school of thought in South Korea, the unification process is likely to result in pockets of volatility, particularly if unification occurs in the aftermath of a North Korean collapse or implosion. In such an instance, the military posture of South Korea, or a unified Korea, could face an abrupt transition into the post-unification era that would result in significant changes in the force structure, command arrangements within the US-ROK Combined Forces Command (CFC), key weapons procurement priorities, and accompanying doctrines and strategies.

[15] If the UNSC considers any type of economic sanctions against North Korea, the key question is whether China and Russia would support them. Assuming that ongoing

diplomatic measures ultimately fail to persuade North Korea to discard its nuclear weapons program, Beijing and Moscow are still unlikely to support economic sanctions against North Korea unless Pyongyang crosses the red line—either by conducting an underground nuclear test, test-firing its long-range Taepodong-1 missile, or a simultaneous move. Under these conditions, Beijing would be hard pressed not to support UNSC sanctions.

[16] In essence, the Nixon Doctrine was an effort to expedite a US disengagement from South Vietnam by accentuating the need for Asian states to assume primary responsibility for their defense. On July 25, 1969, President Nixon announced in Guam that (1) the United States will keep all of its treaty commitments; (2) that the United States will provide a shield if a nuclear power threatens the freedom of a nation allied with the United States or of a nation whose survival the United States deems vital to its own security; and (3) in cases involving other types of aggression, the United States will furnish military and economic assistance when requested in accordance with existing treaty commitments. But Nixon added that "we shall look to the nation directly threatened to assume the primary responsibility of providing manpower for its defense."

[17] See "Korean Response to President Carter's Troop Withdrawal Moratorium," February 26, 1979. Declassified US State Department Document. For an engaging overview of the tense period in South Korea following President Park Chung Hee's assassination in October 1979, one of the worst periods in ROK-US relations, see John A. Wickham, Jr., *Korea on the Brink* (Washington, DC: Brassey's, September 2000), especially the preface and chapter two, "Aftermath of the Assassination."

[18] "Japan-US Joint Declaration on Security: Alliance for the 21st Century," The Ministry of Foreign Affairs of Japan, April 17, 1996, *http://www.mofa.go.jp/region/n-america/us/security/security/html.*

[19] "The Washington Declaration," NATO Press Release NAC-S(99)63, April 23, 1999, *http://www.nato.int/docu/pr/1999/p99-063e.htm.*

[20] New Defense for the 21st Century (Seoul: Ministry of National Defense, 2001), *http://www.mnd.go.kr/english/html02/2001/2-1-1.htm.*

[21] Anthony H. Cordesman, "Military Expenditures and Arms Transfers in Asia," (Washington, DC: Center for Strategic and International Studies, February 2002), p. 6.

[22] "Speech before the Asia-Europe Press Forum," September 12, 2002, Office of the President, Republic of Korea, *http://www.president.go.kr/warp/app/pre_speech.*

[23] "Speech before the Asia-Europe Press Forum," September 12, 2002.

[24] "Speech before the Peace Forum," September 24, 2002, Office of the President, Republic of Korea, *http://www.president.go.kr/warp/app/pre_speech.*

[25] "Speech before the American Chamber of Commerce and the EU Chamber of Commerce in Korea," January 17, 2003, Office of the President, Republic of Korea, *http://www.president.go.kr/warp/app/pre_speech.*

[26] "President Roh Moo Hyun's Inauguration Speech," February 25, 2003, Press Release, Office of the President, Republic of Korea.

[27] "Joint Statement Between the United States of America and the Republic of Korea: Common Values, Principles, and Strategy," The White House, Office of the Press Secretary, May 14, 2003, *http://www.whitehouse.gov/news/releases/2003/05/print/20030514-1.*

[28] "85.7% of Respondents Say That Anti-Americanism Is Not a Surprise," *Munwha Ilbo,* December 12, 2002.

[29] *Donga-Ilbo,* April 1, 2003, *http://www.donga.com/fbn/news.*

[30] "Favorable Ratings of Korean and Americans," *Chosun Ilbo,* March 3, 2002, *http://www.chosun.com/bin/printNews.*

[31] "Big Change in Public Attitudes According to Opinion Poll," August 15, 2002, *http://www.voiceofpeople.org/new/nws_view.html.*

[32] "Perceptions on the Iraqi Conflict," *Chosun Ilbo,* March 19, 2003, *http://www.chosun.com/bin/printNews.*

[33] *Donga-Ilbo*, April 1, 2003, *http://www.donga.com/fbn/news.*

[34] "83rd Anniversary Opinion Poll," *Donga Ilbo*, April 1, 2003, *http://www.dong.com/fbin/news.*

[35] "83rd Anniversary Opinion Poll," *Donga Ilbo*, April 1, 2003.

[36] "James A. Kelly, Assistant Secretary of State for East Asian and Pacific Affairs, Remarks to House International Relations Committee," Washington, DC, February 13, 2003, *http://www.state.gove/p/eap/rls/rm/2003/17754pf.htm.*

[37] "Armitage Urges North Korea Follow Example of Libya on WMD," December 24, 2003, *http://usinfo.state.gov/utils/printpage.html.*

CHINA

US-China Security Relations and America's Pacific Alliances in the Post–9/11 Era

David M. Lampton

What have been the critical changes in Asia's security environment since 9/11? What opportunities and challenges do these developments present for continued and broadened Sino-American security cooperation? What implications does Sino-American security cooperation have for America's Asian partners, particularly Japan and the Republic of Korea? And, what do these developments imply for future American policy?

There have been six post–9/11 alterations in the regional and global security environments most significant for both Sino-American security cooperation and America's alliances with Japan and South Korea:

• China's economic and diplomatic clout in Asia has dramatically increased since 1997, in the context of a Washington preoccupied elsewhere and a less economically potent Japan. Nonetheless, American preeminence in Asia remains the central geopolitical fact, a circumstance reflected in the PRC's priority on maintaining productive relations with Washington.

• North Korean nuclear weapons programs have fostered Sino-American cooperation to a degree few would have predicted in November 2002, simultaneously strengthened US cooperation with Japan, and have had the opposite effect with respect to Seoul-Washington ties.

• Japan gradually is assuming more responsibility for its own defense and beginning to provide limited "global, public security goods," a development that is occurring with American blessings and Chinese wariness. Simultaneously, Japan is developing ever-deeper economic ties with the PRC and Beijing is not making an issue of Tokyo's changing security role, though it is worried. The US-Japan alliance is strong, in part as a hedge against a rising China, and Chinese leaders have partially conceded that the US-Japan alliance has given Beijing a "free ride"[1] on security. The net is that China seems reconciled to a more "normal" Japan and the US-Japan security alliance as long as neither is aimed at promoting the separation of Taiwan or containing China, concerns that never will be fully assuaged. Indeed, both Washington and Tokyo view this ambiguity as part of the structure of deterrence vis-à-vis an attack on Taiwan.

• South Korean–Chinese economic (and to a lesser extent security) relations have grown with remarkable speed since the two nations established diplomatic ties in 1992. Today, Beijing and Seoul often have been closer on inter–Korean peninsula issues than Washington and Seoul. The ROK-US alliance relationship is troubled, raising the issue of its long-term prospects.

• The war on terror (here to include the war in Iraq and counterproliferation policy) has fostered growing and important Sino-American cooperation. While the Japanese wish to see peaceful and workmanlike US-China relations, they also fear an overly zealous strategic embrace of Beijing by Washington as the PRC cooperates in the war on terror. The fear is that if Washington embraces China intimately as a "strategic partner" some important Japanese interests might be affected.[2]

• With respect to Taiwan, the core friction in US-China relations since 1950, micro-nationalism and competitive electoral politics have energized Taipei's increasing efforts to assert autonomy. This threatens Beijing's, Washington's, and Tokyo's interests. For now, this has produced Sino-American cooperation and generated growing friction between Washington and Taipei. American allies and friends are increasingly allergic to a Taiwan Strait conflict and Tokyo and Paris urged restraint on Taipei in the run up to the March 2004 presidential election, as did President Bush on December 9, 2003.

For the most part, these developments have fostered Sino-American security cooperation and strengthened bilateral relations. This cooperation has facilitated Washington downplaying other US-China frictions (e.g., economic and trade and human rights concerns) and enabled Washington to keep its focus on the Middle East, the war on terror, and proliferation threats. For its part, Beijing wishes to avoid external entanglements so it can stay focused on its daunting domestic challenges and continue to enlarge its comprehensive national power over the next two decades or more.

Looking ahead, however, there will be challenges to Sino-American security cooperation and to the post–World War II security structures that the United States did so much to construct. Most fundamentally, China is translating its economic muscle into political clout throughout Asia and beyond; Washington has been relatively distracted[3] since 9/11 and therefore needs to devote far more effort to being economically and diplomatically effective throughout Asia. Paralleling the strains that have developed in NATO after the Cold War, the aforementioned developments have weakened the ROK-US alliance and (though US-Japan relations currently are in the best shape in many years) there are cautions for the future of Washington's alliance with Tokyo as well. The biggest caution is that as the United States bases much of its post–9/11 security behavior on "coalitions of the willing," it inadvertently calls into question the sanctity and mutuality of alliances.

With respect to the US-ROK security alliance, one should be troubled by the attitudes that South Koreans reportedly have toward America and its post–9/11 foreign policy priorities. The Pew Research Center for the People & the Press[4] has found that South Koreans see North Korea as significantly less threatening to "regional stability" than Americans perceive it to be; they view Americans less favorably than many other surveyed US allies do; and they support the war on terror less than any other American ally, with the level of popular support in the ROK less than one-half the level found in Germany, which was only 60 percent in 2003. The chapters by Chung Min Lee and William Drennan in this volume provide additional data in this regard.

Turning to Sino-American cooperation on the North Korean nuclear issue, while Pyongyang's programs have thus far been a binding force since late 2002, future potential challenges to continued US-China cooperation are evident. Though neither Washington nor Beijing desires a nuclear-armed (much less proliferating) Pyongyang, it remains unclear whether or not either capital is willing to do what may be necessary to prevent (or reverse what may already be) the nuclearization of North Korea. As Alexander George pointed out years ago in his classic *The Limits of Coercive Diplomacy*, it takes much less to induce a state to stop doing something (or to not initiate an action in the first instance) than to undo something already achieved.[5] In the event that negotiations with North Korea fail, we can expect Washington to push for more vigorous measures, either to eliminate Pyongyang's programs or to limit the negative consequences of them. If Washington were to push for more muscular measures against Pyongyang under anything like current circumstances, this probably would generate conflict between Washington and Beijing, as well as between Washington and Seoul. Effects on US-Japan relations are less certain, but Beijing's moderating role has, as Kurt Campbell has noted in his contribution to this volume, produced a situation in "which other countries are beginning to look at China as a stabilizing actor in Asia."[6]

And a final challenge to continued US-China security cooperation is Taiwan's current drift toward autonomy, against the backdrop of China's growing power, the reluctance of US allies to become entangled in this issue, and Taipei's resistance to US cautions directed toward President Chen Shui-bian in 2003-early 2004. All this spells trouble for the future if some stabilizing combination of changes in Beijing, Taipei, and Washington is not forthcoming. We shall look at each of these four issues below, concluding with suggestions for US policy.

Chinese Power in Asia and Beijing's New Look

It may sound odd to say, but China has embraced economic and security policies that America has advocated throughout the post–World War II era—multilateral forums, free-trade agreements, and military confidence-building measures, not the least notable being a recent Sino-Indian joint maritime operation,[7] as well as military exercises with Pakistan and Central Asian states. Beijing's policies contrast with a Washington that is distracted, more inclined toward unilateral or bilateral than multilateral security options, skeptical of confidence-building measures, more bilateral in its trade policies, and trying to link every dimension of policy to the war on terror. China is emphasizing soft power, cooperation, and mutual economic benefit as America is emphasizing hard power in a region that prefers at least the illusion of preferences now associated with Beijing. Knowing that its own rapid rise could cause a backlash among neighbors, Beijing seeks to reassure them. Over the longer term most nations on China's periphery wish to foster a balance between American and Chinese power.

A decade or so ago it was at least credible to speak of an Asian economic structure of "flying geese" with Japan as the head of the formation and other regional economies arraying themselves around Japan. Today, there is an emerging regional economic configuration in which most Asian economies are becoming suppliers to China. These economies see their principal growth opportunities in the rapidly expanding PRC domestic market and in China's use of those suppliers' intermediate goods in its own production of exports for North America and Europe. China is becoming a principal export destination for nations and economies in East, Northeast, and Southeast Asia, with large jumps in their export percentages going to China since 1996. For example, in 2000 China took about 16 percent of Australia's exports (up from 9 percent in 1994); about 14 percent of Singapore's exports in 2001 (up from about 2–3 percent in 1997); and about 18 percent of ROK exports in 2001 (up from about 8 percent in 1996). In 2002, China replaced the United States as the largest customer of Taiwan and South Korea,[8] Sino-Russian trade surpassed Russian-US trade in 2003,[9] and in 2002 China became the largest exporter to Japan.[10] As the economist Pieter Bottelier notes, "China's share of exports [of East Asia, minus Japan] to NAFTA and the EU increased dramatically from 25 to 45 percent [from 1985 to 2001].[11] This phenomenon also is seen in the fact that China's share of total US merchandise imports rose to about 11 percent in 2002, about quadruple the 1990 percentage. Meanwhile, the rest of Asia's share of total US merchandise imports fell from about 17 percent in 1990 to about 13 percent in 2002.[12]

While inward foreign direct investment (FDI) to the United States, the world, and ASEAN has been declining in recent years, inward FDI to China has been rising (though a considerable fraction of this is "round-tripping" money from the PRC itself, looking for the benefits accorded "foreign" capital).[13] While China's magnetic pull on FDI alarms much of Asia, another fact does not—China is a growing foreign direct investor in the region, though starting from a low base. About 13 percent of PRC (non-trading) FDI[14] goes to ASEAN and 16 percent to Asia more broadly (including ASEAN), with the International Monetary Fund (IMF) estimating a cumulative total Chinese FDI (worldwide, 1979–2001) of $34.69 billion. These figures considerably understate China's FDI because of unrecorded capital flows (flight) from the mainland over a long period (though this has reversed recently). "The rapid development of outward FDI reflects not only China's increasing integration with the global economy but also its continuing need to expand overseas to secure natural resources (e.g., Australia and Canada) and advanced technology (e.g., the US)."[15]

Beijing has been quick to perceive the power that derives from its growing economy and has embraced a number of policies that, not long ago, would have been associated with Washington. The first hint of this approach came with the 1997 announcement of China's New Security Concept and with the subsequent Asian financial crisis (1997–1998) when Beijing decided against devaluing the Chinese dollar (RMB or yuan), winning gratitude throughout East and Southeast Asia. Moreover, as distinct from Washington, Beijing became proactive by contributing stabilization funds to Thailand and Indonesia via the IMF.[16] Thereafter, in November 2000 in Singapore, then premier Zhu Rongji proposed an ASEAN Free Trade Zone, an initiative finally agreed to in Phnom Penh in late 2002.[17] During his October 2003 trip to Southeast Asia, Premier Wen Jiabao emphasized Beijing's willingness to drop its barriers on some Southeast Asian agricultural exports (e.g., Thailand and China signed an agreement to end tariffs on 188 kinds of fruits and vegetables in June 2003[18]) ahead of schedule—the "early harvest" initiative.

Not only is Beijing seizing the opportunities afforded by economic integration to its south, it also is pursuing similar policies in Northeast Asia. At the Bali Meeting in October 2003, Premier Wen Jiabao proposed the establishment of a "Tripartite Committee" of China, South Korea, and Japan to study a Free Trade Area among the three and cooperation between that group and ASEAN.[19] A recent survey in the three countries indicated that the concept had wide appeal among enterprises in each society.[20]

By way of contrast, as Beijing is pushing free-trade areas around its periphery, in 2003–early 2004 Washington had a two-pronged trade policy. One prong was targeted protectionism against politically sensitive imports during the election season. The other was bilateral free-trade arrangements such as those with Singapore and under negotiation with Australia.

All this means that America's historic friends in the region have increasing interests with Beijing (and vice versa) in terms of supply and investment relationships. Nowhere has this growing interdependence been more evident than in the Sino–South Korean relationship. Seoul has become a major investor in China (US$6.8 billion in 2002, making the ROK the fourth largest FDI supplier to China after Hong Kong, Taiwan, and the United States)[21] and, as noted above, the PRC has become the number one export market for Seoul. In 2002, Seoul's trade with the mainland accounted for 13.1 percent of the ROK's total global trade.[22]

Consequently, South Korea is developing interests with the PRC and sometimes joins Beijing in resisting US policy preferences—most notably the use of force on the peninsula. At the same time that one recognizes the increasing attraction of China for South Koreans, however, one also must acknowledge the mutual anxieties lying near the surface. Chinese investment now is going into the ROK (South Koreans had seen China as a market, not an investor that would gain domestic clout) and there are unresolved territorial issues that Koreans and Chinese alike remember.[23]

Ironically, the United States for more than fifty years advanced the proposition that free trade and interdependence would contribute to a more stable framework in the region and Beijing's integration into that structure would constrain the PRC. This has been true to a remarkable extent. At the same time, however, this development also constrains Washington by weakening the perceived dependence that many Asian societies have on America and by limiting the degree to which Washington can exert economic pressure on Beijing without damaging the interests of friends and allies. Moreover, China's economic integration into the region has produced attitudinal shifts. Every year since 1996, public opinion surveys in South Korea have shown a popular preference for China over the United States.[24] William Watts reported in 2002 that 86 percent of South Koreans expected closer relations with China in the future.[25] Adding this dynamic to the other tensions in US-ROK relations, it is hard to predict that the troubled alliance will soon become less so. Moreover, were Washington to employ its military assets based in Korea beyond the peninsula for purposes with which China and/or the South Korean populace disagreed, this would further strain the alliance.

Currently, with Japanese forces cooperating in Afghanistan and Iraq, the US-Japan alliance appears stronger than it has been in a long time. Nonetheless, there are corrosive forces at work, not the least Japanese desires to see the United States operate more multilaterally and use more diplomacy. Moreover, there is disquiet with the notion of "coalitions of the willing," marriages of convenience arranged by Washington that degrade alliances and international institutions.

On the other hand, there are centrifugal forces in Sino-Japanese relations that strengthen the US-Japan alliance. Among those are Japan's efforts to become a more "normal" country in defense terms (worrying Beijing) and Tokyo's wariness of growing Chinese power. Consequently, it is an open question whether or not the rise of China's power will constitute a glue for the US-Japan security pact or, on the contrary, China's growing economy will prove to be an aphrodisiac for Japan, gradually ripping asunder the alliance.

For its part, Beijing apparently expects the US-Japan alliance gradually to weaken as Tokyo seeks accommodation with China. As Yang Bojiang at the China Institute of Contemporary International Relations put it:

Strategically, it [Japan] undoubtedly balances the bulwark of [its] US ally against Chinese influence. But its [Japan's] high degree of economic internationalization, past decade of depression, the extensive security demand[s] in the Asia-Pacific region, and the emergence of China—all this stimulates it to expand cooperation with China and other nations so as to keep diplomatic equilibrium. Tokyo cannot possibly turn to the single banyan tree of America for its security strategy. For all its mental complexities before and varied reactions to the emergence of China, Tokyo still needs cooperation with Beijing in security strategy and even more so in political and economic fields.[26]

The North Korean Nuclear Programs and Their Implications

Since Pyongyang's apparent[27] October 2002 declaration that it had a covert uranium enrichment program in violation of the 1994 Agreed Framework and other sovereign undertakings, its subsequent withdrawal from the Non-Proliferation Treaty, and the North's other assorted declarations since, US-China cooperation to denuclearize the Korean peninsula has been growing. This cooperation has far exceeded the expectations of most Americans who assessed the prospects for such joint efforts in late 2002. The effect of this cooperation has been to considerably improve US-China bilateral relations. As Secretary of State Colin Powell said at the Bush Library in Texas on November 5, 2003, "This is just illustrative of the kind of leadership role that China is playing regionally and on the world stage in cooperation with us, not in competition with us."[28] Using both carrots (aid and the prospect of non-isolation) and sticks (oil interruptions and threats that China would not come to the North's aid if a war were to break out) in its dealings with Pyongyang, Beijing has pushed Kim Jong-il to diplomatic tables, though with few results thus far. In late 2003, Chinese Vice Foreign Minister Wang Yi was in Pyongyang, winning its agreement to come to a second round of Six-Party Talks early in 2004.[29]

By pursuing a strategy in which negotiations are front and center, and in which regime change in North Korea figures not at all, Beijing has been much closer to the policy preferences of Seoul (and probably Japan) than have the more vocal and muscular among US policymakers. Beijing has increased credibility in Washington (by pushing Pyongyang to the negotiating table in a multilateral context) and in Seoul (and to a lesser extent Tokyo) by pursuing a policy of negotiation instead of regime change and military threat. As in the economic area, there is symmetry of interest between Beijing and Seoul that may contribute to a weakening of the traditional US-ROK relationship.

In the happy event that an agreement in principle with Pyongyang can be reached concerning the verifiable elimination of its nuclear programs, this still would leave a divisive issue on the table, in terms of not only US-China relations but also US-ROK ties. This issue is verification. It is likely that Washington's standards for "adequate" verification will be more rigorous than Beijing's or Seoul's.

If one turns from the relatively happy possibility of "successful" negotiations over the North Korean nuclear programs to negotiations "failing," then continued close Sino-American cooperation ought not be assumed. Beijing consistently has said that it does "not wish to see" a nuclearized North Korea and that its objectives are *both* a stable North Korea and a non-nuclear North Korea. This formulation has left unclear which of these two objectives Beijing would choose, if forced to do so. My hunch is that Beijing would choose stability: China fears a US application of coercive power against the North and precipitous regime collapse there more than it dreads a nuclear Pyongyang. Seoul joins Beijing in this preference, however unpalatable.

While it is unclear how Washington actually could conduct a military option against North Korea with the two contiguous land powers opposed (one of which is a US ally that would pay a steep price), the results of a split between Washington on the one hand and Beijing and Seoul on the other could rupture the US-ROK alliance. Even if Washington did not employ military force against the North, it probably would search for muscular ways to "quarantine" North Korea; Beijing and Seoul likely would resist this course too. This would further strengthen Seoul's ties with Beijing at Washington's expense.

Further, we need to consider the possibility that Washington simply accepts North Korea (either explicitly or implicitly) as a nuclear power, declared or otherwise. Were this to happen, Seoul might increasingly turn to Beijing as a more useful partner in constraining Pyongyang than Washington. For its part, Japan might rethink the wisdom of relying exclusively on the US nuclear umbrella. Tokyo might consider it prudent to move to the threshold of nuclear capability or something approaching Israel's current status, both of which would spur further vertical and horizontal proliferation in the region. And finally, the United States must ask itself: If US troops leave South Korea for whatever reason, how long will the Japanese people be willing to provide the last large, permanent outpost for those US troops that remain in the region, particularly if to do so makes Japan a possible target for North Korea?

Whether negotiations with North Korea succeed or not, Beijing is thinking about whether or not the "Six-Party" framework (North and South Korea, China, Russia, Japan, and the United States) might constitute a promising future multilateral security structure for Northeast Asia. Such a structure could be seen as either a supplement to or a substitute for the hub-and-spokes alliance system in the region today.

Concisely, as the United States is distracted, as its policy preferences on the Korean peninsula differ somewhat from those of North Korea's neighbors, and as the common interests between the PRC and its neighbors grow, it is not axiomatic that the United States' bilateral alliances with the ROK and Japan will remain unchanged.

The War on Terror, the War in Iraq, and Counterproliferation Policy

With respect to the war on terror, Sino-American cooperation has been multidimensional and positive:

• The PRC was extremely helpful in the initial stages of the war in Afghanistan by encouraging Pakistani president Musharraf to cooperate with Washington, by sealing off its own borders to Al Qaeda and Taliban forces, and by supporting (or abstaining on) key UN resolutions since 9/11.[30]

• While Beijing has been anxious about the growing American military footprint in Central Asia, it has created no obstacles to US military operations there.

• With respect to the Iraq war, Beijing voted for the key UN resolution (1441 of November 2002) and did not join Russia, France, and Germany in actively opposing the US invasion. Beijing acquiesced because its interests in Iraq were not great, it hoped to benefit from post-US victory contracts, and it placed priority on maintaining good relations with Washington.

• Beijing has cooperated in the Bush administration's Container Security Initiative (CSI), an effort to inspect containers before they depart the world's top twenty ports that ship to America. These ports account for about two-thirds of US cargo imports, and China controls big facilities on the list—Hong Kong, Shanghai, and Shenzhen (Shekou). These three ports alone account for approximately two-thirds of the PRC's total port trade.[31]

• And, Beijing has continued to improve its nonproliferation export-control regime by issuing regulations in the latter half of 2002. Though Washington has felt obliged to sanction Beijing since those regulations were promulgated, former assistant secretary of state for nonproliferation Robert Einhorn describes the overall situation as follows:

> But by the early fall of 2002, the Chinese had promulgated the comprehensive, missile-related export controls called for in the November 2000 agreement and upgraded controls in the chemical and biological field. Since then, they have made serious efforts to inform Chinese firms of the new regulations and required firms wishing the right to export controlled commodities to register with Chinese authorities. They have also investigated a number of questionable transactions by Chinese entities when the US has tipped them off with intelligence information, stopped a shipment to North Korea of chemicals associated with nuclear reprocessing, and taken disciplinary action against the Chinese entity that the US had earlier sanctioned for missile assistance to Pakistan.

Notwithstanding these undeniably serious attempts to get a handle on the chronic problem of China's sensitive exports, performance remains uneven.[32]

All in all, China's role in the war on terror has had several effects. To start, China is being regarded as a responsible member of the international community, and therefore the anxiety level about Beijing in the region (and in Washington) has dropped. For its part, China enjoys its newfound status, with

President Hu Jintao announcing at a state dinner in Paris in January 2004 that France and China bear "a great responsibility in world affairs."[33] Second, the global counterterrorism effort has left Washington principally talking about counterterrorism in a region that also wants to talk about other forms of US engagement—Washington seems to many in East and Southeast Asia to be a "Johnny one-note." By way of contrast, Beijing has been talking about multilateral cooperation, free-trade areas, and making confidence-building moves. The contrast between a preoccupied America and a dynamic PRC in the region is symbolized by the warmer reception that Chinese president Hu Jintao received from the Australian Parliament than the same body accorded President Bush in the fall of 2003. Third, Beijing's cooperation in the war on terror has helped restore discipline to Washington's demands of Beijing, meaning that while economic and human rights frictions are not ignored, they are not pursued to the detriment of security cooperation. And finally, China's cooperation in the war on terror has contributed to Washington's willingness to resist entreaties from Taiwan to pursue a course that Washington feels could undermine Beijing's cooperation.

Taiwan—An Unanticipated Area of Beijing-Washington Cooperation?

The latter point provides a segue into an unanticipated (limited, and probably temporary) area of US-China security cooperation—the Taiwan issue. When President George W. Bush assumed office in January 2001, one of his first impulses was to more explicitly deter the PRC from using force across the Taiwan Strait. When asked in April 2001 whether he felt obligated to defend Taiwan "with the full force of the American military," the president said that Washington would "do whatever it takes to help Taiwan defend herself."[34] Two other impulses the president shared with many in his political base were to enhance military-to-military ties with (and arms sales to) Taiwan and to treat Taipei with more dignity than had been the practice since normalization with Beijing in 1979. This latter impulse was reflected in ways large and small, not the least by enabling Taiwan president Chen Shui-bian to transit the United States for longer periods in more visible venues, the last being a relatively high-profile visit to New York City in fall 2003. However, these initiatives combined with domestic politics in Taiwan to create an increasingly volatile mix.

In March 2004, Taiwan's presidential election will occur. The incumbent president, Chen Shui-bian, in late 2003 and early 2004 sought reelection against a coalition of the Kuomintang or Nationalist Party (with its presidential candidate being Lien Chan) and the People's First Party (with the vice-presidential candidate being James Soong). This coalition was popularly known as "Pan Blue." In the prior presidential election (2000) Chen had won with a plurality of the votes (about 39 percent) because the Kuomintang (KMT) had split its own vote between Lien and Soong (the PFP did not exist then). In the March 2004 election, therefore, Chen's problem was how to get 50 percent of the vote with a united opposition. Moreover, he had to do so when the economy had not done well during much of his tenure (though it picked up somewhat in the second half of 2003[35]), his initial reform agenda had not made much progress (against an admittedly recalcitrant legislature dominated by the KMT), and cross-Strait relations were tenser than when he assumed office.

Chen apparently concluded that his principal opportunity for victory depended on polarizing the electorate over cross-Strait issues and standing for reform of a political system widely perceived as dysfunctional. By creating wedge issues Chen hoped to mobilize young voters and his political base to get to the polls. He tarred the opposition as pro-Beijing—hence his campaign slogan of "Believe in Taiwan and Insist on Reform."

In pursuit of this strategy, in the last third of 2003 and into 2004 Chen advanced an ever-changing array of proposals, including setting a timetable for constitutional change and a national referendum. Like a cascade, the first proposal for a referendum focused on constitutional change, the second on PRC missiles aimed at the island, and the third on whether or not the island should join the US ABM system and resume cross-Strait dialogue with the mainland. Each proposal in this sequence was designed to energize Chen's political base for the March 2004 election. Beijing became progressively more apprehensive about abandonment of the ROC's "One China" constitution, but was hamstrung by its knowledge that if it openly threatened Taiwan (as it had prior to two previous elections) it probably would help reelect Chen, thereby producing precisely the result China wished to avoid. Consequently, Beijing sought Washington's help in restraining Chen.

These calls did not fall on deaf ears because President Bush was coming to feel that his earlier solicitude of Taiwan, and his several earlier requests that Chen restrain himself in the interests of maintaining stability in the area,[36] were being ignored. Moreover, Washington did not need, and would find it difficult to cope with, a security crisis in the Taiwan Strait given American deployments in Iraq and Afghanistan. Moreover, military sources in the PRC were cranking up incendiary rhetoric about the price the PRC might have to pay to prevent Taiwan independence.[37] In a November 21, 2003, interview with the *Washington Post* Premier Wen Jiabao had said, "The Chinese people will pay any price to safeguard the unity of the motherland."[38]

President Chen Shui-bian was overplaying his hand with a US administration that had assumed office well-disposed toward him. This all came to a head in the December 9, 2003, visit of Chinese premier Wen Jiabao to the White House, when the president said: "The comments and actions made by the leader of Taiwan indicate that he may be willing to make decisions unilaterally to change the status quo, which we oppose."[39] In a CNN interview two days later, President Chen rejoined that he would continue to pursue the referendum he had proposed on December 5, 2003,[40] urging the PRC to withdraw missiles aimed at the island and to renounce the use of force against the island. This rebuff was unwelcome at the White House, but the administration was reluctant to apply much additional public pressure, though Deputy Assistant Secretary of State Randall Schriver made a statement on December 17, 2003, indicating that the administration would differentiate among possibly different types of referenda. There were those clearly of a domestic character, those that bore on sovereignty, and those that were in a gray (symbolic) area. Washington would not express a view on the first type, would oppose the second, and would approach instances in the third category on a "case-by-case basis."[41] This formulation inadvertently encouraged Chen to plumb the limits of the third category. In the short run, however, President Bush's December 9 remarks seem to have reassured Beijing that Washington and it shared an interest in keeping stability in the Taiwan Strait. Chen has continued to push near the limits of Washington's tolerance. And Beijing keeps pushing the administration to get firmer with Taipei in ways Chen's electorate will discern.

For Washington's friends throughout Asia, this US-China cooperation was welcome. These nations all desire to avoid being forced to take sides in a conflict between America and China over Taiwan—in the last extremity, most probably would seek to remain uninvolved. Early in the Bush administration, the discomfort of US friends and allies with Washington's Taiwan tilt was evident. When Deputy Secretary of State Richard L. Armitage went to Australia in early 2002 and suggested that Washington expected Canberra to be at its side in a Taiwan contingency, former Australian prime minister Malcolm Fraser said: "[The Australia–New Zealand–United States Defense Treaty] designed to achieve Australian security is now being distorted potentially to embroil us in a conflict of America's choosing with another superpower [China]."[42] In June of the preceding year, Singapore's visiting prime minister Goh Chok Tong told a Washington audience, "It makes no sense to mortgage East Asia's future by causing the Chinese people to conclude that its neighbors and the US want to keep them down."[43]

In the wake of Chen Shui-bian's moves, the administration has welcomed friends and allies warning Taipei away from a dangerous course. In late December 2003, former Japanese prime minister Mori arrived in Taipei reportedly "carrying a message from Prime Minister Koizumi" informing President Chen Shui-bian "that Japan does not want to see Taiwan hold referenda and hopes cross-Strait stability will be maintained."[44] And, during his January 2004 visit to Paris, French president Jacques Chirac greeted Chinese president Hu Jintao with a state dinner and the statement that "Breaking the status quo with a unilateral destabilizing initiative, whatever it is, including a referendum, would favor division over unity. It would be a grave error. It would carry a heavy responsibility."[45]

In short, President Chen's policies, and US preoccupations elsewhere, have combined to get the United States and its friends and allies back on the same page of Taiwan policy and have fostered US-China cooperation, at least for the moment.

Implications

What does all this mean for US policy, future US-China security cooperation, and prospects for America's alliances with the Republic of Korea and Japan?

• A concatenation of events (the war on terror, counterproliferation efforts, and the North Korean nuclear problem) has recreated a security rationale for US-China relations, a foundation that disintegrated in the 1989–1991 period with the fall of the Warsaw Pact and the Soviet Union and the Tiananmen violence. This more stable basis for US-China relations is welcome by our friends and allies in the region, almost without exception, though Japan and others get nervous if Washington embraces Beijing with excessive ardor. This security rationale, when combined with growing economic and cultural ties between the United States and China, has created a relationship that is stronger than often perceived. If the Taiwan issue can be managed effectively, this situation is likely to endure for a considerable period.

• If the Taiwan issue is managed ineffectively and degenerates into conflict, this would be a solvent to the US alliance with South Korea and might well weaken the alliances with Japan and Australia as well. Beyond cross-Strait stability, therefore, a lot is at stake for the United States in Chen Shui-bian's behavior. The Bush administration and the current US Congress, along with their successors, will face hard decisions about how far to go in backstopping Taiwan's domestic politics. The Bush administration has welcomed the cautions that allies (Japan and France) have expressed to Taipei and more such statements from capitals influential in Taipei should be sought.

• The combination of growing Chinese economic and diplomatic attraction and gradually mounting Chinese power provides America's allies increasing incentive to cooperate with the PRC. In the case of Seoul (when combined with the frictions in US-ROK relations), all this has created a process in which the alliance is weakening. The US-Japan alliance is stronger, given the history of Japan's relations with China, Japanese disquiet with the PRC's growing strength, and Beijing's wariness of Tokyo's slowly expanding global security role. Nonetheless, it is wise to remember that Seoul also has partially sublimated anxieties about what PRC economic and military power may mean for it, despite the current "China fever."

• The developments discussed in this paper raise a fundamental question: Is a new (perhaps supplementary) security structure needed for Northeast Asia? Does the Six-Party framework provide a place to start thinking about such a development?

• A failure to achieve a negotiated settlement with Pyongyang over the nuclear issue could push the United States in one of two undesirable directions. The first would be toward a muscular policy that would strain—possibly break—the US-ROK alliance, push Seoul yet closer to Beijing, and damage US-China ties. The second would be the explicit or implicit acceptance of a nuclear North Korea. This would have ominous long-term consequences for proliferation in the region and beyond and for both US alliances in Northeast Asia. The Bush administration needs to come to some internal agreement on the basis for possibly productive negotiations with Pyongyang. The current policy of near total reliance on China, no positive inducements to the North, and no actions that would stop the North's march down the nuclear road promises a nuclear North Korea, a more influential China, and a proliferating region.

• The United States should diversify its policy repertoire in Asia, moving beyond the war on terror by engaging more with Asia in multilateral economic and security forums and by using its "soft" power as well as its "hard" power. One example would be the problem of visa delays and the obstacle this presents to business and educational exchange. Multilateral trade liberalization would be another avenue, albeit difficult at the moment given electoral and economic considerations in the United States.

• Finally, because Asian economies are becoming progressively more integrated with China's, Washington will find it increasingly difficult to employ economic sanctions against Beijing without simultaneously hurting a broad array of American regional partners, not to mention the United States itself.

NOTES

[1] Jing Huang, "China and America's Northeast Asian Alliances: Approach, Policy, and Dilemma," paper presented at Asia-Pacific Research Center Workshop, January 14–15, 2004, Stanford University, p. 2.

[2] Hiroshi Nakanishi, "The Japan-US Alliance and Japanese Domestic Politics: Sources of Change and Prospects for the Future," paper presented at Asia-Pacific Research Center Workshop, January 14–15, 2004, Stanford University, p. 11. "Japan is concerned that the US-China entente may replace the Japan-US alliance as the key bilateral relationship in East Asia."

[3] Kurt M. Campbell makes this point in his contribution to this volume.

[4] See the Pew Center's "Global Attitudes Project," June 2003, *http://people-press.org*.

[5] Alexander L. George, et al., *The Limits of Coercive Diplomacy: Laos, Cuba, Vietnam* (Boston: Little, Brown & Co., 1971), pp. 22–23.

[6] Kurt M. Campbell, "America's Asia Strategy during the Bush Administration," prepared for the Workshop on the Future of America's Alliances in Northeast Asia, Stanford University's Asia-Pacific Research Center, January 14–15, 2004, p. 4.

[7] See "Editorial," "Naval Exercises Indicate Sea Change in Relations," *South China Morning Post*, November 15, 2003, p. 12; see also James J. Przystup, "China's Great Power Diplomacy: Implications for the United States," carried in *Nelson Report*, October 10, 2003.

[8] Pieter Bottelier, "Atlantic Council Meeting on WTO Compliance across the Strait," October 2, 2003, p. 1; also, Kim Sung-jin, "China Emerges As Korea's Largest Export Market," *The Korea Times*, July 6, 2003.

[9] Moscow-ITAR-TASS in English 1346 GMT 19 October 2003, *Daily Report*, FBIS, World News Connection, October 19, 2003.

[10] JETRO, "Japan's International Trade in Goods (2002/12), "Table 1," "Value of Exports and Imports by Area and Country (2002/1-12)," *http://jetro.go.jp/ec/e/stat/ jpn_trade/200212.html.*

[11] Pieter Bottelier, "Comments," Atlantic Council Meeting on WTO Compliance across the Strait, October 2, 2003, Washington, DC, p. 1 of notes.

[12] Lehman Brothers, "The Growing China," Global Economics Series, June 9, 2003, graph on p. 12.

[13] Guy Pfeffermann, "China's Staying Power," in Letters, *Foreign Policy*, November/ December 2003, p. 6.

[14] John Wong and Sarah Chan, "China's Outward Direct Investment: Expanding Worldwide," *China: An International Journal* 1, no. 2 (September 2003), pp. 273–301, especially Table 3, p. 276.

[15] Wong and Chan, op. cit., pp. 277–278.

[16] Thomas G. Moore and Dixia Yang, "Empowered and Restrained: Chinese Foreign Policy in the Age of Economic Interdependence," *The Making of Chinese Foreign and Security Policy in the Era of Reform* (Stanford, Calif.: Stanford University Press, 2001), pp. 191–229.

[17] "East Asia Trade Bloc to Emerge within 20 Years," *http://english.peopledaily.com.cn/ 200212/01/eng20021201_107737.shtml.*

[18] "China backs Mekong project," *China Daily*, August 20, 2003 (online, eastday.com.cn); see also Michael Vatikiotis and Murray Hiebert, "China Pushes Economic Ties with Southeast Asia," *Wall Street Journal*, July 16, 2003, p. A12.

[19] "Chinese, Japanese, South Korean Leaders Discuss Creating 'Tripartite Committee,'" Beijing Xinhua in English, 07 October 2003, FBIS-CHI-2003-1007; also, "Enterprises Keen to China-Japan-ROK FTA: Survey," *Xinhua*, November 18, 2003, FBIS-CHI-2003-1118.

[20] Beijing, Xinhua in English, November 18, 2003, "Survey Conducted in China, Japan, ROK Finds Most Firms Support Free Trade Area," FBIS-CHI-2003-1118.

[21] Robert Ash, "China and Asia: Towards a New Regional System," draft paper presented for the conference on "China and Asia: Towards a New Regional System," December 5–6, 2003, Elliott School of International Affairs, George Washington University, p. 17.

[22] Jae Ho Chung, "China's 'Ascendancy' and the Korean Peninsula: From Interest Re-evaluation to Strategic Realignment?", p. 6, draft paper presented at Conference on "China and Asia: Towards a New Regional System," December 5–6, 2003, Elliott School of International Affairs, George Washington University.

[23] Anthony Faiola, "Kicking Up the Dust of History: China Makes Novel Claim to Ancient Kingdom, and Both Koreas Balk," *Washington Post*, January 22, 2004, p. A15.

[24] Jae Ho Chung, "China's 'Ascendancy' and the Korean Peninsula: From Interest Re-evaluation to Strategic Realignment?", p. 17, draft paper presented at Conference on "China and Asia: Towards a New Regional System," December 5–6, 2003, Elliott School of International Affairs, George Washington University.

[25] William Watts, *Next Generation Leaders in the Republic of Korea: Opinion Survey Report and Analysis* (Washington, DC: Potomac Associates, April 2002), p. 12, cited in Jae Ho Chung, op. cit., p. 18.

[26] Yang Bojiang, "Bilateral Relations Defined at a Strategic Level," *Contemporary International Relations* 13, no. 11 (November 2003), p. 5. Issue entitled, "What Future for Sino-Japanese Relations."

[27] There is an apparent difference "between what North Korea believes it said and what the United States believes it heard" in October 2002 when the United States asserts it was told by North Korea that it was conducting a covert highly enriched uranium program. John W. Lewis, "Hope on N. Korea," *Washington Post*, January 27, 2004, p. A17.

[28] Colin L. Powell, "Remarks at Conference on China-US Relations," Texas A & M University, College Station, Texas, *http://www.state.gov/secretary/rm/2003/25950.htm*.

[29] *New York Times*, December 28, 2003.

[30] See David M. Lampton and Richard Daniel Ewing, *The US-China Relationship Facing International Security Crises: Three Case Studies in Post–9/11 Bilateral Relations* (Washington, DC: The Nixon Center, 2003), pp. i–x and Chapter 1.

[31] See US Department of Homeland Security, "Fact Sheet: Container Security Initiative Guards America, Global Commerce from Terrorist Threat," March 12, 2003 (viewed on October 3, 2003 at *http://www.cbp.gov/xp/cgov/newsroom/press_releases/032003/033122003.xml*); also, US Department of Commerce, "Spotlight on China's Ports" (viewed on September 27, 2003 at *http://www.mac.doc.gov/China/Docs/Spotlights/ChinesePorts.pdf*).

[32] Robert J. Einhorn, "China's Proliferation Policies and Practices," briefing paper prepared for congressional conference "US-China Relations," sponsored by The Aspen Institute, Honolulu, Hawaii, January 5–11, 2004, p. 7, published in, Dick Clark, director and moderator, *U.S.-China Relations and China's Integration with the World* (Washington, DC: The Aspen Institute, 2004), p. 11.

[33] Associated Press, January 26, 2004.

[34] David M. Lampton and Richard Daniel Ewing, *US-China Relations in a Post-September 11th World* (Washington, DC: The Nixon Center, 2002), p. 17.

[35] The American Chamber of Commerce in Taipei, "Taiwan Briefs," in *Topics* 33, no. 11 (November 2003), p. 9.

[36] David M. Lampton, "The Stealth Normalization of US-China Relations," *The National Interest*, no. 73 (Fall 2003), p. 40.

[37] Huang Hai and Yang Liu, "Military Experts on War to Counter 'Taiwan Independence': Six Prices; War Criminals Cannot Escape Punishment," Beijing Renmin Wang, text in Chinese, December 3, 2003, FBIS-CHI-2003-1203; also, "Luo Yuan Reiterates Once Again: The Day of 'Taiwan Independent' Is the Day of Declaration of War," *Zhongguo Xinwen She* in Chinese, November 18, 2003, FBIS-CHI-2003-1118.

[38] "Interview with Wen Jiabao," *http://www.washingtonpost.com/ac2/wp-dyn/A6641-2003Nov22?language=printer* (accessed November 24, 2003).

[39] David E. Sanger, "Bush Lauds China Leader As 'Partner' in Diplomacy," *New York Times*, December 10, 2003.

[40] Mike Chinoy, "Interview with President Chen Shui-bian," December 11, 2003, provided by Taipei Economic and Cultural Representative Office in the United States, December 17, 2003; also, Keith Bradsher and Joseph Kahn, "Taiwan Referendum to Focus on Missiles, Not Independence," *New York Times*, December 5, 2003.

[41] David M. Lampton, "Notes of Public Remarks by Deputy Assistant Secretary of State Randall Schriver," The Brookings Institution, December 17, 2003.

[42] Agence France-Presse, "Clashes Mar Clinton China Conference in Sydney," February 23, 2002 (via Lexis-Nexis).

[43] "Keynote Address by Prime Minister Goh Chok Tong at the US-ASEAN Business Council's Annual US-Ambassador's Tour Dinner," Washington, DC, June 12, 2001 (Viewed on June 3, 2002, at *http://app.internet.gov.sg/scripts/mfa/pr/read_content.asp?View,1047*).

[44] "Summary of Taiwan Newspapers," AIT, December 25–29, 2003, pp. 2–3, from *Taiwan Daily*, December 27, 2003.

[45] Associated Press, "France Backs China over Taiwan," January 26, 2004.

CHINA AND AMERICA'S NORTHEAST ASIAN ALLIANCES: APPROACHES, POLITICS, AND DILEMMAS

Jing Huang

The most significant phenomenon in the Asia-Pacific after the end of the Cold War is China's ascendancy. This is demonstrated not just by China's dynamic economy, which has become essential to continued prosperity in the region, but, more importantly, by China's increasingly active and prominent role in international affairs, especially in Asia. Thus, it is imperative in our inquiry of the future of America's Northeast Asian alliances to understand China's view on the two US-led alliances and its approaches and policies toward them.[1]

This paper begins with an examination of China's "new diplomacy," based on the newly adopted "development strategy of peaceful ascendancy" (*heping jueqi fazhan zhanlue*), and its implications for China's approach to international affairs. The analysis then focuses on the changes in Beijing's view of America's role and military presence in Asia—from hostile to realistic, and from negative to conditionally positive. Beijing's accommodative approach toward the United States and its conditionally positive attitude toward the US role in Asia have changed China's negative perception of America's Northeast Asian alliances, resulting in a pragmatic and rational approach toward them. I will argue, however, that although China's current policies toward the two US-led alliances seem to be interest-oriented rather than based on ideology or nationalism, China still faces a serious dilemma with regard to them.

Despite their substantial reservations about the two US-led alliances, especially that between the United States and Japan, Chinese leaders seem to have realized that it does not serve China's best interests to challenge or undermine the status quo of the international system in Northeast Asia.[2] This is not only because China's rapid development in the past two decades has resulted largely from integrating its economy into the world economic system, which is market-based, but also because a peaceful international environment is necessary for China's political stability as well as its further development. Chinese leaders have recognized that China has in fact had a free ride on the existing system in the Asia-Pacific, a system which has been secured essentially by America's Northeast Asian alliances and prospered upon a market economy in which the United States and its allies have played leading roles. For China, seeking regional dominance would be economically too expensive—perhaps the essential reason why Beijing refuses to give up the artificial peg of RMB to the US dollar despite the substantial power and credibility RMB has earned in the Asian market since 1997. Moreover, it could also set China on a collision course with America's Northeast Asian alliances.

China's "New Diplomacy" and Its Implications for China's Foreign Policy

The most noteworthy change in China's foreign policy in the post-Deng period has been the adoption of a "new diplomacy," with two "guiding principles" (*zhidao fangzhen*):

> 1. "Actively engaging in international affairs," especially in the Asia-Pacific, with a general approach of "seeking cooperation, putting aside disputes so as to avoid confrontations ... [and] promoting multilateral communication and cooperation."[3]
> 2. "Maintaining a stable relationship with the United States"   this is "the core issue concerning China's diplomacy."[4]

Although China's leaders claim that they still adhere in foreign affairs to the "principles" laid by Deng Xiaoping in the early 1990s, i.e., "observing sober-mindedly, standing firm, and remaining calm,"[5] this "new diplomacy" has in fact departed from Deng's teaching that China should "hide [its] capacities and bide [its] time" (*taoguang yangwei*) in world politics and focus on economic growth and political stability at home, given the difficult situation caused by the May 1989 crisis and the collapse of the Soviet Union in 1991. Instead of following Deng's tactics, which were virtually an extension of Mao's guerrilla strategy—to build up one's capacity while waiting patiently for the enemy to be worn out—the post-Deng leadership has actively engaged in international affairs since the late 1990s, especially in Asia, with "constructive, multilateral, and cooperative approaches." Meanwhile, Beijing has approached the United States with various initiatives after the September 11 terrorist attack in an effort to "seek cooperation" or even a "strategic partnership." All this, according to the Beijing media, is part of a newly adopted "development strategy of peaceful ascendancy," a strategy which is aimed at integrating China positively into the existing world system despite differences in political systems, levels of economic development, and cultural traditions; and at "seeking multilateral and constructive cooperation," instead of confrontation, with the world powers in solving differences and conflicts during China's "ascendancy."[6]

Beijing's new approach to international affairs resulted in large part from several simultaneous "research projects" in 1998–2001. These projects were to "reassess China's international environment" and the role a rising China can, and should, play in international affairs.[7] Although there are differences among Chinese leaders, a common assessment has been reached of the world situation and China's approaches in world politics in terms of its "peaceful ascendancy":[8]

1. China should recognize and accept the reality that the United States has played, and will continue to play in the foreseeable future, a predominant role in both international politics and the world economy. Thus, *maintaining "a stable relationship and avoiding confrontations with the United States" must be the linchpin in China's foreign affairs.*
2. Although China is still a developing country, the outside world sees China as a rising power that could become a threat to the status quo. Thus, *China must strive to cast an image of a responsible power that abides by the accepted norms and principles in international affairs.*
3. The mainstream in world politics is for peace and prosperity; and the current international system is an essential guarantee for such a status quo. It is more effective to promote China's interests from within this system rather than challenging it from the outside. Thus, *China must integrate itself into this system, and be opposed to any attempts to undermine it.*
4. The United States has enormous and increasing interests in the Asia-Pacific. Thus, *"a good and interdependent relationship" with the Asian countries will not only help China's security and development, but also provide China with effective leverage in dealing with the United States.*
5. Despite America's predominance, other major powers have important roles and substantial influence in international politics. Thus, *China must actively engage with the major powers with cooperative approaches in order to develop a "stable framework of big power relations"* (wending de daguo guanxi kuangjia).
6. To sustain economic growth and maintain political stability at home, China needs not only a peaceful international environment but also a healthy world economy, especially in the Asia-Pacific. Thus, *China's long-term development strategy must be constructive for promoting regional prosperity.*

Obviously there is a certain amount of wishful thinking in the above assessments and policy designs; and serious questions can be asked about this "peaceful ascendancy strategy."[9] Yet it is well observed that China's international behavior has changed substantially since 1999: while actively engaging in international affairs, China has become more patient and cooperative in interstate affairs. A subtle but significant change is that Beijing quietly replaced "anti-hegemonism" with "anti-unilateralism" in its diplomatic language after it actively involved itself in the North Korean nuclear crisis. This shows that China has accepted America's predominance in international politics. But it is opposed to US unilateralism, not only because Chinese leaders see the multilateral and cooperative approaches as a more effective way to steer America's predominance into directions not adverse to China's vital interests, but also because they have realized that only by strengthening and operating through international regimes and institutions can China better protect itself and avoid confrontations with the superpower, given the inevitable conflicts of interests between the two countries during China's ascendancy. Not surprisingly, Beijing argues forcefully that US unilateralism not only undermines the existing international system in which the United States is the leader, but it can also damage America's own vital interests.[10]

Changes in China's View of America's Role and Military Presence in Asia

But it is in the Asia-Pacific that we have seen the most significant changes in China's diplomacy. In addition to increasingly active and accommodative engagements in South, Southeast, and Central Asia,[11] China has adopted pragmatic and rational approaches toward the United States and its Northeast Asian allies. The first and foremost change, which is subtle but significant, is in Beijing's view of America's role and military presence in Asia.

Chinese leaders used to be very suspicious of, and to some extent hostile toward, the US role in Asia. They were convinced that after the May 1989 crisis, and especially after the Soviet Union collapsed in 1991, the ultimate US policy goal in East Asia was to contain China in order to keep it under US influence. This view was best expressed by Deng in his talk with a Japanese delegation on December 1, 1989:

The Western world, especially the United States, incites turmoil in many countries. They are in fact carrying on power politics and hegemonism in order to control these countries. They attempt to pull these countries into their sphere of influence. Seeing this point clearly helps [us] to realize the essence of the matter.[12]

Thus, up to 1998 China's foreign policy in Asia was largely centered on its efforts to counterbalance mighty America and to "break the blockade by the Western world led by the United States."[13] Major measures Beijing adopted included:[14]

1. Improving its relationship with Moscow in an effort to form a "Sino-Russia strategic partnership."

2. Initiating "confidence-building measures" with Russia, Kyrgyzstan, Kazakhstan, and Tajikistan to reduce military forces in border areas and promote military exchanges. (Based on these confidence-building measures the five countries established the Shanghai Cooperation Organization on June 15, 2001.)

3. Joining the ASEAN countries in promoting "the ASEAN way" of security concept and practice; i.e., maintaining regional peace and stability through

multilevel communications, coordination, and cooperation among the Asia-Pacific countries.

4. Improving its bilateral relations with Japan and South Korea (especially the latter) in an effort to dilute the perceived threat from the US-led alliances.

5. Reinforcing the "good neighborhood policy" with a conciliatory and even accommodative approach in settling territory disputes.

Although China has achieved some success with these measures according to its "new security concept,"[15] the reality that America's Northeast Asian alliances are crucial to peace and stability in Asia remains unchanged. Nor has the US role diminished in the regional security system. Instead, the US role in Asia has become more prominent since the late 1990s because of the lingering economic recession in Japan, continual tension across the Taiwan Strait, nuclear competition in South Asia, Pyongyang's nuclear weapon program, and above all, the effort to combat terrorism. Thus, the Chinese leadership had to reconsider China's approaches to the United States and its military presence in Asia.

Evidently, Beijing's view on the US role in Asia has changed, although its diplomacy along the lines of the "new security concept" continues, especially in Southeast Asia. Chinese leaders have recognized that the United States has vital *and* legitimate interests in Asia. Moreover, they have realized from their own perspective that US interests in Asia do not have to collide with those of China—it is vital for both countries to maintain peace and prosperity in the Asia-Pacific. Since Zhu Rongji's visit to America in 1999, all the Chinese leaders have repeated virtually the same thesis in their meetings with the Americans: that the United States and China share "important strategic interests" in the Asia-Pacific and the two countries should therefore "put aside their differences but seek cooperation." Even the bombardment of the Chinese embassy in 1999 and the EP3 incident in 2001 did not alter China's conciliatory approach toward the United States, despite strong opposition from the hard-liners.[16] The September 11 attack just provided the Chinese leaders with "an opportunity" to present their case to the Americans.[17]

Consequently, China's attitude toward the US military presence in Asia has also changed from negative to at least realistic, if not downright positive. Contrary to the conventional wisdom that China would be opposed to any US military presence in Central and South Asia, Beijing has in fact been cooperative with, if not supportive of, US military operations in these areas during the war on terrorism. Even the PLA generals, who were known for their hostile stance toward the US military presence in Asia, have acknowledged that the US military has a right to stay in Asia because of vital American interests in the region. Today the PLA even views the US military presence in the Asia-Pacific positively for the sake of military-to-military exchanges.[18]

It is noteworthy that in his speech at the Conference on Security Cooperation in East Asia on December 12, 2003, Wang Yi, a vice minister of foreign affairs in charge of policy planning and Asian affairs, admitted *for the first time* that "the US military presence in the Asia-Pacific is caused by a historical process." Thus, China "is willing to see the United States ... playing a positive and constructive role for peace and stability in the region."[19] This is a significant change indeed, for until 1999 "withdrawal of all foreign troops in Asia" had been a "principle" in China's foreign policy. More importantly, this change has set the backdrop for the changes in China's approach toward America's Northeast Asian alliances.

Changes and Dilemmas in China's Approach toward the US-Led Alliances

Up to 1998 Beijing's view of America's Northeast Asian alliance stemmed largely from the classical explanation of military alliances. That is, alliance building is not necessarily based on identical domestic attributes among the alliance members, but it is motivated by an external threat coming from a common adversary.[20] Thus, a military alliance has a clearly defined goal, to contain or defeat the common adversary. To the Chinese leaders in the Deng period, the continuous existence of America's Northeast Asian alliances, which were established during the Cold War to contain communism, was "not desirable now or in the future."[21] They believed the two US-led alliances were essentially US instruments to contain China, which remained communist (at least in its political system) after the collapse of the Soviet Union. The Chinese leaders were very skeptical about the US-Japan security alliance, especially after it was revised in 1997 with a redefined (or not clearly defined) scope, target, capacity, and roles for its members. They believed that the ultimate mission of the alliances was to contain China by stealth. Thus, Beijing saw the US-led alliances in Asia as "a serious, long-term challenge, if not a threat, to China's national security, national unification, and modernization."[22] Not surprisingly, while the Chinese media was vocal in criticizing the alliances, especially the US-Japan alliance, the PRC government warned repeatedly that America's Northeast Asian alliances had to be "strictly bilateral" and not "intervene in internal affairs of the other countries." Otherwise, they would "cause instability to the neighboring countries and create complicating elements for regional security."[23]

As China's view has changed, so has its approach toward the US-led alliances. It is evident that Beijing has adopted a pragmatic strategy that aims at improving bilateral relations with the members of the two alliances and solving problems through interstate talks instead of dealing with the alliances. The best example in this regard is the changes in China's approach to Japan on the Taiwan issue and the expansion of the Japanese Self-Defense Force (SDF), the two major concerns for China with regard to the US-Japan alliance.[24] Although from Beijing's perspective the two issues have roots in the revised US-Japan security treaty,[25] China has quietly stopped criticizing the US-Japan alliance on these "two most troubling issues in Sino-Japan relations" after the September 11 attack. Instead, Beijing now expresses its concern and anxiety over the two issues directly to Tokyo and handles them in a bilateral framework. In other words, China is trying to manage these issues by putting pressure on Japan rather than on the US-Japan alliance, where the problems originated.[26] Accordingly, the vocal attacks on the US-Japan security alliance in the Chinese media have also quieted down. The occasional criticisms that appear now usually focus on Japan's increasing role in the alliance and the expansion of the Japanese SDF, rather than the alliance itself.

But it is Japan's military development that worries China the most. Ironically it is on this issue that Beijing can appreciate the US-Japan alliance to the extent that it effectively contains Japan's militarism and constrains Japan's role in international affairs. This, from China's perspective, is essential for the regional peace and security necessary for China's development.[27] Beijing feels uneasy about the expansion of the Japanese SDF, both in quantity and quality, not necessarily because of the expansion per se but because such expansion can be justified in the system for cooperative security provided by America Northeast Asian alliances.[28]

China has adopted a similar approach to the US-ROK alliance: improving bilateral relations in order to dilute the perceived threat from the military alliance. China's approach to South Korea has been more successful and fruitful than that to Japan, partly because of the shared resentment against Japan but largely because of the increasing common interests and policy priorities between the two countries in both economic development and security concerns, especially on the recent North Korea nuclear issue. The summit meeting between Hu Jintao and Roh Moo-hyun on July 7, 2003, "has brought the Sino-ROK relationship to a new height." The two sides "agreed that they would lift bilateral [Sino-ROK] relations up to a partnership of comprehensive cooperation [that will] cover political, economic, educational, cultural, scientific and technological, and all other fields."[29] In this new Sino-ROK courtship, however, neither side has mentioned, let alone discussed, the US-ROK alliance; nor has either side addressed the US military presence in South Korea. An intriguing fact is that China has quietly dropped its support of North Korea's demand that "all foreign forces must withdraw from Korea." This seems to suggest that China can appreciate the US military presence in South Korea to the extent that it helps to sustain peace and stability on the peninsula and, ironically, keeps Pyongyang dependent on Beijing. Yet Chinese leaders are understandably reluctant to confirm, or even to imply, this newly adopted view of the US military presence in Korea. Not only is this view inconsistent with China's insistence that the Korean problem must be solved peacefully, but it is also against China's well-advocated policy of noninterference in the internal affairs of other countries. Thus it is revealing indeed that after September 11 the US military presence and the US-ROK alliance have become virtually invisible in the official PRC documents on Sino-ROK relations and on China's policy toward South Korea.[30]

As a matter of fact, America's Northeast Asian alliances have rarely been mentioned, let alone discussed, in the official PRC documents of the past few years. Nowadays it is well-known among Beijing insiders that America's Northeast alliances are among the most "bothering topics" for PRC spokespeople.[31] In his speech on improving "collective security in East Asia" at the Conference on Security Cooperation in East Asia on December 12, 2003, Vice Minister of Foreign Affairs Wang Yi did not once mention America's Northeast Asian alliances.

China's ambiguous and even contradictory views on the alliances and the US military presence in Asia reflect Beijing's dilemma on these issues. On the one hand, Chinese leaders feel uneasy about America's Northeast Asian alliances, not necessarily because they were established during the Cold War in part to contain China, but because they are in fact double-edged swords: they can secure regional peace and stability, which is necessary for China's further development, but they can also contain China if the allies feel threatened by China's ascendancy. Chinese leaders are especially unsure about the US-Japan alliance. It is true that the alliance has effectively deterred Japanese militarism and constrained Japan's international role. But it can also justify and sponsor an increasing Japanese role in international affairs and a dramatic military build-up in Japan if necessary.

On the other hand, the post-Deng leadership has realized that America's Northeast Asian alliances are fundamental to American interests in the Asia-Pacific, and that China also shares these interests to a large degree. In order to "maintain a stable relationship with the United States," China has to respect and accept this status quo. Moreover, the alliances are essential to the regional peace and security necessary for China's political stability as well as its economic development. China is neither willing nor capable of challenging this system, on which it has had a free ride since 1979.

This dilemma in China's approach toward America's Northeast Asian alliances has considerable implications for China's policies toward them.[32] It is evident that the Chinese leadership has made remarkable efforts to improve or at least stabilize bilateral relations with Japan and South Korea. Beijing has taken a generally conciliatory approach toward Japan despite its anger and frustration over Japan's refusal to formally apologize for war crimes against China during World War II and the repeated visits to the Yasukuni Shrine by Japanese leaders, including Prime Minister Junichiro Koizumi.[33] Beijing has also made a substantial effort in recent years to calm growing anti-Japan nationalism. It is noteworthy that since 1999 the major newspapers in China have stopped routinely printing Japan-bashing editorials and commentaries on anniversaries such as July 7 (Japanese troops attacked the Lugou Bridge), September 18 (Japanese troops attacked Shengyang City), August 15 (Japanese surrender), and December 15 (the rape of Nanjing). The conciliatory message could not be clearer given the tight control of the media by the PRC government. China has also taken an accommodative approach to South Korea, although people in Beijing were convinced that Seoul "double-crossed China" on the refugee issue.[34] China has in fact gone the extra mile to promote economic exchanges between the two countries, despite over $82.4 billion US dollars of deficit on the China side since the 1997 Asia crisis.[35]

Yet Beijing has been careful not to let its policies toward the two American allies be seen as an effort to undermine the US-led alliances, not only because this would damage the effort to "maintain stable relations with the US," but also because Chinese leaders are afraid that a conflict within the alliances could have consequences damaging to peace and stability in Asia. Thus, Beijing has made sure that its policy portfolios with Japan and South Korea not involve their alliances with the United States. For example, Beijing has engaged in bilateral talks with both Tokyo and Seoul on the North Korean nuclear issue. The Chinese participants had "clear instructions" that their exchanges with their Japanese or Korean counterparts had to be strictly bilateral, and that they should not involve themselves in any discussions about the US-led alliances.[36] In fact, China has made a painstaking effort to keep itself out of the dispute between Washington and Seoul over the North Korean nuclear crisis,[37] although Beijing does share Seoul's position that the crisis must be solved peacefully and that the key to the solution is to provide Pyongyang with assurances of security and economic development.

Concluding Remarks

China's approach toward America's Northeast Asian alliances is based on its long-term goals of sustaining economic development and maintaining political stability at home. To accomplish this goal, which is an enormous challenge in itself, China needs a peaceful international environment. But only recently have the Chinese leaders realized that China's rise could itself become a formidable threat to the existing international system, not necessarily because history has taught us that a rising power usually means instability, but because a rapidly developing China has brought, and will bring, conflicts and competition over resources, markets, and eventually the value system. Moreover, China's previous efforts to counterbalance "hegemonism" and to break the perceived "containment" by the US-led alliances not only caused further anxiety and suspicion from the outside world, but also helped to reinforce the perception that China is a challenger of the status quo.

Thus, we have witnessed substantial, if not dramatic, changes in China's foreign policy and international behavior in recent years. Not only has China accepted America's predominance through "seeking constructive cooperation" with the United States in international affairs, but it has made remarkable efforts to integrate itself further in the existing world system through multilateral and cooperative approaches. Consequently, it appears that China has also accepted America's Northeast Asian alliances as part of the status quo in the Asia-Pacific.

Toward the US-led Asian alliances China's views are no longer based on ideology or nationalism, but rather reality and objectivism; its approaches focus on bilateral relations, with the rationale that a solid bilateral relationship with the members of the two alliances, including the US, will diminish or even dissolve their potential threat to China's security; and its policies are more pragmatic and interest-oriented.

It is beyond China's capacity to change the reality that America's Northeast Asian alliances have been fundamental to peace, stability, and prosperity in the Asia-Pacific. Moreover, as long as Beijing is convinced that America's alliances are not aimed at containing China, any conflicts between the United States and its Northeast Asian allies do not serve China's best interests, for such conflicts weaken the regional peace and stability necessary for China's development. All this has formed the source of China's dilemma in its approach to America Northeast Asian alliances. On one hand, the US-led alliances are the core of the security system in Asia, a system that has an enormous impact on China security environment. On the other hand, China is neither included in nor does it have any substantial influence over this system. Moreover, any effort by China to change or influence the system could backfire against its own interests. At present it seems that Beijing has not found a way to solve this dilemma, only to manage it with ambiguity—avoiding America's Northeast Asian alliances altogether in international affairs but setting out to improve its bilateral relationship with the members of the alliances. Ambiguity may provide China with more options, but it means uncertainty.

NOTES

[1] In addition to China s rise, how China rises could have an equal, if not more significant, impact on international politics. This is the question raised by Yoichi Funabashi in his recent article China's Peaceful Ascendancy, in YaleGlobal Online, 19 December 2003. This paper does not address this question.

[2] This conclusion is consistent with the one Iain Johnston draws in his "Is China a Status Quo Power?" (*International Security* 27, no. 4 [Spring 2003]) that China is a status quo power rather than a challenger to the existing world system.

[3] This approach was raised in Jiang Zemin's "Report to the 15th CCP National Congress," *Shiwuda yilai zhongyao wenjian xuanbian* [Collection of the Important Party Documents since the 15th Party Congress], vol. 1, Beijing, People's Press, 2000, pp. 42–43. It was restated as a guiding principle in his "Report to the 16th CCP National Congress," at *http://www.cctv.com/news/china/20021117/100187_9.shtml.*

[4] Quoted from Niu Jun, in Song Nianshen, "*Zhongguo zhoubian waijiao fenliang zhong*" (China's peripheral diplomacy carries a heavy weight), *Global Times*, December 12, 2003, p. 7.

[5] Deng raised these principles in his talk with "several leading comrades" in the CCP leadership on September 4, 1989. His original words were *lengjing guancha, wenzhu zhenjiao, chenzhuo yingfu*. See *Deng Xiaoping sixiang nianpu* [Chronology of Deng Xiaoping's Thought] 1975–1997, composed by the CCP Central Department for Research on Party Documents, 1998, p. 435.

[6] Zheng Bijian, executive vice president of the CCP Central Party School, made a speech, "The New Road of China's Peaceful Ascendancy and the Future of Asia" at the Bo'ao Asian Forum, held in October 2003 at Bo'ao, Hainan Province, China. The CCP leaders reached a consensus on this strategy at a "Politburo study session" on November 24, 2003. But it was Wen Jiabao who repeated this thesis of "peaceful ascendancy" during his visit to the United States in December 2003. See Zhang Jianjin, "*Heping jueqi: yige zhongda de* chengnuo" (Peaceful Ascendancy: An Important Promise), *China Economic Times* (published by the Center of Development Studies of the PRC State Council), December 12, 2003, p.1.

[7] Immediately after the 1997–98 Asian economic crisis, several leading research institutes and think tanks in China, including the Social Science Academy, the CCP Central Party School, and the China Foundation of International and Strategic Studies, organized simultaneous "research projects" on world politics and trends in its future development, China's development strategy, national security, foreign policy, and China's position and role in international affairs. The "policy recommendations" produced by these projects have exerted a substantial effect on policymaking, especially after the Hu-Wen leadership took over in March 2003. I authored four policy papers and participated in several workshops for these projects.

[8] See Tang Jiaxuan, "*Zhonguo kua shiji waijiao de guanghui licheng*" (The glorious achievements of China's diplomacy in 1989–2002). This is a speech Tang made at a conference on October 17, 2002, convened jointly by five CCP central apparatus and ministries, including the CCP Propaganda Department and the Ministry of Foreign Affairs. The version at *http://www.fmprc.gov.cn/chn/ziliao/wzzt/2319/t10827.htm* is watered down for "the propaganda toward the outside [*duiwai xuanchuan*]." But even in this version one can see fundamental changes in China's foreign policy in the post-Deng period, especially after 1998.

[9] For example, Yoichi Funabashi in his recent article "China's 'Peaceful Ascendancy'" questions China's willingness and ability to "learn to respect and observe the rule of law on the international stage... [and] to accustom itself to treating others as equals, particularly other Asian countries." He also seems skeptical about whether Beijing can convince Washington that China's "peaceful ascendancy" will not present a threat to the United States.

[10] See He Hongze, Danbian zhuiyi de kunjing (The Plight of Unilateralism), *People's Daily*, August 4, 2003, at *http://www.people.com.cn/GB/guoji/1030/1998190.html*.

[11] In my view, China's diplomatic maneuvers in these areas are more noteworthy in terms of China's "peaceful ascendancy strategy," although they are not the focus of this paper.

[12] *Deng Xiaoping sixiang nianpu* (Chronology of Deng Xiaoping's Thought) 1975–1997, p. 445.

[13] See Tang Jiaxuan, "*Zhonguo kua shiji waijiao de guanghui licheng*" (The Glorious Achievements of China's Diplomacy in 1989–2002).

[14] See Chu Shulong, "China and the US-Japan and US-Korea Alliances in a Changing Northeast Asia," project paper of America's Alliances with Japan and Korea in an Changing Northeast Asia, Asia-Pacific Research Center, Stanford University, June 1999, pp. 8–13.

[15] Beijing began to advocate its "new security concept" in early 1997. It argues that the "traditional concept" that security can only be achieved through military means is wrong because this concept would lead only to arms races in which every country is trying to build up its military for its own security. According to China's "new concept," true security must be "common security [*gongtong anquan*] that is based on mutual trust and common interests, and it cannot be achieved except through communication, coordination, and cooperation among the involved countries." See "[Defense Minister] Chi Haotian's Speech in Japan," *The PLA Daily*, February 5, 1997, p. 1; Editorial Commentary, "A

New Security Model of Good Neighborhood," *People's Daily*, April 25, 1997, p. 1; Qian Qichen's speech at the 4th ARF Meeting in Malaysia, *China Daily*, July 28, 1997, p. 1, and Li Qinggong and Wei Wei, "The World Needs a New Security Concept," *People's Daily*, December 24, 1998, p. 5. But this "new security concept" has rarely been seen in the Chinese media since September 11.

[16] See Willy Wo-Lap Lam, Dynamics of Sino-US Relations: The Perspective from Beijing, Harvard Asia Quarterly 103 (December 30, 2001). Lam s assertion was confirmed by two reliable sources in Beijing in March 2002. According to them, The Center had issued instructions [during both crises] that the [handling of] the event must not interfere with the general direction of maintaining stable Sino-US relations.

[17] According to the same sources, the CCP leadership issued an instruction that China "must seize the opportunity to show [our] sincerity to the US [*zhuazhu jiyu, xiang meiguo biaoshi women de chengyi*]" immediately after the attack.

[18] A senior PLA officer who has a role in China's policy toward the United States told me recently that there has been a "fundamental change [*genben bianhua*]" in the PLA's perception of the US military presence in Asia. He said, "No matter what, we have to accept the reality that Americans will stay in Asia because they have important interests here. Don't you Americans have a saying that 'if you can't beat them, join them'? The fact that they are here makes it easier for us to engage with them in our exchange programs."

[19] Wang's speech is published at *http://news.sina.com.cn/c/2003-12-15/14091346610s.shtml*.

[20] See, among others, George Liska, *Nations in Alliance: The Limits of Interdependence* (Baltimore: Johns Hopkins University Press, 1962); and Julian Friedman, Christopher Bladen, and Steven Rosen, eds., *Alliances in International Politics* (Boston: Allyn & Bacon, 1970).

[21] Chu Shulong (1999), op. cit., p. 21.

[22] Yu Bin, "Containment by Stealth: Chinese Views of and Policies Toward America's Alliances with Japan and Korea after the Cold War," project paper of America's Alliances with Japan and Korea in an Changing Northeast Asia, Asia-Pacific Research Center, Stanford University, June 1999, p. 5.

[23] Comments by Cui Tiankai, spokesman for the PRC Ministry of Foreign Affairs, on the Japan-US Security Treaty, *People's Daily*, June 11, 1997, p. 1.

[24] The PRC Ministry of Foreign Affairs, "*Zhongri mingan wenti*" (Sensitive Issues in Sino-Japan Relations), April 2, 2002, at *http://www.people.com.cn/GB/shizheng/252/7824/7837/20020402/700371.html*.

[25] From Beijing's perspective the revised guidelines redefined the scope, capacity, and target(s) of the US-Japan security alliance. As a result, not only have the guidelines justified the expansion of Japan's Self-Defense Force, they have also reoriented Japan's security strategy from "home defense" to active responses to (the perceived) "external threat" from either an adversary (e.g., China) or a looming international crisis (e.g., a conflict in the Taiwan Strait). See Liu Jiangyong, "*Xin 'rimei fangwei hezuo zhizhen' yu zhongri guanxi*" (The New 'Guideline for Japan-US Cooperative Defense' and Sino-Japan Relations), in *1997-98 guoji xingshi fenxi baogao* (1997–98 Reports of Analyses on the International Situation), composed by the Chinese Society for Strategy and Management Research, Beijing, 1998, pp. 19–21; and Yu Bin (1999), op. cit., pp. 8–10.

[26] A senior official who has a role in China's foreign policymaking said bluntly at a conference in March 2001, "We understand that the US has to intervene [in Taiwanese affairs] because of the Taiwan Relations Act. But Japan does not have such a law. So we have the absolute right to put pressure on Japan and ask them not to get involved [in Taiwanese affairs]. As long as Japan is reluctant to intervene, it will put constraints on the Americans."

[27] Some Chinese scholars call it "hegemonic security" (i.e., security that is based on

US military supremacy and US alliances in Northeast Asia), which China does not really like but cannot do without. See Pang Zhongying, *"Lengzhan hou de zhongguo guoji diwei he duiwai zhanlue"* (China's International Position and Strategy after the Cold War), lecture at Tsinghua University on April 6, 2002, at *http://news.sina.com.cn/c/2002-05-05/1127567001.html*.

[28] Niu Jun, *"Dongyan anquan de chulu he zai"* (The Future for Collective Security in East Asia), *Global Times*, December 26, 2003, p. 15.

[29] See the PRC Ministry of Foreign Affairs, "President Hu Jintao Meets with ROK President," at *http://www.fmprc.gov.cn/chn/wjb/zzjg/yzs/gjlb/1236/1238/t23670.htm*.

[30] For example, at a news conference on July 8, 2003, when a reporter asked Kong Quan, spokesman for the PRC Ministry of Foreign Affairs, if "China's relations with the DPRK are mainly on security because of the bilateral treaty and its relations with the ROK are mainly on economic aspects," Kong repeated the statement "President Hu Jintao and President Roh Moo-hyun... agreed that they would lift the bilateral relations up to a partnership of comprehensive cooperation." Yet he stopped short of saying anything about the implications of this "partnership of comprehensive cooperation" for the US-ROK alliance, nor did he clarify if China's relations with the DPRK are mainly security-oriented. For this news conference, see *http://www.fmprc.gov.cn/eng/xwfw/2510/2511/t22725.htm*. The published documents about the Hu-Roh summit meeting also avoided this issue altogether.

[31] I had a brief discussion on this issue with a person who has a role in China's foreign policymaking on June 30, 2003. He said bluntly: "What can they say about it? We know we need American troops to stay in [East] Asia. But we cannot talk about it because it is against our own official position on this matter."

[32] This paper does not examine China's policies toward Japan or Korea. The author merely wants to indicate the general implications of China's dilemmas in approaching America's Northeast Asian alliances for China's policies toward the two US allies.

[33] Koizumi paid homage to the shrine again on January 1, 2004. China's reaction was prompt but restrained: except for voicing China's anger and protest, no substantial actions were taken. See "China Expresses Strong Indignation at Japanese Prime Minister's Paying Homage to the Yasukuni Shrine," at *http://www.fmprc.gov.cn/chn/zxxx/t57352.htm*.

[34] Quoted from a PRC official who was directly involved in the refugee controversy.

[35] Quoted from the news conference by the PRC Ministry of Foreign Affairs, at *http://www.fmprc.gov.cn/chn/xwfw/fyrth/1032/t23473.htm*.

[36] The author participated in the Sino-Japan Bilateral Talks on Security in October 2003 as a "special observer." The Chinese participants confirmed to me that they could not discuss any issues regarding the US-Japan alliance at the meeting, although they would not object to listening to the comments and discussions of the Japanese participants on the US-Japan alliance.

[37] When the North Korean nuclear crisis began to unfold in late 2002 and early 2003, there was an opinion among Beijing insiders that China should take advantage of the growing gap between the US and South Korea and strengthen the Sino-ROK relationship at the expense of the US-ROK alliance. The CCP leadership soon suppressed this opinion, dressing it down as "myopic and foolish."

CONTRIBUTORS

MICHAEL H. ARMACOST is Shorenstein Distinguished Fellow and director of the Walter H. Shorenstein Forum for Asia-Pacific Studies at Stanford University. He was born in Cleveland, Ohio, and educated at Carleton College (BA 1958), Friedrich Wilhelms University, and Columbia University (MA 1962, PhD 1965). He started his career as a political scientist on the faculty of Pomona College in 1962, and has taught courses at Georgetown, Johns Hopkins, and International Christian University in Tokyo. During his twenty-four years in public service, he held senior policymaking positions in the Department of State, the Department of Defense, and the National Security Council. His assignments included US ambassador to the Philippines (1982–84), undersecretary of state for political affairs (1984–89), and US ambassador to Japan (1989–93). Following his retirement from the Foreign Service, he was president of the Brookings Institution (1995–2002), one of the nation's oldest and most prominent think tanks. He has received the President's Distinguished Service Award, the Defense Department's Distinguished Civilian Service Award, and the Secretary of State's Distinguished Service Award.

Armacost is the author of three books, including *Friends or Rivals? The Insider's Account of US-Japan Relations*, an analysis of US-Japan relations in the post–Cold War world, and numerous articles. He serves on a variety of corporate and nonprofit boards, among them AFLAC, Cargill, Applied Materials, USEC, Inc., the Asia Foundation, Carleton College, the American Academy of Diplomacy, and the National Committee on US-China Relations. He is married to Roberta Bray Armacost, and they have three grown sons and six grandchildren.

KURT M. CAMPBELL joined the Center for Strategic and International Studies as senior vice president and director of International Security in May 2000. He is also the Henry A. Kissinger Chair in National Security Policy. In this capacity, he is responsible for helping develop the foreign policy and security agenda of the center into the twenty-first century. He is also director of the Aspen Strategy Group, a regular contributor to NPR's *All Things Considered*, and a frequent author on the editorial page of the *New York Times*. Previously he served for five years as deputy assistant secretary of defense for Asia and the Pacific. During his tenure, Dr. Campbell worked to develop the framework for the US-Japan security initiative, deeper ties with Korea, military dialogue with the Chinese PLA, more security interaction with ASEAN as a whole, and renewed military contacts with Vietnam. Before coming to the Pentagon, he served as director in the democracy office at the National Security Council, deputy special counselor to the president for NAFTA, and chief of staff (international) and White House Fellow at the Treasury Department. For his work in government, Dr. Campbell has received numerous awards, including the Distinguished Public Service Medal from Secretary Cohen, Medal for Outstanding Public Service from Secretary Perry, Department of State Honor Award, Joint Service Commendation Medal, and the Republic of Korea's Order of National Security Medal.

Dr. Campbell was associate professor of public policy at the John F. Kennedy School of Government at Harvard University between 1988 and 1993. He was also the assistant director of the Center for Science and International Affairs and a director of the South Africa Project at Harvard. He was an International Affairs Fellow and is now a member of the Council on Foreign Relations. Campbell is also a member of the International Institute for Strategic Studies in London. Previously he has been a stringer for the *New York Times Magazine* in southern Africa, an Olin Fellow at the Russian Research Center at Harvard, a Fellow at the International Institute for Strategic Studies in London, a lecturer in international relations at Brown University, a consultant to the Rockefeller Foundation, and a member of St. Cross College.

He received his BA in political science (minors in physics and music) from the University of California, San Diego, a certificate in music (violin) and political philosophy from the University of Erevan in Soviet Armenia, and his doctorate in international relations from Brasenose College at Oxford University, where he was a Distinguished Marshall Scholar.

Campbell was formerly a special assistant on the Joint Chiefs of Staff and served as a reserve naval officer between 1987–95 in a special Chief of Naval Operations advisory unit in the Pentagon. He has also testified on numerous occasions in front of both houses of Congress. He is a member of the US Council for Security Cooperation in the Asia-Pacific and was appointed by the Secretary of the Navy to serve on the Advisory Board of the Naval Postgraduate School.

Campbell serves several companies and educational institutions in a variety of capacities. He is a member of the advisory boards of Civitas, STS Technologies, the O'Gara Company, New Media Strategies, and the Woods Hole Oceanographic Corporation. He is also on the Coordinating Committee of the US-Australian Leadership Dialogue and the Advisory Committee of the International Affairs Program at the College of William and Mary.

Campbell is the principal author of *To Prevail: An American Strategy for the Campaign against Terrorism*. He is the author of two other books, numerous scholarly articles, and many newspaper, magazine, and opinion pieces on a wide range of international subjects. He is married to Lael Brainard and they have two daughters, Caelan and Ciara. Together they maintain Iron Bell Run farm in Little Washington, Rappahannock County, Virginia.

VICTOR D. CHA (PhD Columbia, BA/MA Oxford) holds the D.S. Song–Korea Foundation Chair in Asian Studies and Government in the Edmund Walsh School of Foreign Service, Georgetown University. He is the award-winning author of *Alignment Despite Antagonism: The United States–Korea–Japan Security Triangle* (Stanford University Press), which won the 2000 Ohira Book Prize, and has written articles on international relations and East Asia in journals including *Foreign Affairs*, *International Security*, *Political Science Quarterly*, *Survival*, *International Studies Quarterly*, *Journal of Strategic Studies*, the *Washington Quarterly*, *Current History*, *Orbis*, *Journal of Peace Research*, *Security Dialogue*, *Australian Journal of International Affairs*, *Japanese Journal of Political Science*, *Korean Studies*, and *Asian Survey*.

Professor Cha is a former John M. Olin National Security Fellow at Harvard University, two-time Fulbright fellow, and Hoover National Fellow and CISAC Fellow at Stanford. He serves as an independent consultant to the various branches of the US government, Booz Allen, SAIC, and CENTRA Technology, and has testified before Congress on Asian security issues. He has been a guest analyst for various media including CNN, ABC *Nightline*, *Newshour with Jim Lehrer*, CBS *Morning Show*, Fox News, MSNBC, CNBC, the BBC, National Public Radio, the *New York Times*, the *Washington Post*, and *Time*. He serves on the editorial boards of *Asian Security*, the *Journal of Comparative Governance*, *Problems of Post-Communism*, and the *Korean Journal of International Relations*. He is a regular columnist for CSIS Comparative Connections; *Joongang Ilbo–International Herald Tribune* (English edition); *Chosun Ilbo*, and *Japan Times*.

Professor Cha is currently director of the American Alliances in Asia Project at Georgetown, and is co-author (with Dave Kang) of the November 2003 book *Nuclear North Korea? A Debate on Strategies of Engagement* (Columbia University Press).

RALPH A. COSSA is president of the Pacific Forum CSIS in Honolulu, a nonprofit, foreign policy research institute affiliated with the Center for Strategic and International Studies (CSIS) in Washington, DC. He is senior editor of the Pacific Forum's quarterly electronic journal, *Comparative Connections*. He is a member of the ASEAN Regional Forum's Experts and Eminent Persons Group. He is also a board member of the Council on US-Korean Security Studies and the National Committee on US-China Relations (New York), and a member of the International Institute for Strategic Studies (London).

Mr. Cossa is a founding member of the Steering Committee of the multinational Council for Security Cooperation in the Asia Pacific (CSCAP), a nongovernmental organization focusing on regional confidence-building and multilateral security dialogue. He co-chairs the CSCAP working group on confidence and security-building measures and also serves as executive director of the US Member Committee.

Mr. Cossa is a political/military affairs and national security specialist with over thirty years of experience in formulating, articulating, and implementing US security policy in the Asia-Pacific and Near East–South Asia regions. He writes a regular column for the *Japan Times* and the *Korea Times* and is a frequent contributor to the *International Herald Tribune* and other regional newspapers and periodicals.

Mr. Cossa served in the United States Air Force from 1966 to 1993, achieving the rank of colonel, and last serving as special assistant to the commander-in-chief, US Pacific Command. He served previously as deputy director for Strategic Studies at the National Defense University's Institute for National Strategic Studies, and earlier as a National Security Affairs Fellow at the Hoover Institution at Stanford University.

RUST M. DEMING joined the INSS Research Directorate at the National Defense University in September 2003 as a Distinguished Visiting Fellow on the completion of his tour as US ambassador to Tunisia. Prior to that, he served as principal deputy assistant secretary of state for East Asian and Pacific Affairs (June 1998 to August 2000).

Ambassador Deming has spent much of his career dealing with Japanese affairs, having served in Japan as chargé d'affaires, ad interim, from December 1996 to September 1997, and as deputy chief of mission from October 1993 to December 1996. From September 1991 to August 1993, Ambassador Deming was director of the Office of Japanese Affairs in Washington. He served as minister counselor for political affairs at the American Embassy in Tokyo from August 1987 to July 1991. From 1985 to 1986, Ambassador Deming was detailed to the National War College at Fort McNair in Washington, DC.

Ambassador Deming joined the Department of State in 1966. His foreign languages are Japanese and French. He completed his undergraduate degree in 1964 at Rollins College and received his MA in East Asian studies from Stanford University in 1981. He is also a 1986 graduate of the National War College.

He is a member of the Council on Foreign Relations, the American Foreign Service Association, and the Stanford University Alumni Association.

WILLIAM M. DRENNAN is the deputy director of the Research and Studies Program at the United States Institute of Peace. He joined the institute upon his retirement from the US Air Force as a colonel in 1998. His last military assignment was as an analyst with the National Defense University's Institute for National Strategic Studies from 1995 to 1998, where he concentrated on Korea and Northeast Asia security issues. Prior to that he was a professor of national security policy at the National War College. From 1990 to 1991 he was a military fellow at the Council on Foreign Relations in New York City. He was stationed in the Republic of Korea from 1988 to 1990 as the chief of the strategy and policy division, J-5, US Forces Korea.

In the mid-1980s he served as a squadron commander, and later as the deputy commander for operations of a USAF flying training wing. From 1981 to 1984 he was assigned to the White House as the Air Force aide to President Ronald Reagan. A command pilot, he accumulated 3,300 flying hours during his military career, including over 800 in Southeast Asia during the Vietnam War.

He is a graduate of the US Air Force Academy, holds a masters degree from Georgetown University, and has done doctoral work at the Catholic University of America.

Mr. Drennan's publications include "The Tipping Point: Kwangju, May 1980" in David I. Steinberg, ed., *The Endured and Enduring Relationship: Korean Attitudes toward the United States*, M.E. Sharpe, spring 2004 (forthcoming); "Nuclear Weapons and North Korea: Who's Coercing Whom?" in Robert Art and Patrick Cronin, eds., *The United States and Coercive Diplomacy*, United States Institute of Peace Press, 2003; and "A Comprehensive Resolution of the Korean War," US Institute of Peace Special Report, May 2003.

DONALD P. GREGG is chairman of the board of the Korea Society in New York City. Following graduation from Williams College in 1951, he joined the Central Intelligence Agency, and over the next quarter-century was assigned to Japan, Burma, Vietnam, and Korea. Gregg was seconded to the National Security Council staff in 1979, where he was in charge of intelligence activities and Asian policy affairs. In 1982, he was asked by then Vice President George H. W. Bush to become his national security advisor. He then retired from the CIA, and was awarded its highest decoration, the Distinguished Intelligence Medal. During his six years with Vice President Bush, Gregg traveled to sixty-five countries, and also was a professorial lecturer at Georgetown University, where he taught a graduate-level workshop entitled "Force and Diplomacy." From September 1989 to 1993, Gregg served as US ambassador to Korea. Prior to his departure from Korea, Mr. Gregg received the Department of Defense Medal for Distinguished Public Service, an honorary degree from Sogang University, and a decoration from the Prime Minister of Korea. Recent awards include an honorary degree from Green Mountain College (1996), the Secretary of Defense Medal for Outstanding Public Service (2001), Williams College's Kellogg Award for career achievement (2001), and the 2004 Bartels World Affairs Fellowship from Cornell University.

JING HUANG (PhD, Harvard 1994), is senior fellow in the Foreign Policy Studies Program at the Brookings Institution. Previously, he was associate professor of political science and co-director of the Asian Studies Program at Utah State University. He was a Shorenstein Fellow at the Asia-Pacific Research Center, Stanford University, in 2002–03. He is the author of *Factionalism in Chinese Communist Politics* (Cambridge, 2000) and numerous articles and book chapters on Chinese politics, US-China relations, China's Taiwan policy, the North Korean nuclear issue, and other security issues in the Asia-Pacific region. He is now working on a book manuscript, *Civil-Military Relations in China: A Long March toward Institutionalization*, and a project on China's security policymaking.

KIM JAE-CHANG (General, retired) graduated from the Korean Military Academy in 1962 and served in the Korean Army for thirty-two years until he was retired from active service in April 1994. His major assignments include commanding general of the 9th Infantry Division, commanding general of 6th Corps, assistant minister for policy, and deputy commander in chief of the Korea and United States Combined Forces Command. He also graduated from the United States Naval Postgraduate School, majoring in operations research and system analysis, and earned a master of science degree in March 1976. After his retirement, he studied at the Fletcher School of Law and Diplomacy in Boston, receiving his PhD in November 2002.

From November 1999 to December 2001, he served as chairman of the Defense System Reform Committee, Ministry of National Defense. Since September 2003, he has taught students at Yonsei University.

WON-SOO KIM graduated from the College of Law of the Seoul National University (bachelor of law) in Korea, and received his MA from the Paul H. Nitze School of Advanced International Studies at the Johns Hopkins University. He pursued graduate legal study as a doctoral (JSD) candidate at Stanford Law School. At Stanford, he also worked as a visiting fellow at the Center for International Security and Arms Control (CISAC) between 1994 and 1995, and at the Asia-Pacific Research Center between 1995 and 1996.

Kim has pursued a foreign service career since joining the Korean Foreign Ministry in 1978. He has worked as the second secretary in the Korean Embassy in Washington, DC, and as the deputy director of the North America Division in the Foreign Ministry. He subsequently served as the political counselor in the Korean Embassy in New Delhi, and as the director of the Treaties Division in the Foreign Ministry.

In 1996–97, Kim served as the alternate representative of the Republic of Korea to the United Nations Security Council. During that period, Korea was a nonpermanent member of the Security Council for the first time, and sought to contribute substantively to international peace and security. Kim also worked as the political counselor of the Korean Mission to the UN until 1999.

Most recently, Kim worked at the Office of the President of the Republic of Korea as the secretary to the president for foreign affairs and trade (2002–03), as well as international security affairs (2000–02). During that period, he was in charge of overall coordination of Korea's foreign policy on major issues, including the North Korean nuclear problem and management of the Korea-US alliance. Since September 2003, he has been in residence as a visiting scholar at the Asia-Pacific Research Center at Stanford.

KURIYAMA TAKAKAZU was born in 1931. He studied law at the University of Tokyo, passed the foreign-service examination in 1953, and entered the Japanese foreign service the following year. Ambassador Kuriyama spent two years (1954–56) in the United States under the foreign-service training program at Lawrence College in Wisconsin and Amherst College in Massachusetts. After serving in various posts at home and overseas, he served as ambassador to Malaysia (1985–87), as deputy foreign minister (1987–89), vice minister for foreign affairs (1989–91), and ambassador to the United States (1992–95).

Ambassador Kuriyama retired from the Foreign Service in 1996. Currently he holds the title of advisor to the minister, Ministry of Foreign Affairs. He has taught at Waseda University (1997–2002) and the International Christian University (1999–2002) as a visiting professor.

DAVID M. LAMPTON is the dean of faculty, George and Sadie Hyman Professor of China Studies, and director of the China Studies Program at the Johns Hopkins School of Advanced International Studies. He also is affiliated with the Nixon Center and was founding director of the China Studies Program at the American Enterprise Institute; former president of the National Committee on US-China Relations; and former associate professor of political science at Ohio State University. He received an honorary doctorate from the Institute of Far Eastern Studies of the Russian Academy of Sciences. He received his PhD in political science from Stanford University.

Professor Lampton's publications include *Same Bed, Different Dreams: Managing US-China Relations, 1989–2000* (2001); *Paths to Power: Elite Mobility in Contemporary China* (1986; reprinted 1989); *A Relationship Restored*, co-author (1986); *The Politics of Medicine in China* (1977); *The Making of Chinese Foreign and Security Policy*, editor (2001); *Bureaucracy, Politics, and Decision-Making in Post-Mao China*, co-editor (1992); *China's Global Presence*, co-editor (1988); and *Policy Implementation in Post-Mao China*, editor (1987).

LEE CHUNG-MIN is a professor (tenured) of international relations at the Graduate School of International Studies, Yonsei University, and director, Division of International Education and Exchange, Yonsei University. Prior to joining Yonsei University in 1998, he was a policy analyst at RAND (1995–1998), a Visiting Fellow at the National Institute for Defense Studies, Tokyo (1994–1995), a Research Fellow at the Sejong Institute (1989–1994), Research Fellow at the Institute of East and West Studies, Yonsei University (1988–1989), and a Research Fellow at the Institute for Foreign Policy Analysis, Cambridge, Massachusetts (1985–1988).

A graduate of the political science department at Yonsei University (BA, 1982), he received his MALD and PhD from the Fletcher School of Law and Diplomacy, Tufts University (1988). Dr. Lee is a specialist in East Asian security issues with a focus on developments in Northeast Asia and the Korean peninsula. He has written widely on security dynamics, defense planning, force modernization, WMD proliferation, and political-military crises. Dr. Lee co-authored a RAND monograph, *Preparing for Korean Unification* (1999), and his recent publications include "Reassessing the ROK-U.S. Alliance," *Australian*

Journal of International Affairs (Summer 2003), "East Asia's Awakening from Strategic Hibernation and the Role of Air Power," *Korean Journal of Defense Analysis* (Spring 2003), and "North Korean Missiles: Strategic Implications and Policy Responses," *Pacific Review* (2001). Dr. Lee served as an advisor to the ROK Joint Chiefs of Staff from 1993 to 1994 and as an advisor to the ROK National Security Council Secretariat from 1999 to 2001. He is a member of the International Institute for Strategic Studies (London) and the Seoul Forum for International Affairs.

HIROSHI NAKANISHI has been professor of international politics at the Graduate School of Law, Kyoto University, Japan, since 2002. He was born in Osaka in 1962. He earned BA and MA at Kyoto University, and pursued doctoral studies in the department of history at the University of Chicago before being hired as associate professor at Kyoto University.

He works on international history, historical analysis of postwar Japanese foreign and security policy, and policy studies on various aspects of Japanese foreign and security policy. His recent works in English are "Japanese Relations with the United States," in Ezra F. Vogel, Yuan Ming, and Taniko Akihiro, *The Golden Age of the U.S.-China-Japan Triangle, 1972–1989* (Harvard, 2002); "Toward a New Foreign-Policy Doctrine," *Japan Review of International Affairs* (Fall 2003); and "Military Power in International Politics: Can the Beast Be Tamed?" *Gaiko Forum* (Fall 2003).

DANIEL I. OKIMOTO is a specialist on the political economy of Japan. Professor Okimoto is senior fellow of the Stanford Institute for International Studies, director emeritus of APARC, and professor of political science at Stanford University. During his twenty-five-year tenure at Stanford, Professor Okimoto has served as a research fellow at the Hoover Institution and the Northeast Asia–United States Forum on International Policy, the predecessor organization to APARC, within the Center for International Security and Arms Control. He has also taught at the Aspen Institute for Humanistic Studies, the Stockholm School of Economics, and the Stanford Center in Berlin.

In 1976, Professor Okimoto co-founded the Asia-Pacific Research Center. He has also been vice chairman of the Japan Committee of the National Research Council at the National Academy of Sciences, and of the Advisory Council of the Department of Politics at Princeton University. Professor Okimoto's fields of research include comparative political economy, Japanese politics, US-Japan relations, high technology, economic interdependence in Asia, and international security. He received his BA in history from Princeton University, MA in East Asian studies from Harvard University, and PhD in political science from the University of Michigan.

He is the author of numerous books and articles, including *Between MITI and the Market: Japanese Industrial Policy for High Technology*; co-editor, with Takashi Inoguchi, of *The Political Economy of Japan: International Context*; and co-author, with Thomas P. Rohlen, of *A United States Policy for the Changing Realities of East Asia: Toward a New Consensus.*

YAMAGUCHI NOBORU, Major General, Japan Ground Self-Defense Force (JGSDF), was born in 1951. He is currently the director of the Research and Development Department, Ground Research and Development Command, JGSDF.

Major General Yamaguchi was educated at the National Defense Academy, 1974, CGSC, staff college, JGSDF, 1983. He received his MA at the Fletcher School, Tufts University, in 1988 and was a National Security Fellow, Olin Institute, Harvard University, in 1991. He has been a helicopter pilot in the 3rd Aviation Unit and held a staff postion in the Japan-US Security Division, Ministry of Foreign Affairs. The major general also held the position of senior defense attaché at the Japanese Embassy in the United States.

Some of Major General Yamaguchi's writings include "US Defense Policy Transition after the Cold War," *International Security* (Tokyo: International Security Association, 2001); "The Origin of Civilian Control," *Securitarian* (Tokyo: Defense Agency, March 1993); "Japan's Future Security Role," *Strategic Review* (Washington DC: US Strategic Institute, 1992); "Japan: Completing Military Professionalism," in *Military Professionalism in Asia*, edited by Muthia Alagappa (Honolulu: East-West Center, 2001); "The Security of Northeast Asia," in *The Future of Korea-Japan Relations*, edited by Robert Dujarric (Indianapolis: Hudson Institute, 2001); "Trilateral Cooperation: Opportunities, Challenges, and Tasks" in *US-Korea-Japan Relations*, edited by Ralph Cossa (Washington DC: Center for Strategic and International Studies, 1999); "Why the Marines Should Remain in Okinawa: A Military Perspective" in *Restructuring the US-Japan Alliance*, edited by Ralph Cossa (Washington DC: Center for Strategic and International Studies, 1997).